## Praise for *9 Realities of Caring for an Elderly Parent*

"[T]he A to Zs of elder care including an essential guide to thoughtfully purging a childhood home filled with decades of clutter...the mechanics of caring for a bedbound mother, and the trials and joy of caring for someone until the end."
—Dody Lapworth, Hospice and Palliative Care Nurse

"Ms. Shaffer can feel satisfied on a job well done.... Her playbook for navigating the aftermath of death, including funeral design and estate management, is indispensable."
—Catherine Raye-Wong, Estate Law,
Aaron, Reichert, Carpol & Riffle, APC

"The decision to take on the full-time care of a parent near the end of their life is complicated. Ms. Shaffer movingly and transparently draws the reader into the complex emotions and events that accompany this...in a well-written, compelling self-help book about...before, during, and after courageously...caring for her dying, beloved mother. Reading *9 Realities* moved and enlightened me."
—Robert L. Hendren, D.O., Professor and Vice Chair,
Department of Psychiatry,
University of California, San Francisco

"Very easy to read, well-written, and so engaging—just a smart book! I wanted to read more. Stefania is a spot-on spokesperson for daughters and orphans whose moms have died... and for all who experience caregiving and death."
—Stephanie Amsden, MSW, Grief Counselor and former
Hospice Patient-Care Volunteer

"Managing finances is a critical aspect of elder care that Ms. Shaffer covers in-depth. Relatable examples will remind you why understanding your parent's financial picture today will save you many headaches in the future. For anyone struggling with where assets are held, the insight shared here will motivate you to start your road to financial preparedness now."

—Leonard A. Watson, Financial Advisor

"According to AARP as more people live into their nineties, most of us will face caregiving responsibilities. Forty-five million Americans are finding out that what begins as just helping out a parent can quickly turn into a full-time job. Shaffer's book reads like a novel but shows you how to navigate every critical stage of senior care…so heartfelt and palpable. I truly enjoyed reading. Her voice is clear, her emotions genuine."

—Suzanne Pertsch, M.D., Internal Medicine

# 9

# REALITIES
## of CARING for an
## ELDERLY PARENT

### A Love Story of a Different Kind

## Stefania Shaffer

All my heartfelt wishes
Stefania

PRESSMAN BOOKS

For more information visit stefaniashaffer.com

Book design by:
Arbor Books, Inc.
www.arborbooks.com

Printed in the United States of America

*9 Realities of Caring for an Elderly Parent*
Stefania Shaffer

1. Title    2. Author    3. Memoir

Library of Congress Control Number: 2013907382

ISBN 13: 978-0-9772325-2-9

# TABLE OF CONTENTS

**REALITY 4:** *Managing Health—Both Medical and Financial—Is a Second Full-Time Job*

**PART 4: Damage Control**

**REALITY 5:** *When Your Home and Your Parent Begin Falling Apart, Get Prepared*

**PART 5: Warning Signs**

**REALITY 6:** *A Birth Allows Us Nine Months to Prepare; Death Has No Timeline; Act with Urgency in All You Do*

**PART 6: Death March**

**REALITY 7:** *The Critical Role Bowel Movements and Bedsores Will Play in the End*

**PART 7: Going Home**

**REALITY 8:** *A Preplanned Funeral Is a Gift to Your Family; Binders, and Lots of Them, Are an Executor Trustee's Gift*

**PART 8: Estate Management**

REALITY **9**: *Do Everything You Can to Self-Soothe,*
*but Include Grief Counseling; You Need*
*It More Than You Think*

**PART 9:  Grief Counseling**

# PREFACE

Dear Gentle Reader,

I imagine you are holding this book today for one of two reasons. Either you have been ignoring that nagging question of what will happen when Mom or Dad can no longer care for themselves. Or you are already there at the front of it, or in the middle of it with one or both of your parents. If you have no idea what to expect, this is the book you need now. The guideposts herein will prepare you for what's ahead. They are the nine realities every adult child should expect when coming home to care for an elderly parent until the very end.

If you are at the front, I am so sorry for the pain you are experiencing now and the pain and fear your beloved parent is experiencing too. I am just so sorry. It is quite unnatural for humans to be made to look on while the person you love, who always fixed things for you as a child, is looking at you now helplessly waiting as his or her life unravels.

This will be a gut-wrenching experience for you. I was in your shoes, but I didn't know it. I only knew my mom was falling a lot, but she always managed to pick herself up, dust herself off, and keep her sense of humor intact. We were not on speaking terms when I got her phone call asking if I would come for a visit. I hadn't seen her in several years, but by the time I finished that weekend at her house, I knew she could no longer be alone and that I would be the one to fulfill her wish that she die in her own home whenever the time came.

My mind began racing with questions: How will I purge a home filled with decades of clutter while preserving childhood memories? How can I make her money last, and where are all of her assets? What is this filing system of hers that keeps mail tucked under beds and stuffed into shoeboxes on shelves? What legal documents are still not in place? Is she simply being forgetful, or are we dealing with the warning signs of something worse? What are her wishes to be carried out after her death? What will make her happiest today?

And much later I would be asking other questions. How can I make her comfortable? How much time do we have? How can I possibly say good-bye?

I wish someone had prepared me for what I experienced in this undertaking. I would have still said yes to the job, but I would have had a better idea of what the job entailed. Nobody says yes to firefighting, or nursing, or the FBI, or the army without asking a few questions up front about what a typical day at work is like. Yes, it was stressful. Yes, it was also joyful. Yes, it was scary, and hard—absolutely the hardest bullet point I can now list under "work experience" on my résumé. Yes, it was my privilege. Yes, I did it because I knew no one else could or would, and because I believed my father would have wanted to know his beloved wife of fifty-four years was not going to have to go it alone.

To know of my mother's early buoyancy is to enlighten you as to why the signs at the end of her life were so powerful in hindsight. At the time, I had only the capacity of mind to imagine that she and I would have fun every day until she would go to sleep one night with a smile on her face and simply not wake up the next morning. I could not conceive of it any other way. She was mobile, and alert, and I had never known her to be sick or hospitalized in my forty years. Within five years of my arrival home, she would die at my side.

Now that you are ready to go through it and you want a look—a gritty look—at the realities of caring for an elderly parent, this book will help you. Its nine chapters deal with early topics like how to keep your parent safe in their own home to middle chapters revolving around waiting for death and the important roles bowel movements and bed sores will play in the end. The final third of the book deals with the aftermath, including funeral arrangements that are predesigned, and managing as executor trustee of the estate. Grief counseling for the adult orphan is the last chapter.

This book is written for the person who has no support system in place. The whole job falls to you, and you have nowhere else to get information or help—you are me. I was there. It was hard. If you are alone, without a husband, children, or family members who want to be involved, keep reading. If organizing is not your strength, know that it is mine and I will walk you through the steps you can take to get your house in order. If you do have siblings to account to, I will give you all the communication tips I used effectively. If the house you are managing is one belonging to a hoarder, I will break down for you how to de-clutter room by room and how to compact only the important items as you preserve the memories.

Designed to be an indispensable guide for all decision makers in your family, consider sharing this book with them so you will all be on the same page. The biggest battles within families come when the parent has died and the inheritance hangs in the balance or the estate items are in question as to who gets what. I have the benefit of experience and can walk you down this path so there are no misunderstandings.

My siblings were limited in what they could do to be more supportive. Each of them said they would have put my mother in a home. None of them wanted to care for her. All of them ignored her on Mother's Day and her birthday in the last year of her life. This made an already-tough journey even more difficult. I have since learned through research that family dynamics, even those that are not strained to begin with, can really unravel when a parent becomes ill. The stress impacts each adult child differently. It may be that the sibling who refuses to participate in caregiving simply lacks the capacity to cope with losing his parent. More often than not, families do not share the job of caring for an elderly parent; statistics reveal the job fell to the forty-five million daughters over the age of forty-six just in the year 2012.

If you are the reader who thinks there is still plenty of time before you need to worry about who will take care of Mom or Dad when they can't take care of themselves, answer just one question: do you know anyone who ever died before they expected to? I do. At least three people, and they weren't even senior citizens yet. So, if you are over the age of forty, have these conversations about end-of-life plans with your parents today before they begin to cry in front of you when forced to think about their own mortality as they become frail or sick. The inevitable is more unbearable when a parent is feeling vulnerable. Have this conversation now when everybody is happy and healthy.

And just know that to me, there is no competition in death. I do not believe my mom's death had any less of an impact on me and those she left behind because she died with dementia in her old age and didn't suffer from a traumatic injury or a horrible cancer. I also don't believe there is any comfort in hearing the empty words, "Well, she lived to be a ripe old age instead of having her life cut tragically short." Yes, premature deaths are horrible. I know families who have suffered through them. I have suffered through this myself with someone I loved. But losing a parent at any age is difficult. Becoming an orphan is disorienting. Anyone not sensitive to this has probably yet to experience the loss of a parent.

There are two important thoughts you can take with you right now without even buying this book: 1) Hospice care is available for anyone who meets the criteria that his or her end of life is near. It is not only for cancer patients, which is what I always believed. 2) Get your financial papers in order because if you do not have a separate will, trust, durable power of attorney, and durable power of health (commonly referred to as an *advanced health-care directive*), and the joint paperwork signed that allows you to make decisions without mutual consent, you will be experiencing even further distress before and after you bury your parent.

As far as disclaimers are concerned, I am not an attorney, so I do not share legal advice. I am not a doctor, so I cannot tell you what medical readings indicate. I am not an accountant, so I cannot dispense financial planning advice. I am a seventh-grade English teacher who had the unenviable position of acquiring some basic training along the way. I am Sister One, and this is my story. The names of all participants have been changed to preserve their privacy.

A wise man once told me this would be a thankless job. No truer words were spoken.

E-mail me if you need moral support.

# PART 1

# BEING THERE

## REALITY 1
### *The House Is a Wreck Inside and Out*

CHAPTER 1

# The Rift

Let's open with some sobering statistics that you cannot ignore for much longer. The number of people caring for an aging parent has soared in the past fifteen years, according to MetLife. In 1994, 3 percent of men and 9 percent of women helped with basic care for an aging parent. In 2008, these numbers increased to 17 percent of men and 28 percent of women providing help, which is defined as dressing, feeding, bathing, and other personal-care needs. This goes well beyond grocery shopping, driving parents to appointments, and helping them with financial matters. And it is more stressful as well. In 2011, nearly ten million adult children over the age of fifty provided this care for an aging parent.[1]

In a deeper look at options available for seniors with limited finances who cannot stay in their own homes because they are unable to care for themselves anymore, *USA Today* reports that most families are unprepared for the news that Medicare

---

1   Philip Moeller, "10 Tips for Caring for Aging Parents, Phillip Moeller," US News & World Report, July 18, 2011, http://money. usnews.com/money/blogs/the-best-life/2011/07/18/10-tips-for-caring-for-aging-parents.

doesn't pay for long-term care. The median cost of a year in a private room at a nursing home in 2011 was $77,745, according to Genworth. And only those who have spent most of their assets can qualify for Medicaid to pay for the nursing home. Assisted living is another option, but it's also not cheap and isn't covered by Medicaid. The national median cost in 2011 was $39,135, according to Genworth. With ninety percent of elderly parents preferring to stay at home, according to AARP research, families are left with the agonizing question of who will be stepping up to care for Mom or Dad.[2]

As more people live into their nineties, most of us will face caregiving responsibilities or need caregiving ourselves. AARP says forty-five million Americans perform some kind of caregiving, including meal preparation for older or impaired adult relatives or friends. After A. Barry Rand, CEO of AARP, experienced caring for his own elderly father, he began addressing the daunting problem of caregiving by building the AARP Caregiving Resource Center in January 2012, where caregivers can come together to find experts and advice through local agencies. What starts out as just helping our parent can quickly turn into a full-time job.[3]

As an adult child, the first question you need to ask yourself is, "Who is the most capable and readily able family member to handle Mom or Dad when facing the inevitable—that they can no longer care for themselves?"

2   Christine Dugas, "Caring for an Elderly Parent Catches Many Unprepared," USA Today, March 25, 2012, http://www.usatoday.com/money/perfi/basics/story/2012-03-25/caring-for-an-elderly-parent-financially/53775004/1.

3   A. Barry Rand, "Caregiving Challenges and Rewards, AARP, November 8, 2012, http://www.aarp.org.home-family/caregiving/info-11-2012/caregiving-challenges-and-rewards.html.

Now, be sure to add the following criteria to the list when determining which family member will be best suited for the job, and it is a job, full-time and hard—meaning it will take an emotional toll that hospice grief counselors liken to post-traumatic stress syndrome for at least the first two years following your parent's death: mobile enough to relocate or ability to provide extra bedroom and bath space, trustworthy, alert, non-drug user, non-smoker, reliable, observant, savvy, organized, multi-tasker, patient, creative cook, dietitian, pharmacist, nurse, non-alarmist, soother, committed, non-traveler (at least willing to put off that long-dreamed-of trip to Italy for the unforeseeable future), thoughtful, tender, good reader, great storyteller, very smart, light sleeper, pragmatist, excellent communicator (written and oral), dedicated, and service-oriented.

The answer needs to be predetermined before the next fall turns out to be a pretty bad one with a broken hip, or before full-on dementia sets in, or before the disease that has already begun to show signs further weakens and disorients the parent you always knew.

In a 2007 *USA Today* article on caring for elderly parents, AARP reported the typical unpaid caregiver is a forty-six-year-old woman who works outside the home while taking care of a relative. This is something the National Alliance for Caregiving confirms, estimating that mainly women take time off from work to care for their parents, resulting in a loss of pensions, Social Security benefits, and wages for adult children.[4]

For me, I knew it would never be my task, my charge, my

---

4    Mindy Fetterman, "Becoming 'parent of your parent' an emotionally wrenching process," USA Today, June 24, 2007, http://www.usatoday.com/money/perfi/eldercare/2007-06-24-elder-care-cover_N.htm.

responsibility—my privilege, as my mother would later put it. I was not on speaking terms with my mother, and the story behind this will be left untold. Just know that I never spent a moment of my independent, hard-charging, demanding, freewheeling life thinking that the job of caring for an elderly parent would ever fall to me. Until it did.

No one else was fit for the job except for one person, being that the only criteria she could meet in the checklist was that she had the requisite spare bedroom. But she declined to assume the position, and probably better for it because her family is far more dysfunctional than mine. No one in that hot mess would have been able to step outside of themselves for even an hour to consider the actual care that would need to go into caregiving for an elderly parent.

The turning point came in the form of a phone call one year on Valentine's Day. On the other end of the line was my mother's voice. The voice I had not heard in several years, ever since I moved far enough away from home with dust and pebbles kicking up behind me in the rear view mirror and my far-as-eye-can-see forward lock set on a life of peace and quiet straight ahead. The last thing I had said to my mother was that her loyalties were being divided. Why would she question the dutiful daughter I had been for decades, never ever giving my parents a reason to distrust me, in the face of a stack of lies against me, which she chose to believe instead? That hurt.

In fact I was devastated because my mom was my best friend. I took her on business trips, and we traveled the world together. Even my friends who watched it all unravel could not believe that a mother would turn her back on her own daughter against the word of a stranger. After all that I had done to stick with and stick by this family, it was finally the last time I wanted to feel abandoned. So, this time I did the leaving. Years later the truth did come out, as it always does. There was no end of remorse felt by the people who knew me best but bet against me, trusting a sordid source instead. Now they wanted to make it up to me. At holidays the phone rang often with calls from family members who wanted to make amends and put it all behind us now that they realized the error of their ways. Polite and disinterested was how I remained.

Everyone else had already said their own versions of "sorry" to me, and now the matriarch was calling. I heard she had fallen a few times in her home, my childhood home, but the information was never enough to concern me. This phone call today, an invitation for a visit, was not accompanied by the long-awaited apology I felt entitled to for the years that had been undone between us. So, I could only say I would think about it. I was still too rattled by hearing her voice on the other end of the line, and I wasn't processing with much clarity.

I felt exactly as I did the last time she made me feel hopeful that things could be patched up between us. It was when a package arrived in the mail, and in my haste to see what was inside I tore into it while filling up at a gas station on my way to catch a red-eye flight out of town for another business trip. The only contents were her letters to me contained in a three-ring binder, ranting about how wrong I was and what a horrible person I was. I just couldn't read anymore. I was so disoriented by one more assault to my character that I drove off in a flurry of tears—and realized too late that the gas station attendant was chasing after me. He was frantically waving his arms because I had inadvertently driven away with the gas pump still attached to my tank, now dangling from my car's rear passenger side. I am equally unhinged now.

After returning the phone to its cradle, I have only two thoughts: *I wish I paid for that caller ID feature after all*, but since I never knew her to initiate phone calls, not even through my college years, I didn't want to waste the money. My second thought comes just as clearly: *what's the point of visiting when I also know she never apologizes?*

So I think about the invitation to visit. I decide she has taken the first step by placing the call, and I know this was probably hard for her. Also, I have heard for years through the grapevine that she misses me terribly and is very sorry for not standing up for me. I have to see her face to face to see if she really does feel sorry. I wonder if she has felt sick to her stomach the way I have, and I decide not to turn my back on her invitation—a gesture, an olive branch.

It is early in March, the soonest I can clear my schedule to visit for the weekend and muster up the courage to face whatever additional hurt lay in front of me. The drive in from two hours away seems to fly by, even with bridge traffic. Parking in my familiar spot on the street corner that faces our front door alerts me to the fact that no one is caring for the lawn anymore since my dad passed away. It's been thirteen straight years of sun burning holes into the patches of brown grass with dead weeds all throughout the front yard. No more flowers. No more green. No more manicuring. The chipped paint along the front side of the house where the sun also left its laser imprint and the knee-length brush make this curb appeal look like it is straight out of the savanna rather than in the middle of a traditional suburb of San Francisco. My first reaction is: *why aren't the neighbors doing more to help?*

When I walk up the cement curbing to the front door, nearly tripping over cracked pieces of concrete that have come apart in recent tectonic plate shifts, not nearly full-scale enough to be called earthquakes, I ring the doorbell just once. I don't feel comfortable enough to give it the multiple layering of ding-dongs that is our signature ring reserved only for family members. I feel like a stranger standing at the door.

From the other side, I am met by a stranger with a faintly familiar smile. I gasp, the inaudible kind, but it is loud inside my head. It has been seven years since I was here before, but my mother has clearly aged twenty since the last time we stood together. She reaches out her arms to welcome me in and greets me with her lively "well, hello d'ere!" Most people would just say "hello there" but she is much cuter than that. All of the sudden, I feel more compassion than resentment, and instead of lugging in baggage, I carry with me only the hope for reconciliation.

Her hug is tight around me and robust as she pulls me close into her waist. She is less heavy than I remember and still wearing the baby-blue terrycloth robe we bought her for one Mother's Day in the last century. It seems to be her only one and, all these years later, the toll shows through in the elbows that are threadbare and tattered. The stains from spaghetti sauce and coffee splatters have dried in a formation of drippings all down her front. She is badly in need of a bath, as the stench is one that has been building for weeks, not just a couple of days, and is more on par with the smell of a working man tilling the fields during the dead heat of long, summer days rather than the lady of leisure she has always pretended to be.

Her toenails are overly long and yellowed. Her fingernails are jagged, but I can tell she has cut them to the best of her ability with the sharpest scissors she still owns from sewing days long behind her. Her smile is warm and welcoming as usual, but her teeth are all missing. And her silver hair turned white has thinned, and grown long down her back. It is scraggly and unbecoming for any age. Then I remember she usually wears it up in a twist with one of my old barrettes to hold it in place.

The shock of seeing my mother in this condition strikes me hard to my core, and I am wondering how many days does she look like this, or is today just a lazy weekend? When I was growing up, she was fashionable, always. Her taste in clothes was impeccable and had been ever since she was spoiled as the only girl child in her family. It just seems out of character for her to look like such a disheveled ragamuffin. At least this is my first impression from the first thirty seconds inside the door, which we are now closing behind us. I wonder what is waiting for me around the corner.

# CHAPTER 2

# House Tour

The entire house smells like cat urine. When we step into the living room adjacent to the entryway, I can see that there are dozens of littered messes left by aforementioned cats that have soiled the dingy, gray wall-to-wall carpeting. Delicate piles are dried from days of neglect. Some are still fresh, probably from this morning. How many cats does she have? The answer is clearly more than she can handle. I soon learn a relative gave her three from a litter that had bore themselves beneath their house of the mother cat that had been in this situation twice before. Again, one more household that would not have been deemed suitable to care for my mother in her senior years, since those people care for themselves about as well as they care for their animals.

The house seems so much bigger to me than I remember as she gives me the tour. I am anxious to see my room, the one I grew up in and stayed in until I finally moved away for college. On our way to the back bedrooms, we are first met with the sun-soaked kitchen. It used to be the most cheerful room, with the orange-plaid, floor-length curtains my mother was so pleased with in the '70s. These were never intended to match anything but the linoleum flooring patterned in a lemon and tangerine paisley design. The curtains were now unevenly sagging, unhooked in places from the rod above. The base of the hem is covered in soot at least four inches high. The discoloration from the time I accidentally spit out a mouthful of whipped cream when my elementary school friend made me laugh so hard I couldn't contain myself was now browned by the heat of the sun decades later. The cobwebs above the curtains are thick and have stubbornly stayed put where original webs were probably cast from the silk of spiders that died in the '80s.

But it is not the décor in front of me that has my attention now. It is the countertops in the long galley kitchen, which I cannot see beneath the bags and bags of clutter strewn about, and the massive streak of ants that winds its way in and out of each of these tunnels of garbage mounds. I shudder and check my exposed arms to be sure none of the ants have jumped across the linoleum floor to climb up my leg. Again I wonder why aren't the neighbors doing more to help? Why aren't the relatives who live closer than I do looking at this scene and scratching their heads, and wondering what are we going to do about Mom?

Out of habit, I open the door to the fridge. There is milk, still before its expiration date. There is butter, the really good kind made of only the best cream. There is a half-consumed jar of Ragu. Maybe there will be spaghetti for leftovers. There is Hershey's syrup, already opened, with its rubber, yellow lid smeared in sticky sauce fastened to the top of the can. I don't see lettuce, or any other green items that would belong in the vegetable bin, which is empty for now.

On the counter, there is a twelve pack of Dr. Pepper, from which I am politely offered to help myself. There is an opened pack of English muffins next to the toaster with a lever that still works even without the plastic part to protect your fingers from being pinched when you push it down. I see tangerines in the same wooden bowl we bought our parents for their anniversary when we were in middle school.

The final item I cannot miss is a six-pack of Hershey bars, my favorite kind. The first four have already been eaten, as evidenced by the wrappers entrenched in the ant mess beside me. I am not sure if the counter tops are still the original tiling my parents picked out because not a speck of it is visible beneath the consortium of clutter. There is a breadboard buried beneath plastic bread bags that are stuffed with used paper towels and garbage from wrappers. There are empty Ragu jars, several of them, and I begin to wonder how many nights a week can someone eat pasta. Then it occurs to me, maybe this is all she can cook.

On the other side of the counter, where the stove sits, there are more little bags stuffed with more litter. I wonder when garbage day is, and now I wonder if she has trouble getting the barrels to the curb by herself. I start looking around with different eyes. It is a lot to take in, this old house of mine. She was never known for being a meticulous housekeeper, but she took a lot of pride in running a busy household, and, as I realize now, my mom worked very hard at laundry and cooking multiple times a day every day. By the looks of her today, these tasks take a lot more time to perform, and the simplest chore is not getting done.

We look to the right, across the kitchen and into the dining room, at the oversized table that can easily seat twelve because the leaves have not been taken out since Thanksgiving 1972. I am bewildered by the mass of fabrics covering its entirety.

"Are you sewing again?" I ask, hardly believing the answer could be "yes" since there is no sewing machine in sight.

"I can't sew anymore because I have macular degeneration in my left eye. The doctor says there is a tumor behind it and eventually I will only be able to see vistas."

It's just information she reels off. There seems to be no sadness over the news she has lived with for seven years, ever since she had to stop driving because of it. I used to wonder how hard it would be for her if she could never drive again. She has always been bound and determined to be on the move, especially in the face of her newfound freedom after my father's death. She traveled the globe and still has places she wants to see before she goes completely blind.

So from this pile of fabric, and the baubles that go along with someone intending to sew a new project, I am perplexed as to how long it has actually been sitting here. I wonder why it is on the dining room table when I know she dedicated one of the spare bedrooms as her sewing room. I am going to badger the point until my eyes sweep to the sitting parlor across from the dining room and the parade of *National Geographic* magazines that are spilling onto the floor from four-foot stacks lined up along the walls. Why would these still be in the house?

They have been collecting cobwebs, and in between the piles there are feces and stained pages from visiting critters that burrowed in for safe housing at one time. The contents inside the built-in cabinets, which store the good china and a whole lot of knickknacks no one will ever want have been equally destroyed by spiders that have had time to spin delicate webs over years and years of darkness. Nobody has been opening these cupboards to retrieve serving pieces reserved for entertaining guests at holidays for many, many years.

A picture can paint a thousand words, but when you add in the smells, the sensory memory will never forget. These new images are being permanently imbedded in my mind and will become something I ponder all weekend. Attached to the dining room is the door to the garage. It used to easily house two cars and had floor-to-ceiling built-in shelves along the west wall for neatly storing paint cans and tools my Dad needed for all the do-it-yourself home-repair projects of his retirement years.

There is no room for two cars; not even a single car could park inside. The space to accommodate a unicycle, let alone a bicycle, is nowhere to be found. The garage is a center of chaos similar to the kind of storage units most families stuff into storage units they rent for only a dollar the first month and then forget about because they never really needed any of it anyway. The mess towers from floor to ceiling, and all I can think is, *How did there get to be so much junk, and who is going to sort through it all?*

It has taken nearly forty years to stuff this place, with nary a thing ever being tossed for the "good" reason that some day it might come back in style. Why buy a perfectly good new one when said item is in the garage already awaiting repurposing? This is probably the same rationale my father used for his collection of nuts and bolts and screws. They were stored in a nest of coffee cans in the corner of the garage, just filled to the brim, in case the hardware store decided not to sell them anymore.

I have had enough of the garage. I want to see my old room. It was such a cheerful room, with flowered wallpaper patterned in Gerbera daisies of pink and turquoise and yellow until I insisted I was too old for such cheer and had my father paint over the whole pastel palette in plain white. I wanted to erase my childhood and my youth since I was preparing for college like a big girl. At least white never goes out of style, and I expect that it will still look fresh even after all this time.

Before we get to the end of the hall where my memories were built, we pass the family room off the kitchen. It has a large, open floor plan with oversized, mid-century furnishings spilling out of it into the hallway. The round, dark-oak dining table that can seat six children, away from the adult table in the other room during holidays, is stuck awkwardly in the center of the room because a round dining table will never fit flush against a wall. The matching chairs with their long backs made to look like wood wicker are full of cat hair and old stains on their cushioned seats. There is a pine secretary's desk buried in unopened mail. Notices postmarked five days ago are stacked and rubber-banded in separate piles. She has marked the date she received them with a black Sharpie in her distinct cursive on the front of each envelope.

And then there is the couch. It looks like the remainder of a set that got split up at a garage sale, and this, the little couch that can accommodate only two medium-sized people comfortably, was considered a bargain that day. You can tell others have tried to create additional seating by perching themselves on the sagging armrests, and with some discomfort because the entire left side is dilapidated and sagging. The white stuffing shows through from cats that have used this piece of furniture as their regular scratching post. The cushions have completely sunk in toward the middle of the couch just like an old mattress would beneath the weight of the heaviest person after years of sleepless nights.

There is no space to comfortably live in this room. It is overrun with more clutter in the form of lamps that still don't provide enough good light for reading, and *Sunset* magazines that have been saved for decorating ideas and recipes, but have piled up faster than the last issue could be devoured. There are numerous plants, from African violets to green clippings all well watered, but never dusted. A vacuum cleaner has not been run in any recent time as evidenced by the trail of bread-crumbs that are encircling the couch.

Looking out the living room window, which is really an entire wall of glass, I see the greenhouse my father built in the '80s when my parents decided to take up botany and horti-culture as a hobby in their retirement years. That oversized shed made of heavy-duty Plexiglas was once a really cool place to sleep under the moonlit sky. I could never see the stars through the thick, corrugated, waxy plastic since its purpose was to heat the plants without allowing the sun's rays to burn them. But I could tell the sky was illuminated.

The plants that were once full and wild and lush have become dead brambles over time. Mostly the greenhouse has become a place for storing hundreds of clay pots with the intention of reviving this forsaken hobby. Layers of brush creep down from the shelves, entangling anything that comes into their path along the floor. It will take nothing short of a machete as the first tool needed to begin the clearing in here.

Finally, the first of five bedrooms in this twenty-seven hun-dred square foot house is the master bedroom for my mother. It has not changed since my high school years, but there are more piles of mail in identical stacks like what I saw in the family room. They are all bound by rubber bands according to the date received and marked in her cursive with a faded, black Sharpie. There are at least twenty piles, but these have been opened and re-stuffed with the original contents. Is this her filing system?

Her attached bathroom is another spider hole, and I can barely stand to look at the pot, which is neither sanitary nor flushed. The bathtub is dry and dusty and filled with cobwebs. There is a deep, stainless steel mixing bowl being used as a washbasin. It stands on the sink counter where a washcloth has been wrung out to dry. A wardrobe hanging in the adjoining walk-in closet permeates a slight waft of perspiration.

*Oh boy* is all I can manage in my head because the kaleidoscope of images is still not coming in to focus for me. But I am beginning to detect what the full picture will become by the time my eyes have adjusted.

Before backing out of this room, I do a full visual sweep one last time. I see the disarray of curtains sagging from their rods just like in the kitchen, with filth stained spots from cat spray on the dusty, rose-colored fabric. The bedspread, tattered and not long enough to cover the metal bed frame, allows me a peek at some wooden boxes being used for storage beneath the bed. I can see just the tips of white envelopes—what I suspect is more mail tucked away here.

Four bedrooms left to go. The closest to the master is the sewing room. I remember my mother was fastidious about the storage space she would require to house her many collections of expensive fabrics from the renowned Britex store in San Francisco. She has a sophisticated Bernina model sitting on her sewing table, sandwiched between two high towers of white shelving. These take up all the wall space and are the brightest parts of this dank and dreary room, which only sees early morning sun before it is hidden away in darkness for the rest of the day because of the overhang that blocks the light.

I push the door open past the first four inches with ease, but now it resists against my weight. I finally manage to open it halfway and squeeze myself through the narrow entry. I gape at what lies in front of me. There is my old childhood bed, once a bright-white laminate frame with three lemon-colored drawers for under-bed storage now dulled and faded like most of my childhood memories. I loved my little bed. It had a secret compartment that ran the length of one side, perfectly suited for this lithe little girl in a game of hide-and-seek. When I really wanted to win, I could pull my mattress out just enough to drop inside the coffin of space under the removable particleboard. No one could find me for hours. I loved lying there in wait while hearing friends or family call my name and begin to wonder aloud where I could have gone. Once my secret spot was found out, I declared it off limits for anyone else to use in future games.

My poor little bed is now besieged with piles and piles of fabric and bedding that belonged to children of thirty years ago. There are yellowed pillows without cases that reek of more cat destruction and decayed pellets that seem to have belonged to something other than a cat. There is a corkboard with yellowed clippings of great sewing ideas and Vogue patterns that have been hung as inspiration for the next great dinner-party costume to be worn no place because there are no special occasions anymore.

There are barrels, steel tight drums actually, of yellowed baby clothes in no condition even to donate along with more gaudy fabrics of dated looks from decades past. Expensive fabrics in full bolts are tightly stacked inside the darkened cans for preservation—cans that would have made much better hiding spots in my childhood games if they had been empty. A peek inside one reminds me that there is no place in this house safe from cats or critters who are patient enough to burrow through an unsealed lid to find the haven of plush Pucci fabrics for their new nest.

I am reminded of all the good intentions my mother still has for her last years of retirement from the to-do list hanging on her wall. She wants to sew but can't see well enough to thread the eye of a needle. She is still reading voraciously and is thrilled that she is able to complete the new 768-page biography of John Adams before she has to succumb to large-print books. She waits for the dawn arrival of the newspaper every morning to scan it for headlines only because the small print is too small to see even with her magnifying glass.

I look at her and envision the capable, fearless mother I always knew. I want to dust her off and replace her batteries, and then maybe she will be able to run circles around this house like she once used to. Her spirits are really good. She tells me she hasn't fallen in a while, but the last one that happened in the kitchen, forcing her into the splits, sounds like something I should be paying more attention to. Instead, I am laughing at the way she tells me about it with her head bobbing backward when she lets out a good hoot at how scary it really could have been.

We continue with the tour, moving farther down the long hallway to my dad's den. It remains intact exactly the way it was left, in mid-sentence of a letter-writing campaign. My dad was committed to writing to senators and Congress leaders monthly. His desk is crowded with stationery and office supplies. The outdated company letterhead is still sitting ankle-deep in a pile on the floor. We didn't need expensive, clean paper for doodling when there was perfectly good scratch paper for free flooding every drawer in the house.

This den is well lit from an oversized, white skylight that illuminates more cobwebs cast in corners. Homemade shelves made of plywood are sturdy enough for stacking a collection of books by James A. Michener, whose latest, *Texas*, is still sitting open on my dad's reading chair. The chair still rocks, but if you lean back too far, you can feel the springs pushing up through your spine. Nothing has been moved.

My parents have always been simple people who invested well but never lived above their means because they were from the Depression era. I never minded having older parents because they were really good parents, good to me—and good for me. I never knew my grandparents, so I was always grateful for the opportunities I had to do service work with elderly people. When I moved away to college, I got involved in a project befriending some of the seniors at an assisted living home. One man named Herman became a surrogate grandfather to me. When he finally moved away to live with his daughter in Arizona, I had a hard time saying good-bye even though we promised to write. We were pen pals for nearly a year before his letters stopped coming. I knew what that meant, but he never told me that his sickness had gotten worse. Maybe it was because he was trying to spare me any worry.

Later, when I graduated from college and moved into my first apartment in the city for the first time without a gaggle of roommates, the little old lady downstairs who sat on the porch reading soon became my new best friend. On Saturday nights, she would invite me down to watch Lawrence Welk reruns on PBS, and we would enjoy a batch of her homemade rice pudding together, my favorite. Sometimes I would be late, and she would telephone to say, "Steffie, are you coming? I have your rice pudding ready on the stove!"

It warmed my heart, and I never felt like I was missing out on anything else that dating could have offered because I had Mrs. Fleischman, and we enjoyed each other's company immensely. I became close to her family, who looked in on her from time to time. They repeatedly expressed their gratitude to me for being a regular companion to her, and their relief in knowing that she wasn't alone. They gave me their phone numbers at work and at home in case I ever needed to reach them, and it has never occurred to me why they were so thankful until I look at my disheveled mother now. I wish there was a Steffie looking out for her today. I wish she wasn't so alone.

Years after my move out of the area, Mrs. Fleischman and I kept in close contact by letter. It was hard to talk on the phone because her hearing was getting worse. When I did get the phone call from her daughter telling me that Mrs. Fleischman had died peacefully in her sleep at the age of ninety-six, I emitted guttural sounds of heaving sobs. The sadness came over me in a sudden wave. I had no idea it would hit me so hard. Maybe in part it was too soon after the sudden passing of my father just one month earlier. His was the first death I had ever experienced, and I had no idea how to grieve because I was so busy with my career.

When my boss told me to take as much time as I needed, my mom and I planned a trip to Carmel for the two of us to revisit the places where she and my father had lived while he was stationed at Fort Ord during World War II. The day we were leaving, my boss phoned to find out how much longer I thought I would need. It had been four days, but there were clients who needed my attention, and if I wasn't coming back soon, did I think he should let someone else in the office handle their business? This is the worst news a salesperson working off commission can hear. People's sympathies stretch only so far, and then it's back to business as usual. If you can't get back to it, be prepared for others to jump right in and earn your commissions instead, or worse your clients' future business. My mom and I enjoyed our drive and the minimal time we had to spend in her old stomping grounds. Memories were made, mother-daughter bonds were forged, and Carmel became our special place to retreat many more times in our years together.

CHAPTER 3

# Rosebud

As we leave the den, I shudder at the massive amount of heavy labor that will be required to pull this room together. Next, I enter the bathroom across the hall that was built with large families in mind, with its separate Jack and Jill toilets and double sinks. The extra-wide linen closet has the now-familiar scent of cat urine. All of the pink floral sheets that once tucked me in at night have also been ruined by animals run amuck in this household.

The closet's five long shelves are brimming with old towels that were never big enough to wrap me completely when I was shivering from an afternoon swim in our unheated pool. The good linens, saved for overnight guests we never had, have been defecated on by cats, and there are several heavy, king-sized blankets still in plastic pouches that were purchased on sale and never used. The vibrant floral patterns are clearly Marimekko fabrics that were popular in the '80s. None of them have been opened, which is a shame because the bedding throughout the house is sorely in need of replacing.

The bathroom that used to be mine is grossly unkempt. The window treatment my mother made on her sewing machine is still in place but very dusty. The once ivory linen is now dingy and gray in a way that antique linen is never meant to look. The memory of a bathtub that never drained prior to filling water to one's knees while showering begins to wash over me. A little voice of doom whispers in my ear that someone is going to have to oversee a gut job on this place someday and I so do not want it to be me. I have to get out of this mess because the toilet reminds me of boys urinating but missing the bowl. The smell is seeping through my imagination and burning into my nostrils. The sensory mind never forgets.

There are two bedrooms left. One is mine, and part of me knows that it must be in perfect condition because I left it that way when I moved out and because it was the only room in the house that got a makeover decades earlier. I can't wait any longer. I want to burst into my old room, but the door is fighting me now. I can hardly push it open. I wonder what could possibly be blocking it from behind. All I can spy through the open crack is the old, rickety card table. Its emerald-green inset made of vinyl prevented careless burn marks from misplaced cigarettes during games of gin rummy my parents held in the '50s. Its waxy coat also protected against equally thoughtless smears from greasy chicken wings consumed during poker games in these same post-war days. The last time I saw this table was when I was a small child hosting tea parties with my dolls. Now it is an office desk for my mother since my father's den is overly occupied with clutter that hasn't been touched since his passing thirteen years ago.

This table is similarly overrun with the same envelope mess I saw on the secretary's desk in the family room. Behind the table, there are shoeboxes stuffed with mail, stacked in layers on the bookshelf. More piles of statements spill onto the floor, where they sit abandoned until another logical place for long-term storage can be created. What is all of this mail? I can't tell if it is important or if it is in the process of being filed away, or if I am looking at the only filing system already in place. I eye the familiar scrawl in the same black Sharpie marking the dates and contents enclosed in the envelopes. They have been opened, read, restuffed, and most likely not responded to.

With a few more hard shoves on the door, I am able to fling myself fully inside. There is a heaping mound of a blanket monstrosity coiled at my feet. Its tail has wound around the backside of the door, creating a barrier behind it, which is why my first efforts to glide inside were thwarted. I recognize this mess because the intestines of it are my favorite ones from childhood embroiled with some other unrecognizable lace draperies that were undoubtedly part of some great but long-forgotten scheme to redecorate.

I see my quilt, which is made of the softest cotton in chocolate brown with a pattern of butterflies framed in white squares. I loved monarchs when I was a little girl, so when my mother found this fabric she wanted me to have a quilt of it that I could hold on to for all the years ahead. She wanted me to remember the hobby she and I shared together of collecting butterflies for my butterfly book. The only part I am unable to recall is how my butterflies died. Was it from being trapped in a jar thoughtfully built from netting so they could breathe? Was it because they were no longer allowed their freedom to fly? Were they murdered in time for my return home from school to find one more addition in my collection book? I hope their deaths were natural, because I would not have enjoyed admiring the beauty of their wings taped into my book if it were any other way.

I reach down to untangle the twists of my quilt and realize I have unearthed a waste station of petrified cat poop briquettes. I jump back and am at once disheartened that my prized possession from my little-girl years has been reduced to a pile of cat crap. Plus I am not even sure which decade of cats can claim these pieces that have been left behind. I am disgusted that this entire house is in ruins and nobody has noticed long enough to do anything about it. Two different relatives resided here for a short period of time while on the hunt for temporary housing in the area. Surely, they saw what I am seeing today. How is it possible they were so busy they couldn't do anything to help? They were probably spending every waking hour looking for ways they could get out of here as fast as possible.

The trundle bed that was fun for sleepovers but not so fun for jumping from one bed to another in the dark is still in place. So is the scar on my shin from when I missed the mattress and its metal frame sliced the first four layers of skin off my leg.

I stop to watch a spider crawl up the corner where my built-in study carousel once stood. My dad constructed it all by himself and then reluctantly dismantled it when I wanted my big-girl room to have more square footage so I could put in a white wicker sofa for lounging in front of my new ten-inch television. The only items still hanging in my closet that ever belonged to me are a couple of my favorite prom dresses, the belle skirt from my wedding dress in the twentieth century, and a photo album with some great memories of the boy I was so enchanted with as a teen I could hardly believe he became the selfish man I would grow up to divorce. The rest of the clothes in this closet are my mother's.

This place is a catastrophe. We have owned this house for the better part of forty years. It has been thirteen years since my father passed away. I have been gone for seven. Still, in the time when I did live nearby, I don't remember the house ever being in the shambles it is today. I do not know how long it will take to get this house back on its feet, but I am tearfully wondering now who will be doing this job when it comes time to sell, and yet I am dreading that I already know this answer.

Next to my closet, running the length of the wall, is a seven-foot, rectangular dresser with four deep drawers. I try to open the first one, but it is stuck. I move to the next drawer and with its heaviness, I can only pull it slowly because it is not seated on its tracks and struggles with awkward skids as I bring its contents out into the light. There are even more bundles of envelopes, rubber-banded like the others, and piled in deep stacks according to year. The ones I am looking at now date back to the year of my dad's death. Good grief! She does have a long-term filing system, and I am looking at it.

What is in these envelopes that still needs to be kept?

I tug on the third drawer and it too is off its tracks and squeaks with regret that its coffin lid is being raised. There are more heaps rubber-banded together by date, and more cursive markings in black Sharpie. She is efficient in labeling the envelope contents before hiding them away as if the problems will be taking care of themselves. Out of sight, out of mind. These are the problems that I can see. What are the ones that I cannot?

I turn my back on my old room and walk two steps to

the fifth bedroom next door, the one in which my dad was intended to die. It is dark and smallish, but when my dad got weaker with his congestive heart failure and the warranty on his pacemaker about to expire, my mom dressed it up a bit by papering the room herself in rolls of ivory with satin stripes of taupe running vertically. She painted the closet-door panels in a sand color to match and left the square borders trimmed in white gloss. The old stereo that played my dad's records, including "Sounds That Got Us Through WWII" and other gems from eras gone by, is still in place.

Here is the cassette-tape player my father used for recording his autobiography during his last year upon this earth. I had submitted a list of life-history questions for him to answer, and he went above and beyond by interjecting his humor and infusing stories from his boyhood and, war times, and how he met my mother. I treasure these recordings and play them when I make the long drive to visit his gravesite every Father's Day and Thanksgiving. On these days, he is my passenger, and I never feel alone. Every tender word he ever spoke to me in life is measured by the father's counsel I have on these tapes. And every single time I get to listen to his voice, I am more comforted than grief-stricken.

The cats have not spent much time ruining this room, but the spiders have. There is no natural light on this side of the house because of the same overhang that darkens the sewing room, too. This is another dungeon, and evidently a perfectly inviting place for spiders to weave their webs with no signs of life to disturb their work. As it turns out, my father died at the age of seventy-five on a fishing boat with his favorite captain. He had a massive heart attack while reeling in the big one. It was his only wish that he die this way, and again I take comfort in this detail because I feel it was his reward for living such an honorable life and overcoming more travails than any one person should have to bear.

This room is not cozy. It is in disarray with a queen-sized bed positioned diagonally, unmade with rumpled sheets. It is surrounded by overstock furniture that makes it feel more like a warehouse of Goodwill items than a room for weary travelers. That is, until I spot the small bud vase with a lovely clipping from the red rose tree out back. It is my mother's gesture—she has set this room up to welcome me as her overnight guest. I do not know how I can sleep here in this filth, and I already have hotel reservations in place for this weekend.

But, I look at this beautiful rose, and I am reminded of my favorite bedtime story she would tell from memory about Rose Red and Snow White. They were sisters who took in a bear to warm his fur by their winter fire only to discover he was really a prince Rose Red would marry in the end. It touches my heart and I am torn between leaving her here and ignoring her effort to welcome me back home and sleeping comfortably in a place where I can breathe in something other than cat odors.

This concludes the tour. Five bedrooms, four of which are being used as attic space, plus a garage that has hosted its own share of uninvited guests judging by the little reminders left in dark crevices. This place does not feel like the home I kept etched in my mind. But being with my mom again is slowly bringing back memories of all the fun we used to have together. I remember the trip we took to New York for the first Christmas after my father died. I told my mom it was my treat, and since I had been there a dozen times already, I knew how not to look like a tourist in Manhattan. I gave her regular pop quizzes on the rules she would need to follow: don't look up at buildings, don't wait for the light before crossing, don't read a map on the street, do keep an urgent walking pace—tips so she would not give us away lest we get mugged.

I planned all the Broadway shows and made reservations to have Christmas Eve dinner at the Russian Tea Room before we would catch *Cats*, which left us both cold. Out of the theater and on our way back to the hotel, a tall man with dreadlocks past his shoulders wanted to hail a cab for us. This had not been my experience on previous trips since I was always perfectly capable of catching my own cabs. But he wouldn't get out of the way, and when a cab did pull up to me, he insisted, "I gotchyour cab, I gotchyour cab! Give me some money."

I told him I hailed my own cab, swiftly opened the door, and proceeded to shove my seventy-three-year-old mother into the back of it. The man would not relent and continued with his rant of "I gotchyour cab, I gotchyour cab!" But this time he put his hand on my arm close to where my decoy purse was dangling—I knew enough to always keep my money belt around my waist and tucked into my pantyhose.

I said, "Sir, if you don't take your hands off me now, your kids will be Christmas orphans!" And before he had a chance to respond, I jumped on top of my mom, who was still trying to situate herself in the backseat, while the cab driver, who was savvy to all of this, took off before I even closed the door tightly.

It wasn't until we made it safely back to our hotel room and flopped down onto our beds that my mom let out a howl, imitating the man: "I gotchyour cab, I gotchyour cab!" And then she repeated the line that would be used at parties and gatherings as our inside joke for years and years to come: "Let go of my arm, or your kids will be Christmas orphans!" Oh, what a good time we had, squealing like piglets until tears streamed down our faces from laughing so hard.

I sit down with my mother on the lumpy, sloped couch. Our shoulders are touching because there really is no way for two people to sit on either end without falling toward each other. So we meet in the middle.

"It's good to see you, Mom," I begin.

"I am sorry. You were right. All of the things you told me, I should have believed you, and I didn't find out the truth until it was too late. You were right. And I feel like such a damn fool for not trusting you." With eyes cast downward in a sheepish glance at her knees, she looks humbled and sincere. And this completes the apology I never thought I would hear. It is enough for me because I can tell she means it. And then she speaks again.

"I know you wrote a book. I bought a copy and I think you are very talented. Do you need a new computer to keep writing? I would like it to be my gift to you and your future writing." And this is the retribution. It feels like it is a sacrifice on her part because I cannot tell what her financial situation is today, despite the fact that my father left her fairly well off upon his death, which was all spelled out in the trust that had been in place since we were children.

"Oh wow, that sounds exactly like what I need. I truly appreciate this so much. But mostly thank you for the apology, Mom. It means a lot." After a long, awkward pause, I continue, "I'm sorry we lost all these years. I guess everyone learned the hard way." I can feel a catch in my throat, and slowly I eke out the only inadequate words I can manage: "Thank you very much again for the computer." And, before my face is about to break, "I'm just so sorry we've lost so much time."

With this I move in for our second hug in seven years—both in the same day.

# CHAPTER 4

# The Solution

I decide the kitchen cannot wait any longer, and while my mom lies down for a nap, I make myself useful—plenty useful. I remember there are always cleaning supplies in the garage cabinet, and I find them easily. I make a mental note for later that this is a closet in need of inventorying because I see enough Windex to clean an eighteen-story glass office building, and at least a dozen unopened reams of Saran wrap, not even the strong, clingy kind. Underneath a pile of furniture polish and dusting rags made of old T-shirts and underpants, I find the Hefty sack garbage bags that will help me clear out the kitchen. I make a run to the grocery store for supplies. After buying four cans of ant spray for fear those army ants will have troops coming to search for them, I get to work.

The kitchen doesn't require more than a couple hours of solid elbow grease. The counters are easy enough to sweep clean because the mess there is all just bags and bags of garbage. I decide to clean out the fridge as well since there isn't much in there in the first place. The freezer is full of frostbitten tubs of vanilla ice cream that have been eaten down to the bottom except for one. This container, only half depleted, shows signs of strange spoon carvings laced in smears of chocolate spit throughout the center. She tells me later that sometimes it's just easier to take a few spoonsful instead of having to dirty a dish.

With the job of the counters behind me and the appliances cleaned, I take a visual snapshot of what's inside all of the cupboards. There is more Tupperware here than any Tupperware party from the '70s ever hosted. There are mismatched plastic plates and cups stuffed in front of other mismatched serving trays and pitchers and old-fashioned milkshake makers. There is no end, so I shut the cupboards quickly, and we order in Chinese.

I call the hotel before dinner to cancel my reservation. That rosebud beside the guest bed, staring longingly at me from its simple water glass, the kind she used to keep her teeth in so she could easily find them, beckons me to stay with a voice so loud I can hear nothing else except the sounds that creep into the night in a place that is still unfamiliar. I do not sleep, but I probably would not have slept much better in a hotel either because all I can think about is what we are going to do about Mom.

I am relegated to sleeping in my dad's room as is and hope I will be warm enough if I leave on my bulky fisherman's sweater. I have no clean sheets because of the messes that are in the linen closet. I have no extra blankets because they too have been abused by the animals. I find the corner of the bed that is the least dirty and pull the covers to my shoulders, but it smells so much like dust, I do not want it too close to my face. Then I remember the blankets that were new thirty years ago and still safe in their zippered pouches. I grab the Marimekko and wrestle with its king-size girth until it is unfolded and I can find shelter beneath its plastic smell.

I know this won't even be the worst part of my overnight stay; the dreaded shower that floods the tub will be my nemesis come morning. I don't even know if there are clean towels in this house. At least there is detergent in the garage, and I can wash towels in the morning if need be.

I deem this house unfit to live in. My mom's appearance is not much better. I don't know how she is managing. And in the midst of trying to lull myself to sleep, I hear a sound I cannot place, but my brain knows I should have the answer to this one. It's like a scratching on a vinyl surface, as if someone is smoothing wallpaper to make sure there are no crinkles. I get up to explore as this whoosh moves quickly and urgently. I nearly bump into my mother at the front of the house who is ready to mow me over in her path.

I ask what she is doing up so late, and she tells me this is how she gets her exercise. She walks the length of the house in the pitch of night by feeling her way down the walls. This way she can get out of the house if there is a fire and she is blind. It does make sense, but it is also three in the morning. The vinyl wallpaper runs the length of all the bedrooms in the back of the house. She tells me she can do this ten or twenty times a night and that it relaxes her. She's a night owl, which I had totally forgotten, except now I am remembering how hard it was to come in after curfew because she was always sitting in the chair by the front door, waiting.

"Okay, Mom, I'm going to head back to bed," I say because I am not a night owl. Once she finishes her hour of pacing the house, her light goes on and her first hand of solitaire begins. The shuffling of the cards, and their quick snap of plastic hitting plastic, is so rhythmic, I feel my eyelids getting heavy, and I finally drift off.

The next morning, I am awakened by the smell of hot oil and the stove fan whirring on high. My bedroom is pitch dark, but the noises beckon me to the kitchen where it is sunny and bright. I see she has made her famous pancake batter from the Bisquick box mix, and the oil splattering from the heavy, cast iron frying pan is telling her it is time to spoon in a few ladles.

She is full of good cheer and greets me in the same blue robe I saw her in yesterday with a vigorous, "Well, good *mooorning*, dear heart. Are you ready for some pancakes?"

It is seven o'clock, and after a rough night's sleep, breakfast sounds good, especially when somebody else is making it. I look at the kitchen again, and I am happy with the progress I made yesterday, but I am reminded of the unearthing that still needs to be done inside the cupboards. I know I won't have time for this today.

My mom has also thoughtfully made instant coffee, the kind my friends won't even be reduced to drinking when they camp. We sit and enjoy some comfortable silence over pancakes thinned by a watery mix. We have hot syrup made of brown sugar and butter melted together on the stove. And we have each other's company, which I enjoy the most. I am intently studying her face. She is almost completely unaware that there has been any distance of time between us for the better part of a decade.

A lot has happened for me within this span: I changed careers, trading the prosperity of my successful corporate-America sales job for education, where I spent a chunk of my life savings obtaining my teaching credential, all the while paying bills and subsisting until my first paying teaching position came along. When I was offered a contract making less than I did my first year out of college, I happily accepted because initially I had planned to live in a hut in a third-world country working with the Peace Corps, making four hundred dollars a month. Perspective matters.

Sometime after lunch the front door flies open with the brother I've never been close to breezing through. I am taken aback that he doesn't ring the bell first, but I quickly discover that he sees this place as his flophouse away from his bossy wife and screaming kids. I smile, I grit my teeth, and I bear it while he plops himself onto the couch and asks if I can make him a sandwich. I haven't seen him either in the seven years I have been away, and I enjoyed every single one of those days free from his malevolence.

Now here he is asking me to make him a sandwich, a request to which I politely oblige only because this is my second day on the scene and I want to toe the line of least resistance. Yet it is all I can do to keep from imagining the long-overdue satisfaction I would have of hurtling either the sandwich itself or, preferably, the dull butter knife I used to spread the mustard on it across the room at his chest. I am so not looking forward to this visit.

"How have you been, Stef?" he asks in a chipper voice. "The kitchen looks great. I can finally see the counters."

"Yep, I picked up all the cat poo too. There was a lot of it in the living room." I avoid giving him the evil eye directly, hoping instead to convey my disdain telepathically for how he could leave our mother in such a pathetic state for all these years. The brutal memories I have from our adolescence remind me that confronting his wrath is not something I want to tango with today.

"Oh, those cats are sneaky. But Mom's getting up there in age, and it's probably too much for her to take care of three of them."

"Don't you even think about getting rid of my animals! They are my animals after all, and this is their house!" she pipes in feeling as if she needs to defend the pets once again from a possible suggestion of finding them a better home. I can tell she sees this as a potential mutiny, so I disarm her immediately.

"Mom, do you want to get out this afternoon and go shopping at Bed, Bath, and Beyond? I remember how much you used to love that store."

"Oh yes, we'll go later this afternoon. I want to visit with your brother for a while and hear what's going on with that darling daughter of his. How is she, and what has she been up to since I saw her at Christmas?"

She last saw that baby at Christmas? The baby who lives five minutes away? Christmas was three and a half months ago. How often does she get to see her granddaughter? These are the thoughts that begin to develop in my interior monologue, soon to be filled with other puzzling questions I will have to figure out myself. For starters why is Brother One here without his family? I soon learn he is on call for work on Sundays, but instead of taking his break at his house, he crashes here. This is their ritual every Sunday.

My brother brings up the couple times since Christmas that my mom fell in the house when she was all alone. I heard about these from another relative, and I heard my Mom retell the stories in her funny way, but when he brings them up, I can tell he is worried.

My mother's favorite story is the one about the kitchen fall.

"You should have seen me, down on the floor, practically in the splits, with a swollen ankle like you wouldn't believe. It was my own damn fault for washing the kitchen floor. Next time I won't use soap—it's just too slippery."

But then, I wonder, how will the floor get clean? Seeing that there is soot on the draperies and ants climbing all over the counters, I'm pretty sure we should be using soap to clean the floors.

My mom is on a roll now with two people held captive in her audience, so she continues with the time she fell in the bathroom.

"That was a big one. I don't know how it happened. One moment I was up, and then I was down. And that one hurt too. You should have seen the bruising all up and down my left leg. I still walk with a limp. Dr. Goodcare says I am lucky I didn't end up with a broken hip. I tell you, he is a great doctor. He sees to it that he's going to keep me alive. I'm lucky to still have him. We've been together since he was an intern almost forty-five years ago," she boasts as if she practically put him through medical school herself.

"Mom, you are so lucky nothing worse happened. What would you do if you were really hurt and no one was here to help you?" The question needed to be answered while the mood was still light.

"Well, I would just lie there on the floor until someone came looking for me or the neighbors could smell the stench." She laughs easily at this one. My brother reminds her that he usually comes to check on her a couple times a week and brings her groceries on Tuesdays. So she offers without missing a beat, "Next time I fall, I'll try to plan it for a Tuesday or a Sunday!"

"You know, Mom, in those homes I go into, they always

have Big Leroy standing in the living room, guarding all the little old ladies in their chairs telling them, 'Nope, don't you do it, don't get out of that chair there. You just stay right there, and Big Leroy will be right back with your nice meds. Nuh, nuh, nuh, don't you try and get up. Stay right there.' Is that the life you want to be living, Mom?" My brother paints such a vivid picture. He's telling it like a dinner-party story with all the expected laughs filling in his well-timed pauses. She and I are both entertained because he has caught his rhythm, and I can tell this is not the first time he's had such fun singing this tune.

"Oh no you don't! That's the quickest way to get rid of me. I don't want to be in a home. I plan to die right here in my own house—with all three of my cats!" she says with such defiance we can tell she means it.

"It is a bit of a worry, Mom. What if you are outside walking the length of the swimming pool and you fall in?" I tread carefully.

"Well then, I'll swim to the shallow end and drag myself out."

"Well, what if you fall on the concrete and hurt your head?" I nudge ever so delicately.

"Well, then I got to die in my own home, didn't I?"

"Come on, Mom, we're just trying to think of ways to keep you around for a long time," I say, trying to soothe her.

"Oh, I'm not going anywhere. I'm only eighty-five. My mother lived to be a hundred, and I have no intention of dying before then!" she says while folding her arms firmly across her chest, indicating she has had the final word on the subject.

"Well, Mom, what about going to live with Sister Three? She always said she had that big bedroom for you." I probe gently because I know for a fact that she and Sister Three are on the outs, and no one besides the two of them knows why.

"Oh, I am not going to live with her. I am staying right here. I know every single square inch of this place. That's why I walk the entire house in the dark at night for an hour. I do it with my eyes closed so if I ever go completely blind from my macular degeneration, I can still get around, and I won't be an invalid. The fastest way to get rid of me is to kick me out of my own home!"

"She is fiercely independent—that's what the doctor says about her anyway," Brother One says while he pats her back and caresses her shoulder. She purrs next to him because this is how she has always typecast herself, and he knows how to stroke that ego.

"Well, Mom, you keep falling like this and you are going to end up getting me as your roommate!" I jest.

And there it is. A morsel on the table that is so delicious, she laps it right up like a starving dog that has just come upon a holiday turkey. In the fifteen seconds since it has floated from my mouth and hung in the air, she has devoured this idea to the bone. With her lips still whet with desire, she spits out the words, "Oh, now I love the sound of that. How soon can you be here?"

It's just that quick: another life-altering decision made in haste but not without good reason behind it. The most sickening part of this whole deal will be that this house, in all its great decline, will be mine to resurrect, and I will have to do it with the brother who was never anything but cruel beside me. The less sickening part is seeing the look on his face while my mother is squeezing the life out of me, cooing, "Oh, Steffie, you've made me so happy."

All he can say with a look of shock in his expression is, "Wow, I didn't even know this was an option."

We never make it to our shopping this afternoon. All of our energy is spent on getting reacquainted and planning the items we will tick off our to-do list when I return next weekend. Once my brother leaves, my mom and I have a long talk and agree that the house is in disrepair and that she too could use a little more caring for.

I break down the care of home and the care of her into three important categories: safety, health, and style. She has to be safe in her home. We need to get a health regimen in place regarding her diet, her personal care, and her med routine. My brother had to take over dispensing prescriptions ever since she nearly overdosed once while self-medicating. She just couldn't see the labels well enough to read dosages or pill names. And if we could do all of this while incorporating a little bit of style in her home, her wardrobe, and her grooming, then what would be the harm in that?

She agrees. To be more specific, she agrees to turn a blind eye to anything I feel needs to be thrown out after decades of nonuse, which is a huge change in mindset for her. She agrees to let me cut her hair an inch at a time. She agrees to be agreeable. (The details of what else she agrees to and the transformation that ensues in her and in her home, as well as the labor of love it takes, are laid bare in Part 2: Safe House and Part 3: Paring Down.)

For the entire two-hour drive back to my house, I sort my thoughts into categories that need to be dealt with: urgent details to prepare Mom's house for my arrival; urgent details to exit the life I have worked so hard to build; and, the most haunting, Thomas Wolfe's one liner—"you can never really go home again." All the lists I build in the coming days end with this foreboding whisper in my ear. And yet, when I finally resolve to tell my principal I need to quit, and he asks why I have to be the one to leave, and do I want to think it over for a while, the only answer I can give him is, "It is the only decision I can make. There is no other choice. I have to go."

And with this he swiftly pulls out his big reference book, a kind I have not seen in any library, and turns to the roster of schools in my mom's area. He asks me to point to the top five where I want to work. He calls each of my dream schools—the ones I know to have the best reputations—and talks me up with each of the principals. I am beyond grateful that he gives me this precious time because I know the kind of effort cold calling requires. And all of these principals I follow up with tell me they have never had an administrator go to such great lengths to secure a position for a teacher he is losing—they say I am obviously good, and that he would certainly feel the void in my absence.

In June, saying good-bye to the staff I teach with is harder than what I have mentally prepared for. Only six months earlier, my principal gave me a spot on the meeting agenda because I had a surprise announcement I wanted to make. I led up to the news by reminding my beloved middle school colleagues that they were in the business of making dreams come true, and that whenever there is someone who goes on to achieve remarkable success there is usually a teacher on that long path to be thanked.

And so I shared with them that my dream came true, and I pulled from a manila folder my first published novel, *Heroes Don't Always Wear Capes*, about the plight of a student saddled with horrible teachers save for the extraordinary few who became her heroes for life. My colleagues are so astonished and so elated for me that at once they collectively jump to their feet as if on cue from a conductor and give me the longest roaring standing ovation I have ever witnessed.

I cry right there on the spot, and then they follow me to my classroom after the meeting to buy their own copies from the stack still packed in the brown box that arrived on my doorstep yesterday. That will remain one of the top heartwarming experiences of my life. Now, when they learn I am leaving in June, they plan a good-bye party for me and make sure I have a generous gift card to the office supply store and a colorful new binder to organize something. They know me so well.

The other good-bye I need to say is to my boyfriend of five years. I adore him dearly, and still I cannot find a reason for us to get married because of the lingering "but." He is lovely, *but*. He is funny, *but*. He is supportive of me, *but*. He is great looking, *but*. The "but" always seems to fill me with indecision, so I will not allow us to pass "Go." But he is my friend, and he counts on me when he is in need, and I have counted on him when I have been in need as well.

This time is no different.

# PART 2

# Safe House

---

## REALITY 2
### *Fiercely Independent but Can't Cook, Drive, or Bathe*

---

## CHAPTER 5

# Help Wanted

The next weekend I return as promised. It is mid-March and I am still pondering my life-altering decision, and letting it seep in slowly while I take quick action on my bursting to-do list for attacking my mother's home-refurbishing needs. I figure a realistic goal is to renovate one room a month until I move home in June, when my school will let out.

Another reason that makes me the perfect candidate for being the one to take care of our mother is that I have gained a lot of experience cleaning up messes. One of my most insurmountable undertakings came from a community-service option a judge gave me for a moving violation ticket of the non-speeding sort. I was very willing to pay the hundred-dollar fine and perform the hours of service to keep my record spotless. So when I showed up to the court-appointed address of a women's shelter in a run-down neighborhood, I was pleasantly surprised by the white Victorian and how cute the inside was when I was given a tour.

I wondered how I would be spending my service hours there and thought maybe I would be doing room makeovers or giving baking lessons, since I can make a killer coffee cake. I asked if the kitchen cupboards had enough space to accommodate all of the donated items the director kept referring to, and I could tell by the twinkle in her eye that I had said something that was going to be hysterical to us both in about two minutes.

She walked me through the back door and across a narrow, gravel parking lot to a small cottage. She said this was where the donated items were dropped off. I immediately thought a small cottage would take me maybe four hours to organize, and I could do it on a Saturday morning and still have time to catch a movie matinee. Then we walked through the door and down the stairs to an underground warehouse running the length of an elementary-school field, and I realized this was the job the judge had in mind for me. Holy moly!

"Surprise!" the director said, and that was when she began to laugh hysterically. I was still trying to pick my jaw up from off the floor. What a catastrophe. Yes, they did receive generous donations, but the only items neatly tucked away on shelves were the canned goods. Everything else, from women's business clothes to toddler coats to pots and pans, shoes, curling irons, sleepwear, and toys, along with everything else one needed for living, had been shoved into piles that went all the way back. And like any dump site, the mounds just kept building on top of each other. There was only a narrow groove left that could be considered a walking path for a new mother joining the house to retrieve items she might want for herself and her kids.

"Our sponsors are generous, but what we really need is a system to inventory what we have so we can put out requests for what needs still need to be met," she said seriously and watched my expression to gauge if this is a commitment I was willing to see through or if I would be among those who flaked in the face of real work. "Don't worry about the canned goods on the shelves. We go through the groceries nightly, which is why they are at the front of this storeroom. I need you to organize the rest."

Whenever I hear the word *organize*, a little spark ignites within me, and I get lost in the vision of what a place can look like after I am finished. So I agreed, and I was not even the least bit reluctant about what I said yes to because I know I am task-oriented, and I am a finisher. I was only worried about rodents I might encounter because they like dark places where they can build nests, and that place was a rat family's dream.

For the next two weeks of my summer off, I showed up at 8:00 a.m. and worked until 5:00 p.m. every single day. I did more than my required twenty hours of community service because, again, I am task-oriented, and I inherited my father's work ethic; I won't leave a job undone—or done in anything other than the most superior way I know how.

By the time I was finished and I brought the director in to admire my work, I had created a grand showroom. I gave her the tour of what had once been just a dump site and was now something reimagined from Macy's bridal registry. The first aisle took the careful shopper along a wall of staged pots and pans, all sized to fit within each other, and if there wasn't a complete set then they were grouped together according to color scheme.

Like any smart kitchen, similar items were sorted together: wooden utensils stood united in a porcelain flour jar that was missing its lid; metal spatulas and wire whisks were grouped with twenty other gently used serving spoons to lounge inside a shallow pitcher that said "Lemonade."

I had used the wall space to hang more pots on wire mesh

secured from pothooks I had bought for a song. When space is limited, always build up vertically to make the room look larger and to access your things more easily even if you will have to use a step stool for out-of-reach items.

Along this same aisle to the left was a long zip line I used as a clothesline. Outfits were strung in sizes ranging from children's to teens' to adults', color-coded, with shirts hanging together according to sleeve length. Women's clothes were coordinated to show how loose scarves previously strewn about the floor could make a strong first impression if paired with certain outfits. This would make shopping easier for women who were coming out of very stressful situations where sometimes they left with only the clothes on their backs.

The next aisle to the left featured my best imitation of the shoe department at Nordstrom. Shoes were on display by color, then arranged by heel height, with purses and bags mixed in to create the best professional looks. Behind this, bath products were all together, with hotel soaps and shampoos each in their own sand pails filled to the brim. Hair products, from brushes to pink foam curlers to electric curling irons and straighteners, were all on a separate section of the shelf. Toothpaste, toothbrushes, and travel-size mouthwashes overflowed the glass fishbowls I had found buried beneath some toys. Diapers, toddler pull-ups and feminine products were all tucked separately into three broken suitcases that didn't zip anymore.

Even with the swaying lightbulbs hanging by strings from the rafters above, this place looked like a department store in which any respectable woman would be happy to shop. And that was exactly what the director said. She also said I had provided these women with a new sense of dignity because they could shop in a place that was thoughtfully prepared to meet all of their needs; they could feel like they were being respected and not relegated to digging through dump piles of some other person's trash to find items that would take them into their new lives. This was the best compliment I had ever received and the best way I could have worked off that ticket.

In addition to this job, there was one more nightmare project that landed in my lap, equally preparing me for the task of coming home to get my mother's house in order. It was the worst classroom I had ever inherited. It was filled with abandoned lesson plans and materials from five previous teachers. The only direction the administrators gave me was to throw whatever I didn't want into the hallway for the custodians to haul away.

It sounded so simple, but in hindsight this was a really lousy way to welcome the new teacher because it shouldn't have been my job to clear the room before I could set it up. I had to do it in the heat of the summer, in an upstairs room where the punishing sun beat against the windows—and I had to do it all without any air conditioning. I could only manage to suffer through ten minutes at a time before I felt as if I might suffocate in this closed chamber of heat.

Finally, after an entire week of this, the hallway was stuffed, and my room was done and looking beautiful. The point is I have gained a lot of experience tackling the jobs no one else wants when it comes to purging, sorting, and redecorating.

The first priority this weekend at my mom's is determining the money situation, and I have no way of knowing for sure what it is because the checkbook register lists only check numbers that have been written out, not the amounts. There are no duplicate receipts to determine outgo, so I have to call the bank, and luckily I find out there are sufficient funds in the account. I don't know what amounts have been written against this balance, so I decide to spend my own money until a few days can go by and I can reconcile her account. She assures me she will pay me back for anything I put on her tab that goes toward the house. So we go shopping.

Both bathrooms need attention, and so does the guest room with the little bud vase, which now holds a yellow rose to welcome me back for my second weekend. What I expect to be a fun trip to Bed Bath & Beyond starts off easily with a flurry of dialogue about ideas we have picked up from decorating shows and what she learned when she studied home economics in college. It's a beautiful day, a bit on the warm side though, and when we get to the store, we are happy to be inside where it is air-conditioned.

I am armed with my list of needs: for the guest room two sets of sheets, pillows, cases, a few decorative throw pillows, and a throw blanket, plus a bedside lamp for reading; for the kids' bath, I need towels, shower curtains, a bath mat, an area rug to go in front of the double sink, and storage baskets to hold the few good items that will survive the clear out in that oversized linen closet. I still need to inventory those shelves, but I have done enough reorganizing of houses and messes to know what necessities one must keep on hand in any home.

We are not in the store for more than a half hour because I know it like I know the back of my hand, and I don't like to meander while shopping. The hard part comes when we are waiting in line to check out, and I have two carts to manage in tandem while keeping my mother close because she is constantly looking for a place to sit down. This is not a department store where husbands usually find comfy wingback chairs waiting for them outside the women's dressing rooms. While we are standing in a deep line with other customers eager to get home to their own redecorating projects, my mom moseys over to the next checkout counter, where there is no line and no cashier, and decides to take a rest of a different kind since she can find no chair. She lays her torso across the rubber conveyor belt intended only to move towels and spatulas a distance of fourteen inches so the cashier doesn't need to stretch too far. Everyone in my line looks askance at my mother, whose primary concern is to make herself comfortable; only my cashier looks curious enough to wonder perhaps if she has had a stroke. I step out of my line to go to my mother and ask her if she's feeling all right, to which she replies only that she wants to lie down.

I fret about putting her in the car because it is so hot outside the heat coming through the windshield will only make her more uncomfortable, and I am mindful that elderly people suffer heat stroke easily. So, with my mother's elbow locked firmly within mine, and my two carts overstuffed with the complete list of items I needed to get two bathrooms and one guest room crossed off my to-do list today, I can only say to the cashier that I have to take my mother home and I am very sorry to abandon the items in these carts. And we leave.

I didn't feel I had the few extra minutes it would have taken to leave my mom in the car so I could check out. I have this overwhelming sense of urgency when it comes to addressing her needs because I don't know if she is just tired or if this is something worse. I do know about her falling episodes, and I do not want the next one to be in the Bed Bath & Beyond store. So my to-do list has to be put on hold until I can get my mom into bed and assess the situation.

Once we are safe at home where she can take a nap, I wrap

some ice in cool cloths and dab the back of her neck, since this is a pulse point that holds heat. She feels much better within minutes, and I feel more relaxed, so I venture back to the linen store to shop on my own. I find that I have to reload my entire two carts of contents because someone has already re-shelved my list within the half hour I have come and gone, and come again.

Finally I am home for a second time and motoring through the eleven trips it takes me to haul the oversized bags back and forth from the car to the house. I can see my mom has been awake and in the kitchen in the time I have been gone because I find a candy-bar wrapper sitting on the freshly cleaned counter along with a pot on the stove that has been boiling so long only vapors remain, making singeing hisses.

"Mom, are you awake?" I ask gently while standing over her.

"I hear you," she retorts without opening her eyes.

"Do you know you left a pot on the stove to boil and it has burned completely through?"

"I wanted some coffee." She is awaiting a scolding because this was my father's greatest fear that she would burn down the house by leaving the stove unattended during one of her naps.

"Well, that pot is a goner. Do you want me to make you some coffee now?"

But she decides she would rather sleep this time instead, and thanks me anyway. I make sure she is comfortable, and not too warm, and I open the sliding door that lets in enough of a breeze to prevent her from overheating. I make sure she knows that I will be down the hall in the back of the house paring down rooms if she needs anything.

For the rest of the day, until it is dark and we are hungry for dinner, I spend my time unloading the linen closet that takes up the space of a five-foot wall with floor-to-ceiling shelves. I fill half a dozen of the Hefty sacks with every single piece of cat-stained bedding I come across and save only the ten percent that is still salvageable. Behind more cat poo buried in the deepest part of the shelves in the way far back, I unearth dirty magazines that were never meant to see the light of day. I develop an even greater disdain for the family members whom I suspect owned these at one point, and not just for the sake of their trash, but for the extra burden they put on me to clean up their filthy messes.

It takes me only a couple of hours to excavate the linen closet and launder and fold the new towels. I bought white wicker baskets that are one foot high and nearly two feet deep. Their purpose is to prevent future cat nesting. I label one "Guests," as I expect there will be times when someone will need to stay with my mom so I can catch a break for a weekend. In this basket I put fresh towels and sheets, all in taupe to match the décor of the guest bedroom, which I will set up temporarily for me today to use while I commute for the next few months. Eventually I will gut my old childhood bedroom and move in there, but not yet.

I fill three more identical baskets with labels that read "Master," "Lemon Room," and "West Room" with the clean linens I just purchased, washed and folded. This way I know there will always be matching linens and towels for each of the bedrooms when they are ready for permanent living.

I label a final basket "First Aid" and fill it with essentials we might need if my mother ever does have a real emergency. I keep the heating pad and the hot water bottle I found in the closet and add a basic first aid kit, a sling, an Ace bandage, and two new digital thermometers. I include a jar of Icy Hot and a nice knit blanket for extra warmth if my mom ever gets the chills. There is also a thick sheet that could be used as a barf towel or, unfolded to its full width capacity, to help carry her if I need a stretcher of sorts. I saw that in a movie once, and I figure since I already have it on hand, it might be practical for later.

# CHAPTER 6

# The Awful Bath

My attention is diverted by a noise I hear from my mother's end of the hall. It is a rhythmic clanking upon glass, and I cannot place what could be making this sound. I peer around the corner of the bathroom and see straight into her bedroom, where her blankets are still smooth because she likes to sleep on top of the covers and only uses a down comforter to—well, comfort her. This way, her bed always looks made. Perhaps she figures it is one less chore she can feel victorious over having completed as soon as she awakes. Where is she, and what is she up to? I wonder.

I continue down the hall, around the corner into the open family room where I catch her sitting on the couch spooning Ragu from a jar. She is enjoying it fully, and now I have a better idea of how all those spaghetti sauce stains got splattered onto her old, blue robe.

"What are you doing, Mom?" I inquire nonchalantly.

"I got hungry, so I'm eating sauce," she says while trying to lick the remnants from the side of her cheek. I can tell by how well she navigates that tablespoon that this is not the first time she has wrestled the deep to get the last of the sauce out of the belly of the jar when one's wrist is too wide for its opening. Apparently, turning it upside down works every time.

"Well, do you want me to make you some spaghetti?" I ask.

"Oh, I'll eat when you eat," she offers. She is still focused on the last bit of sauce clinging to the sides of the jar as it travels its upside down path to the waiting hole that is her mouth.

"Mom, what did you make yourself for dinner this week?"

"Oh, I don't know. Pancakes, I guess." She gives me that wide, toothless grin of hers, then she smacks her lips together. "They're my favorite!"

I can't help but smile because she is so childlike in this instance. But soon she will remind me that she is every inch the matriarch in her own home.

"But, is there anything else you'd like to eat for dinner this week?" I ask. "I can get the groceries you'll need until I come back next weekend."

"Oh, I like my pancakes. It's hard to cook for one, but now that you'll soon be living here with me I am happy to pay for groceries if you will be the chef." The lilt in her voice tells me she is so excited by the idea that I am going to be her live-in help, and she can live in the manner she feels she should have always been accustomed to, with servants who will take short orders.

I also now know the answer to my earlier question of how much pasta one person can eat in a week as evidenced by the several empty jars that were stacked in the middle of the ant mess last weekend. There has been no cooking of pasta or anything else in this house except for pancakes. You should know what your parent is eating. Brother One has been dropping off grocery bags every Tuesday with her shopping list of Ragu,

Hershey bars, Dr. Pepper, a jar of olives, roast beef, limburger cheese, white bread, real butter, instant coffee, and salami. He doesn't cook. He stays for the ball game. It's his company that she desires most. It doesn't matter that she will later spoon-feed herself Ragu from a jar and call that dinner.

If someone is dropping off groceries, then who is actually overseeing the cooking? And who is making the grocery lists? Taste buds change. Convenience becomes tantamount. My mom doesn't cook anymore; who has wondered about any of this for the years I was away? Even Mrs. Hoover, the generous neighbor who takes her to the store because my mom doesn't drive, never thought to ask how meals were being prepared. I suppose it would be precarious to be the person who offers to look in on someone and then begins to wonder if the person is still fit to care for herself alone in a big house. I was at the front of discovering just how much elder neglect there was here. It seemed the care needed for both my mother and her home were being ignored.

Sister Two told me a funny story about a recent time when our mother went to church and couldn't see well enough to determine that her grey pencil is not what she had used that morning to darken her brows. It was instead the red lip liner that carved an arch and filled in their length so she had a sweeping expression of sheer madness crossing her forehead. Her closest friends had a good laugh with her in on the joke, and it did sound funny to even hear her tell the story again to me when I bring it up. But it just goes to show she needs a little help.

"Mom, I will run to the store to pick up some hot slices of meat loaf and mashed potatoes from the dinner bar. We can eat in twenty minutes. How does that sound to you?"

It takes nothing more than this to please her. She is so excited for a change of pace in her food, she is purring.

"And should we give you a bath before I go or after I get back?" I need to put it out there, and I figure she has to pick one. No bath is not an option—not on my watch.

"I bathed this morning. Maybe not the fancy way you do it, but I am clean," she says in a rather dignified tone. To her a bath consists of a washbasin that she carries from the kitchen sink to her bathroom counter and a cloth with some very mild soap. The soap needs to be stronger, and the bath needs to include some bristle brushes and lye shampoo. She is this dirty.

"Mom, I can smell you, and you stink," I say with a sweet smile and a twitching nose. "Let's get you fresh and pretty and into a nice, clean cotton nightie so you can be comfortable tonight." I coax her with everything I've got.

"Well, I might need some help getting into that tub. It is pretty deep, and my leg gives me trouble, so I don't think I can manage it by myself."

We have a deal struck. I agree to get the meat loaf first then tackle "the awful bath," as she puts it, after dinner.

Dinner is delicious, and I am so glad the grocery store is nearby and that it features a hot dinner bar for busy moms because I feel like I am one right now. My mom has a hearty appetite and even enjoys seconds. The mashed potatoes aren't quite as good as the ones she used to make, but they are hot, and stiff, and slathered in butter and gravy.

Once we've eaten and I have the kitchen cleaned, I have the job of scouring the bathtub, which has a few good cobwebs from the work of some talented spiders. The shower curtain is new, and I hang it from the spring rod I also bought today. There is a new bath mat so she won't slip when she gets out of the tub, and freshly washed, brand-new fluffy towels in a soft pink to wrap her in when she is clean. I even bought her a nice, quilted robe with easy front snaps so she can have a replacement for that tattered blue one she loves so much.

We have a plan, and it seems like a pretty good plan. It isn't as hard as I expected to get her to strip off her clothes and attempt to get into the dry tub. I figure I will fill it with the water while she is already seated because, knowing in advance that she has a stiff leg from too many falls, I want to prevent against a horrible bathroom accident from slipping in a tub of water.

I remind her that my whole goal is to maintain her dignity, and I try to keep her covered as much as possible with a towel as we each put one foot in a synchronized motion into the tub and be sure that we are firmly rooted before we even think about making a second move. Thank goodness there is already a handrail mounted on the tiled wall. Without it I don't know how I could have convinced her to trust that she will not fall. Slowly she lifts her leg over the tub to stand with her back against me. We did it. It is only slightly harrowing because I can tell she has not done this by herself, and I can see why. She is putting her complete faith and confidence in me that I will not let anything happen to her. I give her every assurance because I am as sure we are safe as I am surefooted.

Now, what comes next—the squat into the tub—is the only part of this plan I did not see coming. Instead of bending her knees to lower her center of gravity then bringing her bottom to the bottom of the tub and leaning slowly back toward me so I can position her comfortably against the neck pillow I bought for her long, leisurely soaks in a lye-filled tub, she suddenly aborts this plan while still standing and just falls back onto me in the way that someone fainting would, expecting to be caught. My knees buckle beneath her full weight, pinning me under her with a towel sandwiched between us. At least I am there to break her fall. She is fine but a little winded, and she never, ever wants to try this again. And neither do I. Good God, we are lucky she didn't break a hip—hers or mine.

It takes us a lingering moment to determine if we are both okay and to assess how we will get out of this confounded mess without a crane. If I were on top of her, I could easily—well, not without some difficulty in wrestling against her girth, but *more* easily prop her up and get her out of the tub. But I am trapped beneath her, cradling her between my legs as a couple would sit together in a romantic bath. Only this tub is not built for two, and I weigh at least seventy pounds less than she does, and she is sure she cannot manage to prop herself upright with her limited upper-body strength.

The word *conundrum* comes to mind here. So, I wriggle, and I think, and I wriggle some more, determined that I can unearth myself from her hold if I can swing my leg out over the tub, skimming the toilet, which is just too close, making this difficult to negotiate. I have successfully planted my left leg on the new, pink floor mat with a rubber underbelly that is supposed to securely hold it in place when I realize the rubber is mostly decorative, and it slips beneath me, causing me to lose my footing for only a frightful moment.

The bare floor is safer, but I now wish I had sterilized it a little better since my naked feet are touching it. Putting off until tomorrow what should be done today leaves one in undesirable situations such as this. I wriggle my right leg out from beneath my mom's midsection, where her right arm rests on my knee, and I manage to scooch her forward so I have room to move my foot behind her caboose and stand up on one leg like a flamingo until I am balanced and out of the tub. We both look at each other and nearly laugh, but we know that a bath must still be had, and plan A is not to be attempted again.

The next best thing I can propose is to try the shower head, but I am too petrified she will slip while standing. So, I decide to get one of the old, wooden child's chairs we used to sit on at the dinner table and see if it will fit in the tub; this way she can be seated while I give her a bath. However, the chair's feet are too wide to fit inside the tub, so I must think of another way. I find a wooden stool in the garage that has a narrow base but seems secure enough to try. Nope, it slips when the feet get wet. Out it goes. It will only be in hindsight that I realize I overlooked an obvious purchase: an industrial, nonslip rubber mat for inside the tub, the kind most hotels rely on to keep their patrons safe and their liability insurance costs down.

I think about patio furniture, and I find a simple lawn chair with rubber slats that will allow the water to rush through so we can clean all her parts. It is the right size and fits in the tub, and for now it seems like a pretty good solution. It doesn't work perfectly—she has to sit sidesaddle, which is not the ideal setup, but for tonight she has her bath. I suds her up twice with a really good sponge and wash her hair twice too. While she is clean and wrapped in a nice, warm towel that I had tumbling on low in the dryer the way she used to do for me when I was a child, I think now might be the perfect time to give her hair a trim.

"Mom, what do you think about styling your hair a bit and taking off some length?"

She looks askance at me as if I am going to lay her hair on the breadboard and hack it with an axe.

"I promise I will make it look pretty, and it will still be long enough for you to put up in a twist."

"What are you going to cut it with?"

"The sharpest thing you have. How about your sewing scissors? I have cut plenty of people's hair, and I even like to cut my own, so trust me, it will look good. You'll be happier with a little length off. It'll keep you cooler too." *Am I overselling it a bit?* I wonder.

She sits very still on the kid's chair I tried unsuccessfully to use in the shower, and we cut her hair inside her walk-in closet. She doesn't breathe, she doesn't move a muscle, and she stays like this for the complete three minutes it takes for me to lop off the four inches that needed removing. Her hair still falls past her shoulders, and she looks more youthful already. I blow it dry on the gentle setting, and she smushes her face into the warm air. I lay out her cotton, floral nightgown and offer her the new lavender, quilted robe I found on sale earlier today. Her face is leathery and in need of some good lotion, so I try my Oil of Olay on her, and she loves it. It takes a generous amount to soak into her skin, but she sure feels pampered.

"Mom, how about tomorrow we go get our nails done?"

Another squeal of delight, and she is finally in her element. I saw a nail salon near the grocery store when I picked up dinner earlier, so I hope they will be accommodating and compassionate for a first-time customer who is clearly overdue for some tender loving care.

It is getting to be so late, and today has been overly full. I feel like I accomplished so much, but my list is still very, very long. I decide the best way to manage my time is to take inventory of the mess in each room of the house, the exterior curb appeal including the exterior pool area, and that dreaded garage. I get a long, yellow legal tablet and create a page for each room with a dividing line down the middle. I write a "Need to Do" header on the left column and a "Need to Buy" header on the right column, leaving room for two more columns on the right labeled "EST" (standing for "estimated expense") and "ACT" (for "actual expense"). At the bottom, I make a box for the "Estimated Total Budget" and a box below that for "Actual Total Budget."

Furthermore I know it will be important to keep receipts in order to be transparent so everyone feels comfortable with the flow of the finances. So I do. I keep every single receipt and label each with a note about the purpose of the expense, then secure them with Scotch tape in a spiral notebook, numbering each receipt in chronological order. At the end of the month, I attach an Excel spreadsheet that does all of the math for how these expenses add up along with a receipt showing that my mother reimbursed the expenses accrued on my American Express card.

This is the system we agree to. My mom likes how she can run a tab, and I like that everything is accounted for in one statement. We never have any disputes over amounts in question or items purchased. Everything we buy for her home is a joint decision, and she signs all her own checks. This method also makes it a lot simpler for her checkbook accounting records.

I can also keep a running tally of how category expenses stack up month by month and determine how many months and years we can project out with our budget intact against what I know to be in the bank today. I know there are other small accounts that need to be liquidated, but it will require some work, and I will tackle them down the road. By the time my caregiving experience ends, I will have accumulated several shoeboxes of receipts, although I do not keep them in a shoebox, and I keep doing my due diligence taping them into multiple spiral notebooks.

My system keeps me transparent to anyone who wants to know about the income or outgo for the household. I make sure to share the numbers with my mom monthly, a chore I remember her shying away from whenever my dad tried to do this with her when I was very young. I want her to be educated and to share ownership in the process of how we spend her money. It makes a difference to her because she feels empowered and comfortable knowing what her finances are. There are no more surprise phone calls letting her know a payment has been missed or a utility is about to be shut off. She finally feels in control with someone to help her manage.

This is different from Brother One's method. Once he discovered a few bills went unpaid and a couple of accounts lost their good standing, he set up certain bills to be withdrawn electronically from her checking account on a monthly basis. Our mother does not have a computer, nor does she understand how electronic banking works, and she doesn't want to be involved because it is just easier to let him do it for her—out of sight, out of mind. She gave her power away. And when you are not involved in your money decisions, you need to trust that the person who is in your pocketbook will not end up robbing you blind.

This is a very precarious position to be in, especially for a senior citizen who can neither see well enough to record numbers in a check register nor hear well enough to listen to automated recordings trying to tell her which numbers to push in order to get her balance. It was too much for her to handle.

I am glad Brother One did what he could. But do I find some not-so-little discrepancies when I take over the accounting? Yep. Are they in my mother's favor? Nope. Do I bring it up? Yep. And let's just say that when people are caught red-handed with their fingers in the till, the response is always the same, some form of incredulous denial. Now that he knows that I know what went on when I finally do comb through her statements for the prior year, my relationship with Brother One becomes tentative at best, volatile at worst. But I am getting ahead of myself.

# CHAPTER 7

# The Fall

I can't believe I am still awake. It is so late for a non-night owl. And I am beyond tired, but my mom is catching her second wind and raring to talk some more. So, we sit in front of the television with the sound muted on one of her favorite PBS presentations of an aria sung by a famous opera singer I do not know by name.

"Sometimes it's much more interesting to look at the staging of a performance than to hear it," she says before admitting her secret desire to have been a producer. I am fine to close my eyes and rest while she welcomes in the night with the darkened sky.

I am not going to last much longer. The day itself has been one of Herculean accomplishments, and I am very pleased with what I have crossed off my to-do list, but I need the energy a good night's sleep will bring so I can get half as much done tomorrow before I drive back home so I can teach on Monday.

"Mom, I think it's time for us to hit the hay, and I think we've had a pretty good night after our adventures in the tub!"

"Oh, I'd say you're right about that. Ye-ow, that was no fun!"

"Okay, good night, Mom."

"Good night, cherub."

I make sure the front door is locked, and while I am turning out the lights in the kitchen, I hear a thud coupled with an ear-piercing scream

"Steffie! I've hurt myself!"

I am already sprinting when I hear the thud, and halfway down the hall before my mom finishes her sentence. When I see her, she is on the floor of her bedroom in a face plant, lying extremely still. The metal frame of her bed is exposed, so I logically assume she has misjudged the distance of her mattress with her poor eyesight and somehow hit her forehead as she fell to the floor. I ask if she can hear me, if she can see me, if anything is broken. Yes, yes, and no, not that we know of. I know every medical show says not to move the victim when she is injured, but I want to turn her face up, and gently, ever so gently, I slowly begin to roll her one centimeter at a time until her legs are stretched out in front of her, and I can cradle her head in the crook of my elbow as she rests on my lap.

I do not want to leave her. I can tell she is dying in my arms at this moment. Her entire left eye is swelling before me so rapidly she looks exactly like Rocky Balboa after he takes his final beating in the ring. Once he has won, he is calling for Adrian, and his face is an unrecognizable mass of purple flesh bulging over a marble-sized eyeball that is now forcibly closed shut because of all the bruising. If my mother had been hit on the side of the face with a baseball bat, it would have looked the same.

"Oh, Mom," I whisper in a hushed tone reserved only for a very grave instance when there is still so much to be said but no time to say it because this will be our last moment together.

"Oh, Steffie," she echoes with such a push, forcing out these two words with all the weight of the sentiment she intends for me to feel behind them. And then she says it: "I love you."

She looks up at my face longingly, as if she is my baby. She is vulnerable, and I am feeling the heaviness of this moment and my responsibility to her. There is not enough time to finish our conversations. We will not have the chance to move forward in our relationship. Tears begin welling up inside me, and I know now how much I truly do love her, and even though I have not quite come to terms with forgiveness, I really do not want her to die here in my arms. Her face is becoming more grotesque, and it is happening so quickly. I need to make some decisions if I am to save her.

"I love you, too, Mom." It is sincere and urgent, and the best I can manage because I have been newly thrust into this life where I have a mother once again. They are the right words that need to be said at this moment, and the feelings that are supposed to come with them are buried deep down beneath layers and layers of protective insulation. "Mom, does anything below your neck hurt?"

"Well, let me see." She pulls her left leg off the floor a little and challenges it to extend fully and then contract, to see if her knee will bend. So far so good. She does the same thing with her right leg, and still no signs of anything broken or paralyzed. She slowly pulls her left arm away from her and bends her elbow, and she can do the same with her right. Appendages are clear for takeoff.

"Mom, I think the most damage has been done to your head because you have a big bruise." I leave it at this because I don't want to scare her, and I don't know what kind of shock she might be in right now.

"Well, that wouldn't surprise me. I fell straight onto my cane."

That bamboo cane looked really cool hanging in our hallway coat closet when we were kids. But for an eighty-five-year-old to fall face-first against it from a standing position, its look is now more threatening as seen from the mark that has been made with its mighty strength. There are knots on the dense wood spread evenly every two inches. This cane has been in our family since the 1950s car accident when my dad was severely crushed after being hit head on by a drunk driver, who nearly killed him, leaving him in the hospital for the better part of a year to learn to walk again. And tonight this cane has mortally wounded my mother.

"Mom, we need to get to the emergency room. Do you think you can walk?"

"Well, there's only one way to find out. Let me do it by myself." She rolls onto her side and pulls her knees into herself while using her arms to gain leverage. She grabs on to the chair nearby and finally lifts herself up slowly. This is a rigorous, multistep, choreographed move that she has obviously rehearsed before when she has been in similar situations alone. She makes it up to the bed and onto her hindquarters, and says she doesn't feel bad.

"Did you get dizzy before you fell?"

"No, I didn't get dizzy. I never get dizzy. I tripped over that damn rug with my lazy toe that got caught in the loop." She is so maddened by this because it seems like such a ridiculous reason to land her in the emergency room late on a Saturday night.

"Are you sure? Your little toe is lazy, and it got caught in the loop on this rug? How do you know you have a lazy toe?"

I have never heard of a lazy toe, and I don't know if she is self-diagnosing or if this is a new term from Dr. Goodcare.

"I can't feel things in my little toe, and I couldn't feel that damn loop. I caught it just right for a perfect face-plant onto my cane, which happened to be in the perfect spot to disfigure me!" She always manages to keep her sense of humor intact. And thankfully for this, I am also less teary and feeling more confident that I can get her to the emergency room by myself, so we won't need to call an ambulance.

*Thank goodness she's had her bath* is the next thought running through my mind. I put on her robe and realize she has no cute slippers to go with it, so I find the walking shoes she has traveled all over the world with, and away we go, but very slowly, ever so cautiously.

We spend the night in the emergency room waiting to be seen by a doctor. I express every concern I have to the nurse. I am worried about internal bleeding, and I want to stay with my mother, and how long will it be before she can be seen, and she is eighty-five you know, and look at her eye.

The problem with trying to get admitted into an emergency room on a Saturday night is that all of the teenagers are there from doing drunken, stupid feats. However, in just a few short minutes, the nurse takes us back and I help my mom out of her comfortable robe into her new hospital gown, which we leave open in the back, and drape her quilted robe around her shoulders for warmth. She is in good enough spirits for someone who looks like she just took a good whack in the face. I still haven't let her look in the mirror. But she can feel the goose egg and knows it must not be very pretty because the swelling blocks her vision, allowing her to see only partially out of her left eye.

The nurse asks what kind of medications my mom is taking, and I have no idea because Brother One sets up her med tray every Tuesday when he comes over; he also orders the prescriptions when they run low. I look to my mom for the answers, and she rattles off a couple of names but is sure there are others she just can't think of right now, and she can't begin to tell me the dosage or strengths of these medications. The nurse makes sure I know to get this information together and to keep it in my purse for all future doctor appointments.

I will do just that, and later on I create a spreadsheet (see Part 2, Chapter 7: Prescriptions Chart in the Notes and Resources at the end of this book) that even her primary physician is impressed with. It's one of the first compliments he gives me, which says a lot coming from a gruff, old man. I love my little pill chart so much, I laminate several copies and keep one in my purse, one in my mom's purse in case she needs to show it to someone during the week when I am teaching, and another copy for Brother One to keep on hand in the event he has an emergency with her when I am not in town.

We are released within two hours, and my poor mother's eye really has suffered. We are so lucky she didn't break a hip. And I am so grateful she did not die. I feel like tonight has marked a new beginning for us because it forces us both to recognize how precious our time together will be. It also puts me into an even more urgent mindset about managing this time. I need to make her house safe for her, and the first step is getting rid of anything that has loops to catch lazy toes.

On Sunday morning, she sleeps and sleeps, and I am grateful to have some time alone to assess this house and safe-proof it the way a parent would for a new toddler. I walk through the house with my legal-sized tablet and, like an inspector, I scrutinize all of the hazards that are in our walking paths, and analyze what are the pieces of furniture that have sharp corners if she does fall again.

Starting in her room, the culprit rug that she tripped on last night gets rolled up right away. I will worry about how to cart it away later because today there is no more room in the garage, so I start a dump pile in the courtyard hidden from view. Aside from that there is too much poorly placed furniture in her room. When she wakes up, I will rearrange the pieces so the walking path has more flow and the tripping hazards are deleted.

The dining room has another identical looped rug, and this one takes quite a bit of my time to carry out. I grunt as I lift each end of the heavy, wooden table on top of it; I heave the head upward with my back like I am balancing a sack of rocks from a quarry while trying to push the rug toward the center with my feet so I can turn it and slide it out. This is not as easy as it sounds, but I manage, and once the rug is rolled up, I toss it too onto the dump pile out front.

In the family room, the marble-top coffee table and two matching end tables are a bloody forehead waiting to happen. These mid-century pieces have sharp, unforgiving corners, and the end tables are placed poorly in front of and on the side of the couch, blocking the traffic flow. I reckon that marble is a natural stone, so these should be able to weather the weather just fine outside, where I decide to place each with a set of lounge chairs so that it will actually look like we have usable pool space. I have to add lounge chairs to my list of things to buy when I am at Target next.

The actual moving of these granite slabs is so difficult for me, though, that I have to be more resourceful. I resort to using one of the old blankets that has been the least abused by cats to assist me in dragging the tables out. Positioning a blanket under all four legs makes heavy lifting very easy because it allows you to drag or pull instead of lift or push. Plus it cuts down on the noise of the tables scraping on the concrete pool area. I feel so much better about what I have been able to do already.

The flooring in this family room also has oversized area rugs trimmed in the same hazardous loops, so I know these are destined for the dump pile soon. However, I need replacements first and, most likely, a new couch, so I have to put this on hold for today. Thankfully the loops are flush against the wall and not a direct threat to lazy toes.

I rearrange the whole living room, after picking up more cat crap I find in a corner. I make a note on my legal pad to buy a much bigger litter box that will accommodate three grown cats, as I believe there are no bad pets, there are only bad pet owners. Clearly these cats don't like their tiny box, which is really big enough for only two small kittens.

The double set of built-in bookshelves makes the living room feel like an inviting library. My parents collected the classics since they were in college, and they remained avid readers. There is a lifetime sitting on these shelves. I scan the titles of hundreds of books they moved from place to place through the post-war decades. All I can wonder about is how long it will take me to sort through them once it comes time to sell this house.

When my mom wakes up, we are both fairly hungry, but there is not much food in the house and the pots and pans are in a junk pile covered in cobwebs beneath the stove. So we go out for breakfast, her favorite thing. Over pancakes and eggs, we talk about our three goals for the house.

I reiterate that first it has to be safe. My mom is happy with my rearrangement of the living room and says it makes so much more sense this way, she doesn't know why she didn't think of it herself. She can live without the looped rugs I have rolled up and removed for future carting away. And she is ready to say yes to a new couch, something splendid, and is open to seeing what kind of new area rugs we can find if they are not too unreasonably priced.

The next priority for the house has got to be health. This is where I fear it might get tricky, but I have to suggest new carpeting throughout the house because my mom cannot live in cat feces and urine. I think we can do better than that for her, and I suggest we go carpet shopping when I am in town the next weekend. She is quite amenable and very excited to decorate a new life for herself.

The final goal for the house is to incorporate some style. Again, this sounds like just the opportunity she has been waiting for—a chance to freshen up her household and get rid of things that have been bogging her down. I am so relieved and utterly surprised to hear this because while her house is not anything like those I have seen on hoarder shows, where you can barely traverse a path from the front door to the kitchen, I know she is a pack rat, and I know she grew up in the Depression era, when people were scrambling to keep hold of what little they had. So I was really prepared for more of a fight from her about inventorying the house and purging what has no purpose or meaning to her or to anyone inheriting anything from her.

I called Brother One this morning when I awoke to tell him about Mom's visit to the emergency room last night and to make sure he knows it was only because of tripping, not fainting, that she fell onto her cane. I did not want to be an alarmist, but I did not sugarcoat the fact that she got a pretty good shiner out of it, and that was putting it mildly. He used to play ball, so he understands that even the worst facial injuries will heal in time. I was also sure to ask him how he wanted me to notify him if there were any future emergencies. Should I call in the middle of the night from the hospital or call in the morning? He said if Mom's dying to call in the middle of the night; otherwise morning is fine.

As if on cue, when we return home from breakfast Brother One is already at the house, just about to let himself in by rounding the two back gates that should have locks on them to prevent burglaries. This reminds me to make another note on my legal pad about security and house locks.

He is so jovial, it is hard for me to remember why I dislike him so much. So I try to scroll through my memory bank for tarnished images of some of the worst things he did in his youth that pained our family tremendously, and yes, there it is—I can feel the familiar groove of that bitter pill lodged comfortably in my throat once again. I just don't want to be associated with him. And the slithering smile, complete with dimples, that he has used to charm his way through life registers something altogether different for me in a gut-check. He has always been a taker, self-serving at the expense of others.

But I am willing to carve out a new thought in my brain that says no one wants to be judged for their childhood when they are living up to their potential in adulthood. Maybe he really has changed.

"Hi, Sis. How's it going, Mom?" He pulls up a chair and reaches for the remote. He has convinced my mother that she loves baseball; he even took her to a game at the stadium on the bay where, unfortunately, she was so unbearably cold she couldn't wait to get home.

"So you wrestled with your cane, and the cane won, eh, Mom?" He is trying to bring levity to the little purple face we see in front of us.

"If I didn't need that cane so badly, I'd let you chop it up into kindling for the fire," she says half-heartedly.

"Mom and I were just talking about getting some new carpeting since the animals have pretty much destroyed the house, and she can't live with filthy cat crap everywhere. It's just unsanitary."

"I know a guy from my AA meetings who owns a carpet store nearby. I am sure he'd be happy to help you out, and he may even give you a discount. We try to take care of each other's families when we can do something. It's our AA way." Brother One is quite happy to make a contribution to the redecorating effort, and supplying the name is a good start. I hope this is a trustworthy person.

"Well, we're going carpet shopping Saturday when I come back, so I'll set something up with Malcolm for then." I thank him for the name and leave him and my mom to their bonding time. "Oh, I almost forgot, do you have any suggestions for how I can get rid of the garbage piles I am starting? Do you want to take them to the dump?"

But he has an even better idea. "There is a guy named Pip who I have used for years every time we move. He owns a hauling business and I've got his number. His rates are reasonable. He will take away whatever you need hauled usually within the same day you call."

Now this sounds like a handy suggestion—one I will be able to use. I leave them to their bonding while I plot in the garage just how much I can actually get together for the first dump load on Saturday.

March culminates in laying plans for the next eleven weeks

before school will be out and I will move back home. It still sounds like I have failed at something every time I utter that phrase: *move back home.* So when saying good-bye to my neighbors, I am sure to include the important detail that I need to take care of my mother because she cannot be alone in her big house anymore.

Invariably people ask a litany of questions: Is she sick? What kind of disease does she have? How old is she? And I feel so sheepish when I tell them she only falls from time to time. But it's the potential of what could happen if she falls and breaks a hip and no one finds her for days. I just don't think people appreciate the degree to which worry and dread play parts in making life-altering decisions.

PART 3

# PARING DOWN

---

## REALITY 3
### *Getting Your Physical Home and Your Financial House in Order*

---

# CHAPTER 8

# Keep, Toss, Donate

I have come home now every weekend since that first visit in early March to spend the rest of the month formulating the plans for what the house actually needs. Now in mid-April, we are able to get the ball rolling on one major exterior transformation. The only request I have is to put up a fence in the front yard to protect my dog, Daisy, from getting hit by one of the neighbors whipping around our prominent corner house.

Daisy is a little black lab who thinks she can outrun anything. I've only seen her chase a car once, and that was enough for me. She is the only dog I've ever owned, and what I have discovered about her is that she doesn't think of herself as anything other than human little girl. She is very pretty, demure at times, and beyond cute when she covers her face with her paw because she still wants to nap. She is also quite excited to greet anyone who comes to my house with a proper face-licking.

She has figured out that if she stands on the arm of the couch positioned by the front door, she has the advantage of becoming full height and meeting her unsuspecting guest at eye level. The next step is really a true test of friendship because with great gusto, she will then proceed to doggedly hold the hostage—rather the guest—in place by straddling the person with her two front paws firmly planted on their shoulders while kissing them hello with her big, wet tongue sprawling all over their face for what can be a few rather thrilling minutes.

The friends who are dog lovers tend to laugh so hard they make the unfortunate mistake of opening their mouths to let out their guffaws, which Daisy will take as her cue to clean their teeth too. I have been on the receiving end of this myself many times, and I will say it never gets old. There is something hysterical about a dog who is either so happy to see you she wants to shower you with this kind of affection or so fastidious she wants to clean you properly before you enter her home.

Brother One feels he knows the construction industry well enough that he can spearhead the outsourcing of putting in a wrought-iron fence and creating a more modern elevated brick curbing around the dead grass, which would be resodded, to make the whole yard look gorgeous. I can't grasp the vision, so we drive around the old neighborhood and find a few homes that have done just this, and yes, they look nice, but their properties are much smaller, so I am pretty sure when it's all done, our changes will have a much more grandiose effect. Pretty soon, within the first summer I am home, the ugliest house in the neighborhood becomes the prettiest one on the block because of this curb appeal work. Looking ahead, it would only take me five years to get the inside to match. The time line is about right for having the yard finished before I move back home, and it feels like Brother One and I are forging a bond at last through working on this house together.

In all actuality, *bond* might be too hopeful a word. Simply put, we are not getting in each other's way. He oversees the outdoor projects. I take care of all the indoor needs. There are twelve interior rooms, plus the garage, plus the four exterior areas bordering the house that have problems in each and every zone. It will take me many weekends to overhaul my mother's home so it can be fit for her to live in within what I presume would be the base-level minimum of any health inspector's standards.

When I say I finish the kids' bathroom in March, what this really means is that it is now sterilized and purged of unnecessary items that were stowed and abandoned for decades. However, this bathroom is still a far cry from being styled. The outdated wallpaper has begun peeling away from different corners of the walls, and my fingers are itching to see how much I can tear down if I give it a good, hard tug. I am not ready for this kind of project yet for fear that it might turn out to be like my friend's experience when tugging, yanking, and spraying could not conquer stubborn paper that was cemented down.

In order to do an effective clear out of any room, it is important first to establish a zone for housing items being removed. Any professional organizer will tell you that at least three staging areas are mandatory: Keep, Toss, Donate. You can also add in a designated area for items to Sell, or you might decide you have enough good stuff to Regift. One of the best shows I've ever seen on how to de-clutter any hoarder's house was called *Clean Sweep* on TLC with host Peter Walsh, who has since gone on to acclaimed fame, earning a rightful place in *O, The Oprah Magazine* with quarterly features. If you like makeovers of any kind, you would have enjoyed watching him get tough on hoarders who still couldn't find reasons why they need to purge twenty of their twenty-two collectible rooster-themed cookie jars.

Peter would set out three sheets on the lawn, or front patio, or any place there was space, designating each area for one of three priorities: Keep, Toss, Sell. When the hoarders saw that their Toss piles were microscopically small compared to their Keep piles, Peter intervened, doing ten-minute psychological, brass-tacks sit-downs to figure out what the root of the issue was and what the stuff symbolized and took place of emotionally. There is my shout-out to Peter Walsh, and I recommend reading whatever he has written if you need further guidance beyond what I can share from my personal experience here.

Additionally, whatever categories you deem necessary beyond the first top three will be determined as your needs change. Depending on the project, for instance, when I am organizing bundles of paperwork with no sorting system in place, my categories change to Shred, File, and Action. But managing paperwork will be covered a little bit later in this chapter.

My go-to zone for bedroom clear outs is, ideally, the garage. However, our garage is still in need of clearing out itself before I can establish any zoning areas within its confines. After calling the hauling guy, Pip, who Brother One recommends, I have a pick-up time set for tomorrow, which gives me today to corral whatever I can to create some order in the garage.

This two-car space is fully enclosed, with a floor-to-ceiling, built-in storage unit dividing it in the center. It boasts plenty of open shelving alternating with closet doors all the way down its length. A car used to be parked on the west side, but that hasn't been possible in many years. The east side has always been reserved as a laundry station with an additional workbench.

I start with the easy and the obvious. Anything that looks like an upright gardening tool will be gathered and stowed standing in one of the unused aluminum garbage cans stashed in a corner taking up valuable space. I find a perfect cutaway within the built-in that will accommodate this barrel. I use all my might to twist and shove it tightly into place, denting it just a bit on one side to get it to fit.

Any electrical tool that looks rusty or broken goes outside in the courtyard where our wooden fort used to stand. This pile is out of view of any passersby, and it begins to grow with each passing hour. I do not find enough junk that has any potential, in my mind, of earning money at a garage sale, so anything that can be used by someone else is going to be donated. For instance, my mom gave up driving several years ago, and with no more car to maintain I am pretty sure she doesn't need the turtle wax or the special chamois towels that are needed for drying the windows before water spots set in.

Anything else that looks like sports equipment from Little League days is dropped into the zone for donations. Old nuts and bolts, collected and sorted into coffee cans, go onto the Toss pile that Pip will haul away tomorrow. Rusty wrenches and a plethora of screwdrivers are also tossed. Once I sort through the won't-ever-be-used-again items, I start to unearth the memory-lane items belonging to different members of the family. I feel a great responsibility for these because I do not wish to rob anyone of his or her childhood memories. I plan to preserve everything I can, but I quickly discover this garage is housing enough memorabilia to drown all of us in a river of cascading junk.

I sift through old yearbooks, and trophies, and college papers that belonged to both of my parents. I rifle through our baby clothes that have yellowed with the good intention of being saved for our own children. Letters that were written home during our years away and cans of dried-up paint remind me of a father who stayed on top of things, including home projects and the progress of his children. I envision exactly what it will take to transition the garage from the disaster zone it is into a thoughtful center containing all of the memories that made their way into the Keep pile. I have heaved enough bulk to the courtyard dump pile, which frees up enough floor space for me to push a broom around.

It is only a matter of a quick run back to Target and Staples for storage crates and office supplies. It's important to note that you can waste a lot of money purchasing storage containers before you actually itemize the inventory that needs to be contained. So, just be patient enough with the process to sort first, then purge. Once you are left with the items that need to be kept, eyeball the amount of volume you have to contain. Be sure to estimate the space where it is to be stored so that you have the right dimensions when buying storage products to ensure a proper fit in your space. Once you have all of this figured out, then you can go on the hunt to find the containers to house it all.

After doing all of this, I decide I need oversized tubs for each child in the family and that these tubs need to accommodate not just what I find today but what I anticipate finding in the other four bedrooms currently being used as attics. Ergo, storage tubs with room to grow. For the sensitive documents my mother evidently emptied from safe-deposit boxes after my father's death, I will need some kind of colored plastic pouches to seal them in.

Do not leave out in the open important identity papers such as Social Security cards, school records, juvenile delinquent reports, awards, acceptance letters, and the ever-popular letters of rebuke or encouragement, depending on the recipient and the scenario said child got himself or herself into, written in triplicate so there was a copy for Mother, child, and Mother's friend who would share in commiseration. I already burned all of the copies I found having to do with me. The ones filled with condemnations designated for other siblings will be forwarded so they can review their own letters of heartache privately.

I buy five grey tubs on wheels—they are forty-five-gallon totes measuring thirty-seven inches long and twenty-seven inches high. I write one sibling's first name in all caps across the front of each tub and then line them up beneath the built-in shelves that start midway up the wall.

In the gap of space beneath the shelves, I can easily stack a trifold board lying flat on each of the sibling buckets for the purpose of holding our artwork from kindergarten. The indiscernible blobs of blue and pink paints that are probably the makings of flowers have all been saved by loving parents who wanted to freeze us in time and keep us with them for longer than the good years of our childhood would last.

The final purchase to preserve those important papers I found earlier is a colored document pouch with a plastic zipper across the top accommodating any paper measuring the standard eight and a half by eleven inches. Anything I find like floppy discs or small electronics can also fit inside, and this avoids the hazards of losing loose items that can disappear into crevices of large drawers and end up getting thrown out with bundles of old clothes.

With these three items—oversized tub, trifold cardboard, and zippered pouch—I am on my way to having a good sorting system in place for the siblings when the time does come that they want to go through and evacuate their personal belongings. It also makes my future sorting go much more quickly because when there is a dedicated place for everything, it is absolutely easier to find what you are looking for within a minute.

Old luggage and picnic coolers that are no longer needed and can't be identified by Brother One as anything he is storing for his family make their way into the Donation pile. I cannot focus any more of my limited time today on the garage, and I know I can not do the rest without some help, so until another day the garage is done enough.

The guest bedroom I am using until I can tackle my old bedroom next door needs immediate attention. The bedding has been arranged for temporary comfort. The room and its striped wallpaper of satin taupe and ivory, which were thoughtfully picked out by my mother so my father would have a soothing environment to rest in, still seem fresh. Outside of the clutter of all the extra furniture, there is a lot of potential for a pretty little guest room here.

This is the room where my dad would record his words of wisdom for posterity, and I am so grateful he started this project when he did because within a year and a half of his beginning it, there was no more Father left to record. But here sits all of the electronic equipment he used for his whole lifetime. The layers of dust that have built up on the clear encasement of the portable stereo remind me of dusty minivan windows with crooked lettering written by a tiny child's fingers that says, "Wash Me." The albums of music, from classic Beethoven to *Big Band Sounds* by Glenn Miller, were often playing on low whenever my father drifted off for afternoon naps in the years when he was slowing down. Dry readings in a documentary format of the fighting that went on in the Pacific during World War II were part of his quiet reflections as well. At times I would see him dab his eyes when I would ask what he was listening to.

"The battles of Okinawa are hard to describe," he would say, "but I still have awful memories of how wretched man can be during times of war."

My beloved, old Cinderella album is still here along with some Elvis Presley vinyl. There is enough old music to stuff into two bankers boxes, and with this chore done, I immediately start a new spot in the garage on the shelf space I have just cleared, and I reserve this for "Errands." I know there are many charities willing to send their own drivers to pick up whatever I have to donate that is in good condition, but I am pretty sure I will need to do the legwork to find a store that still trades LPs like these gems. I label the box "Donations."

Labels and signs become my way. Color-coding becomes my other way. It seems natural to divide the shelving into three sections: "Errands" to do at my leisure when I am headed in a particular direction in town; "Short-Term" for projects that need attention within the next two months; and "Long-Term" for projects, like sorting my parents' loose college photos into an album, that can be done way down the road. Every bankers box to hit that shelf is labeled on the outside as to what the project contents are inside. The more vague your titles are, the less likely you are to remember what was so important you decided to box it for future, probably never to return to it again.

For pieces of life that are worth remembering, be sure to safeguard them in one box—not twenty different ones, but one box large enough so that when you are in transition again after your parent passes, the box can easily come with you and you'll have a good idea of how to tackle what is inside when you are ready to pull off the lid. Concrete, short titles on a label that sticks to the outside will be your saving grace later.

Now that the garage is in starting position for becoming a sorting center for the remnants found in the other rooms of the house, I can start the real purging. The rest of the furniture in the guest room probably contributed very little to making my father feel more comfortable in his surroundings. They were overflow pieces that didn't fit anywhere else in the house, but there was no place else to put them, so they landed here.

The long, mid-century credenza with a built-in stereo that hasn't worked for many years is on its way out. Even if I use it for its tabletop alone, it is still not worth the space it eats up. So, this behemoth joins the albums in the garage that have also outgrown their purpose in a modern age where everything seems to be shrinking. Two more captain chairs that were removed from the dining room table will be moved to the living room, which can more easily accommodate single chairs.

The old table that has a drop leaf on either side will stay, as it brings back memories of little fingers being pinched every time I volunteered to climb beneath its legs to help with the rickety extension of the stubborn springs. This table will fit perfectly in the corner, and now I have a place for my little television to sit.

The even older cedar hope chest that my mother's grandfather built more than 150 years ago will definitely stay, and it will be one more thing I eventually promise to handle with great care and never let anything happen to. It rolls, thankfully, so all the contents inside do not need to be inventoried today. I sit on the floor and push it across the room with my feet to its new position at the foot of the bed. Across its lid I lay a pine-green chenille throw and pull one of the books from the shelves in the living room that has a matching green jacket with a title any guest might enjoy reading before bed: *An Incomplete Education*, complete with encyclopedic anecdotes on every subject imaginable.

A tall bedside table lamp with a glass tray encircling the golden rod pierced through its center is borrowed from my old bedroom next door. Its modest table holds the requisite items needed in any guest room: an alarm clock that glows in the dark, a glass of water with a decanter, and, of course, a bud vase with a beautiful flower awaiting your arrival.

The bedding I am bringing from home will work well in this room with its golden hue complementing the satin walls. The shams to match, along with the extra throw pillows incorporating earth tones, will make this room inviting for the next person we invite to stay over after I reclaim my old room next door once again. The closet is also filled with clothes my mother has bought and never worn, as evidenced by the price tags still hanging on the sleeves. I carry all of these back to her master-bedroom closet in two sweeping armfuls. It is obvious that I need to reinvent a system for her wardrobe because her walk-in is completely overstuffed.

With what she still has hanging in closets in the hall, plus two other bedrooms brimming with her seasonal wardrobes, I suspect she has been self-soothing through shopping ever since my father's demise. Every anniversary has been spent making commemorative trips to the mall, marking the occasion for the department store's sale, not actually the date of my father's death.

With the kids' bath already behind me, and the guest room now off today's to-do list, my tally of two rooms down, ten more to go still seems daunting.

# CHAPTER 9

# My Old Room

Before Pip arrives tomorrow to haul away all the garbage and junk, I need to do a clean sweep of the pool patio because there are a hundred broken clay pots that are overgrown with weeds, and I really want this first pick-up pile to count. This is not a modest area of space since the patio runs the entire length of the house. If we ever did fill in the pool, there would be enough terrain to build four generous bedrooms to create a back house and still have a nice, open atrium sandwiched between it and the main house.

The best way to navigate my way through these mounds of botany experiments is to get out the old, rusty wheelbarrow, which used to be a friend to me in races against siblings on their tricycles. I could push anyone who wanted a free ride, and we could still make it across the finish line faster than any rider on that one three-wheeled bike. Now I load the wheelbarrow with pot after pot and wish I had gardening gloves like Martha Stewart to protect my hands from being muddied and cut. After two solid hours of work, I am starving, and my mother thinks cold cuts sounds pretty good. A trip to the store for a late lunch and plans for a light dinner of Chinese delivery again mean I can continue working for a few more hours before it is bath time for my mom and, finally, bedtime for us both. While I am at the store, I do happen to find the cutest pair of gardening gloves trimmed in a vibrant lemon yellow with a pattern of tiny daisies on a white background covering the hands and fingers.

"You work so hard," my mom says to me while we are eating our homemade sandwiches of turkey and roast beef deli meat. "It feels so good to get all of this junk out of the house. I have been working at it for years," she says in all earnestness.

*Working at creating more of a mess* is what I am thinking, but I am just so appreciative that she is willing to turn a blind eye and trust that I am taking care of the house the way a house should be taken care of.

"Well, I know you will feel so much better when you have surroundings you can breathe in with less clutter and be free from tripping hazards too," I say, pulling a cobweb from my hair.

I look at my ragged fingernails, and I look at her ragged fingernails, and I remember that we never did make it to our beauty appointment after the excitement of last weekend's emergency room visit.

"Hey, Mom, do you want to go to the beauty parlor tomorrow to get our nails done? Toes too, my treat?"

She coos at this suggestion, mostly because I will be paying, but we have a mother-daughter date, and I know she will feel wonderful after getting the pampering she is in sore need of. Now, with a lunch mess I can quickly toss out and a kitchen that is still free of ants, I am free to continue my work, and my mother is off for her afternoon nap.

The challenge of getting my old bedroom in good order has left me frozen in my tracks. I am tired. Looking at everything in front of me, there is just more to tackle in this room than I have the energy for today, so I decide a nap sounds like a pretty good idea for me too. I go to my little guest room, which still smells like dust despite the open window. I put my head down on the pillow I brought with me from home and feel my bones ache from the feverish pace of today's tasks.

I close my eyes, but sleep does not come easily because the list of all that needs to be done before I move in keeps running through my head, and time is running out. April is flying by. I still need to get my taxes done within the next week. Then there is spring break, which means we are behind because we should already be scheduled to lay new carpet that week, but we didn't get to the carpet store today since I needed to get ready for the hauling guy who is coming tomorrow. After doing the taxes, I need to start putting together my résumé so I can be prepared to interview before the school year ends.

I muse about how great it would be to take the year off from teaching to really get a grip on this house and enjoy some time with my mom, but I know the siblings will think I am freeloading, and I am nervous about the pitfalls of being without gainful employment in the fall. So, I ration, since I am going to miss out on a few weekends before June and time is what I am desperate to have more of, I get out of bed after a mere five minutes.

Standing in my old doorway, I see so much potential for a gorgeous, grownup room. But the path from here to there is layered with a hoarder's haven of laundry piles and paperwork stacks. The hardest items to throw away are the precious possessions that have been soiled by cat residue; my favorite butterfly blanket is without hope of rescue and becomes the first of many recovered items that must be piled into the Hefty sack for Pip's haul away. I continue sifting through to see what is salvageable, and even if the cats haven't destroyed some things, the time warp has. Loud, floral-patterned blouses that were fashionable in the '70s are probably not coming back in style, and by the time they might, no one in this house will fit into the ones here on this floor. Out they go.

This is the problem of holding on to things that might someday be en vogue. Either wear it now and enjoy it or send it on to someone else today. If you are the kind of person who is still trying to lose the same five pounds so you can fit into those pants at the bottom of the heap, it is more likely that those five pounds have amassed to fifty, and if you do finally lose them, just go out and reward yourself with a new trendy pair of jeans.

I don't know how many different sizes of clothes are in my old room or exactly how many people these clothes have belonged to, but the collection is worse than what you would expect to find at a church rummage sale, and I don't have the energy to sort and fold the outfits we all wore in the last century. The ruined ones go into the dump pile for Pip; everything else will go into my growing donation pile.

The trundle bed that used to belong to a sweet little girl—whom I vaguely recall as the sister I shared a room with for a few short years until she became a tragic figure in her own drama and moved out before she could be kicked out—finally meets the same fate. This is one heavy bed, so I lug it out in pieces. First, the old spring mattress makes its way across the hall, through the bathroom, and out the back door. Then the bed frame is easy enough to shimmy between doorjambs until it too is resting on the dump pile.

The hardest part about moving this trundle is the popup spring that keeps popping up when I try to turn it on its side so I can slide it across the floor and out the door. It is mechanically impossible for me to keep it closed, and I am spending more time wrestling with this dastardly piece of furniture than it took for me to say good-bye to three decades' worth of wardrobes only an hour ago.

I wonder if there is rope in the garage to tie the spring down. Nope. Is there a tie in my father's den to hold the clasp together? Nope. Is there a fabric belt from one of my mother's blousy tops that just got discarded? Yes. After some digging through old clothes soiled by cat crap while thankfully wearing my new Martha Stewart-lookalike gardening gloves, I find some sashes of silk and tie on the spring guard, then finally move that hulking bed to the dump. As much as I love the immediate gratification of clearing a room full of junk, there is something equally satisfying to my heart that comes from dismantling my childhood, keeping only the pieces that bring me memories of joy, which total only a select few.

After emptying most of the furniture from this bedroom, I start to imagine the useable space that can be turned into a gorgeous junior suite. The card table is wobbly and at this point just another unnecessary piece of history that no one wants to hold on to. It makes its way to the donation pile because I can't bear to put it in the dump. The white bookcase makes a fine addition to the laundry side of the garage where I will store backup supplies of detergent and the tackle boxes reserved for my eldest nephews, who were my father's fishing buddies from the time they were toddlers.

With the first half of the room picked up, the second half is still drowning in bundles of financial statements. Pieces of mail are stacked tower high or stuffed into the four drawers of a dresser that is four feet tall, but its seven-foot length makes it unwieldy to extricate from where it has been wedged. The other trick will be getting it through the doorframe and down the long hall, where it will need to turn on a dime around a narrow corner to travel the remainder of the house. Once it makes its way through the open floor plan, it will carve a path to the garage where it will survive because of its useful storage drawers. I am convinced that if it made it in, it can make it out. I also know my limits, and they tell me that more than one person put this in place. The dread of moving this dresser will have to be shared when I have at least two other people to help. So it sits, the last remaining item in this bedroom clear-out.

The tall bookcase in the corner, hovering in front of the shuttered windows, is full of the same sorting system seen throughout the house. There are bundled envelopes from years gone by, stuffed inside shoeboxes this time and stacked upon each other on all five shelves. I decide the fastest way to clear this room of the paper nightmare is to separate the mail by dates.

The good thing about my mom's system is that I can find some logic in it. I can tell it was important to her to at least open every statement to see what she owed or what the balance in the bank account showed because she recorded these amounts on the fronts of all the envelopes and then restuffed them with the original statements. She would also write the months and the years next to the amounts.

It is easy enough for me to track spending through the past years, but it is the more recent months I am most interested in reviewing. An entire month's statements are bound together and stored in one box. I don't actually know if they have been handled prior to filing or just hidden away as if they could simply take care of themselves. At least the house is already paid for, so we don't have to worry about her losing the only place she has to live. I can just picture my mother toiling away at the rickety card table, trying with her failing eyesight to record amounts and dates in her best handwriting. It is all she can think to do in order to keep an accounting system of some type. Why hadn't anyone seen this mess for what it was—a cry for help.

Anything within the past twelve months goes into my bankers box marked "Action-Statements-Current Year," with each word written on its own line in all caps on a sticky label. Until I know which accounts are active and in good standing, or active and not in good standing because they are either delinquent or awaiting a response from my mom, I need to have easy access to these to review their ninety-day history before I can establish a good filing system.

Any other bundles I find that are dated from the last year or earlier will be filed accordingly into three other bankers boxes labeled "Archives-Statements-Prior Years 1-5," "Archive-Statements-Prior Years 6-10," and "Archive-Statements-Prior Years 11-13" (insert your own years, of course; for instance if you are in the year 2040, then your box will read "Prior Years 2039-2035"). This takes my mom's assortment of financial statements and bills back to thirteen years ago, when my dad passed away.

I realize quickly that I do not have enough bankers boxes here, so I drive back to the office supply store to pick up twenty more because I am sure they will be needed when my scavenger hunt to find all the mail in the house is finally complete. Just as a side note, I do not recommend bankers boxes for permanent storage because they will not weather water damage or rodent intrusions. Even though we have neither today, there is evidence that we have had both in the past, so use only plastic crates with secure-latching lids to store anything long-term.

Once the bookcase is emptied and the labels are on the bankers boxes, I start a corner in the garage that has been newly swept, designating it for paperwork that needs to be sorted, and the towering of boxes begins.

I am pretty sure it will be okay to shred documents from thirteen years ago without losing any critical information, but I need to see the history of accounts at different financial institutions because I only know about one account, and I am sure there are others. My father was a whiz at planning his financial future, which meant diversification. And he did it without a broker, so there is no one else but me to piece together the paper trails for accounts at institutions that have changed hands and names over the decades. The challenge in reading old statements is distinguishing between identical amounts. For example, $5,700 appears on two differently named financial statements. Do we have two separate accounts with $5,700, or do we have only one asset in this amount, which was renamed by another financial institution in a company takeover years after it was established?

I like to be informed, and it will help me to know I have covered all of my bases if I can sleuth through all the financial papers in this house. By the time this entire process is finished, I will have amassed enough loosely stored papers to fill eight-five towering boxes tucked into a narrow corner of the garage. I need to follow the money trail to uncover what assets my mother has, and I need to find her tax returns, which will tell me everything else I need to know.

I know Brother One has started online banking for some

of her household accounts. But there are credit card mysteries glaring me in the face. I still don't know why a particular 1-800 business has recurring charges on her MasterCard for products she receives but says she never ordered and does not wish to keep. There is a suspicious pattern appearing quarterly from what I can glean, but this is going to have to wait until I can go over her finances with a fine-toothed comb when I move here in June.

Be awfully careful to not throw away any financial papers until you are absolutely clear you understand what they mean to the financial picture. I cannot stress this enough. I found money in places disguised as junk and could have unwittingly tossed the whole pile if I weren't paying closer attention—which is precisely why it took me so many days to weed through approximately two hundred empty checkbook boxes. The third one I haphazardly un-lidded was stuffed with cash. Once I realized this was a popular hiding spot for seniors, I had to open every single empty carton just to be sure our entire inheritance wasn't hidden within. Unfortunately, I didn't find more than $50, but I was in no position to know for certain.

Do your due diligence. Take the time it takes to sort through your mess without being hasty even though you feel overwhelmed. Scour thoroughly. It could pay off in the end. Even it if it doesn't, you can relax knowing you weren't careless.

It is easy enough to shuttle all the bundles into my labeled boxes and lug them back out to the garage. I can't wait to set up a permanent filing system, but what an undertaking this will be. Just as I am putting the last box in place in the garage, the doorbell rings, and I meet Pip, the hauling guy. He is not what I expected, but I didn't really have any indication of what to expect. Still, I am pleasantly surprised.

# CHAPTER 10

# Her Closet

I reminded my mom this morning while she was poring over the headlines of the Sunday paper with her magnifying glass that Pip is coming today.

"He's hauling away the dump pile I started, so you can stay in the house if you want, but if you are going to come outside to see what they are doing, you have to be dressed and not in your blue robe. You need proper street clothes."

"Well, do you want to pick something out for me? That way if I do decide to leave my comfy bed, I won't be improper."

"Mom, it's not that you're improper, it's just that I don't want you to be vulnerable, and we don't know these guys. Until I am living here, I want you to be safe. We don't need to be advertising that a little old lady lives here by herself," I add with some caution.

"Oh, I can take care of myself. I've got my cane," she says with such assured independence it makes me laugh so hard. She looks somewhat like the stubborn pixie Shirley Temple when she would put her little hands on her hips and purse her lips. Mostly I am laughing because it has taken me every weekend of the past six weeks to take care of a house that has been as badly neglected as she is.

"Okay, Mom, I'll find you some pants to put on if you come out later."

As the doorbell rings again, I can only hope that shabby, blue robe does not end up making a public appearance today.

Pip has an easy smile with the sort of beautiful, white teeth reserved for Pacific Islanders, and I soon discover he is from Fiji. I learn about his children and discover his young son is finishing sixth grade, so naturally he is interested when I tell him I teach seventh-grade English. It all makes for an easy rapport and good first impressions. He has brought along his brother, Marley, and his elderly father, who is still very prone to doing hard work. Pip is tall and affable and likes my brother a lot, so we talk about how they met while he eyeballs the mess that is in the courtyard for him to haul away.

I am wondering how much this is going to cost my elderly mother when a moment later he tells me the huge pile in the courtyard can be hauled to the dumps for $175. I am blown away that the entire wreckage I have created in four days can be completely swept free for less than I might spend on a good pair of back-to-school shoes. It's a deal! Pip and his crew get to work, and I make sure to bring them chilled bottles of water because I don't know what the protocol is when workers come to your house and it is hot outside. They are not quite guests, but they are people I can imagine inviting back, and they are hot, so why not provide them with cold beverages? Isn't that the mannerly thing to do?

It turns out my mom is interested after all. She pokes her cane along the pathways carved out of the debris to inspect how efficiently they are working. She is good-natured and properly dressed in the outfit I selected, fortunately—not her blue, tattered robe. After smiling a lot and making it known that she approves of their work, she returns to her lair.

I really like Pip and feel like I can trust him to take care of the messes I need cleaned up. So I ask him, "Hey Pip, is there any way you guys would be able to help me move a heavy dresser down the hall into the garage?"

He seems open to taking a look, and before I invite him in through the back door that comes off the kids' bath, I run inside to let my mom know, but mostly to check that she hasn't changed back into that embarrassing robe of hers.

It is uncomfortable to have men I do not know in the house, but Brother One knows Pip well, so I keep telling myself it's okay. Pip grabs hold of that monster of a dresser and figures he and Marley can manage it fine with just the two of them. Another problem solved for me. The dresser is on the move to the garage, where it will be used as long-term storage for the siblings. I decide to reserve one drawer for each of us by painting each of our names above the pull handles.

This will be the overflow space for items that are not quite big enough to warrant storing in the grey crates but will fit perfectly into these drawers, which are the standard size of a small carry-on suitcase. This is also where I will store the zippered pouches holding important documents. Everything is together in one place, segregated so it is easy to find. This will save me many headaches down the road.

After thanking Pip profusely, I ask him if he would be available for another pick up when I put together a second load for hauling in a couple of weeks. I come to find out that Pip, or Phillip as his father calls him, is available to help me with same-day service whenever I need, with really fair pricing. He even has suggestions for how I can get rid of all the toxic left-over paints that are flooding a utility storage shelf hidden near the pool heater under the cabana.

My mother's sons are too busy with their own lives to do manual labor for her, so it is nice to have someone reliable to call. Today is the beginning of many fruitful trips Pip will make to our house, and when I am in need of a handyman, it will be Pip's trusty brother Marley who lends a regular hand. I love more than anything else knowing that there is someone waiting to haul away the junk as fast as I can pile it up and willing enough to help me move a heavy piece of furniture here and there. Pip turns out to be a lifesaver in more ways than one by the time this story is all said and done.

When I finished clearing out my old room yesterday, I moved the rest of my mother's wardrobe into her overstuffed closet. If you have a need for multiple closets, you have too many clothes. Her walk-in is already a burgeoning collection of a clotheshorse who considered herself to be a leader in fashion trends in prior decades. But with apparel that doesn't fit now and will likely not fit again, and shoes that are just too high to be worn by someone who trips in bare feet, it is time to take a pragmatic approach.

"Mom, let's take a look at your closet. I notice you've got clothes in every closet of the house. Are you wearing all these outfits still, or can we start evaluating which are your favorites so we can redesign your closet in a whole new way?"

She takes the bait and sighs as if she is being oppressed. "Well, I am using all of the closets because I have important seasonal outfits I like to keep outside of my regular day-to-day clothes."

The only reason this has little bearing is that she no longer goes places other than to church when she can get a ride. As far as her closet goes, I do not wish to throw away everything she owns in one fell swoop. So I introduce the idea of a slow purge.

"How about we organize what you have in your master walk-in and then worry about the other closets later? Let's sort your clothes according to color so we can inventory what you have. All of your scarves can be paired with the outfits you wear, and we'll get some uniform hangers so we can fit more into your closet. Some of these heavy, wooden coat hangers take up too much space."

The best way to sort a closet is to pull out everything at once. Give yourself a two-hour window, and have your sorting crates in order. You can stuff the clothes you no longer wish to keep into an old piece of luggage you want to donate, a sizeable box, or a Hefty sack. I start with Hefty sacks because we still have enough on hand and because I know my bankers boxes are a precious commodity for the heaping mounds of paperwork I still have to unearth in this house.

This is how the rest of our morning goes. My mother is seated on her bed as if she is the queen of Sheba with her newspaper spread out in front of her. A venti Starbucks cup, filled with her favorite hot cocoa-coffee concoction, teeters on her nightstand. When her mocha becomes the one thing she will shriek for every Saturday morning for all of our years together, I will be reminded that it is I alone who created this monster.

I dive in with gusto. The first armful of clothes I heave out gets me closer to a wardrobe makeover. I ask her to tell me when the last time was that she wore an item and if it's a piece she feels great in and gets compliments on. Her reply is, "Who compliments an old lady on her clothes?"

The things she loves are completely stained and nearly

ruined, but she can't quite see them the way I do because of her macular degeneration. We decide to let the dry cleaner salvage what they can, and what they can't we agree will go by the wayside. I must admit, I am pretty pleased with my mother's newfound will to clean-sweep her house and give her life a makeover. I never thought I would see the day when she would give me carte blanche to instruct her as I see fit.

Out with the old. Out with the even older. Take your rotten, your dirty, your tired, your filthy, and toss them in the Trash pile. She is feeling lighter, I can tell. She is having fun telling me which pieces she absolutely will never give up, no matter how hideous I think they are, because she feels great in them and they have history with her. Some of these pieces were bought while on trips around the world, so far be it for me to tell her she can't have the turquoise beaded necklace from New Mexico or keep the cape she bought in Ireland or the purple smock she found in Israel. The memories of how a piece came to speak to you are what make a wardrobe special. I don't deny that. But you really need to be more selective if you feel like every piece speaks to you in every store you shop.

Out of the four zones we created—Keep, Donate, Dry Clean, Toss—we can see that there is a much bigger pile to donate than to dry clean, so we have a promising start. I think that somewhere in the back of her mind, she might have the idea that if she empties her closet, maybe we can go shopping for some new, modern clothes. I may have planted this seed, but for now we are making tremendous headway, and she is very amenable to change.

With the shelves cleared and the rods emptied, everything we have sorted is now strewn about her room like a tornado has touched down. This look never worries me because it is only temporary. I have seen it a thousand times before, and it does nothing short of inducing an adrenaline rush most athletes have to run five miles to achieve. I get mine without the sweat or, sadly, the calorie burn. A pretty set of drawer dividers will keep me up all night until I can get all the stockings, socks, and tights organized into tiny, color-coded balls befitting such an efficient space. These are the little things that relax me when I am overstressed, which is frequently. Some people overeat. I over-organize.

When I have bagged and tied six Hefty sacks of clothes designated for donation, I get busy redesigning the space. I imagine a lot of designers will tell you the first trick to a streamlined closet is to use matching hangers. I agree. Their uniformity makes it essential for recreating the tailored look we all envy when perusing magazines. However, the real secret to this look, if you carefully assess those magazine photos, is not simply using the uniform hangers but rather having all monochromatic clothes and keeping them sparsely arranged, as if a regular woman could subsist on six interchangeable outfits and call that a wardrobe.

Most of the closets I've ever visited don't look like this at all. For me it has taken several incarnations to get pretty close to perfecting this image by using three different color palettes in my wardrobe and sorting each piece within its same hue. These details make all the difference and in the end produce a very photogenic closet.

My favorite supplies for setting up a good closet space are always the same: thin, suede hangers; a good shoe organizer that hangs over the rod with twelve shoebox-sized compartments dropping vertically; two storage boxes with lids; and finally a double-hang rod that will allow you to maximize vertical space by hanging blouses and blazers above your trousers and skirts.

The shoe cubby I pick is sable brown with an ivory piping trim. There are many shoes we will need to say good-bye to if we are serious about scrutinizing everything in this house based on our mantra of "safety, health, and style." Therefore, a dozen compartments ought to be plenty for a Wisconsin dairy-farm girl who really still prefers her own bare feet to anything else.

I am quickly drawn to two oversized boxes with a pink rose pattern, one of which will be used for putting away items that are cluttering her sink counters. The other will be used for keepsake letters and cards she receives from friends and family because she loves to reread what people have written to her. More than anything, she loves knowing people have thought of her.

I put sixty minutes on the oven timer, and I race against the clock. This is one of the surest ways I know to work through any problematic mess. It keeps me motivated, and I always like to best my time so I have bragging rights although nobody else really cares how long it takes so long as the job gets done and they don't have to get their own hands dirty doing it.

I'm off. In front of me, I move the two tall dressers painted a high-gloss lemon color with gorgeous, white porcelain knobs to the far left corner. Baubles are stuffed into the first three tiers of narrow drawers that widen down to the base. Bigger drawers means more space for throwing in loose photos that are piled in between stacks of report cards from our youth and lots of old supplies of capped needles from the days when my mom took insulin for the diabetes that has since gone away.

There is a virtual pharmacy in four of these drawers, with expired pill bottles, medicine bags for travel, and old instructions from her doctor. And, of course, there are but-tons—an obvious collection for a seamstress. My mom was always at the ready with an unusual replacement for the button that had just popped off a coat, and there are handfuls and handfuls of colorful, multi-sized ones scattered everywhere.

"What are you doing in there?" she bellows from her bed.

"I am just taking a look at what you have stored inside all these drawers because these dressers are heavy to move." I try to reassure her that I am not snooping to be nosy; I am just purveying the scene so I know how much more crap there is tucked away in this house of hidden clutter.

"Well, those are my drawers, so they are my business. Get outta there."

She doesn't need to ask me twice. "Okay, Mom, I am just trying to put everything into corners so we can open up the closet and it can welcome you in instead of you tripping over furniture when you enter," I say.

Finally she is assuaged, and my clock is still counting down from fifty minutes. I give her the job of hanging the pile of clothes I put on her bed with the simple instruction that all crooks of hangers should be facing the same direction and all garments on hangers should have necklines facing the same direction.

"You are a good helper, Mom," I coo to her as she manages to insert hangers in clothes from two of the piles I have cleared off the floor. The last four piles I hang myself, and we are done before the ringer dings. Her closet has been completely trans-formed. There is even room for a little chair where she can sit while she struggles to put on shoes or when she gets tired, or while she endures the fun I have styling her hair during the blow-dry sessions after her bath.

I bring her in to admire her new space, and she lets out an

excited gasp with a mock gesture of her jaw dropping to the floor. "Oh Steffie, you work so hard. I love it." Her eyes scroll from right to left and up and down, and her grin gets wider and wider.

As I give her the tour, I point out that all of her clothes are color coded in sequence from light to dark with all of the white fabrics together, beige next, then her light pink, moving through the rainbow and ending with light greys and blacks. Within each color grouping, items are hung by style so that all collared blouses are separate from all tees, and finally everything is sorted by sleeve length. All of the skirts and pants hang in a corresponding rainbow on the rod beneath.

"This way, Mom, you can see how much you already own of one particular color, so you'll know when you are shopping," I add.

"Well, I think someone promised me a shopping trip," she says, and the banter begins. We agree that while she does have some good staples now, it would be fun to pick out a few new additions to update her wardrobe, and we can probably look forward to doing this in the summer once I am here permanently.

"I do think you deserve a treat, so how would you like to go get your nails done now?" I say.

"Now? I can be ready in five minutes," she says excitedly. The clothes come off and the hair gets combed and the new clothes come on, and she is waiting for me by the front door with her cane before I even have a chance to brush my hair and teeth.

My first impression of the nail salon is it seems fancy for a strip mall. We are welcomed in without an appointment, and I am glad for this because they are much busier than what I would expect on a late Sunday afternoon. I discreetly tell the owner that my mother has never had a pedicure and she is in need of some extra attention, and I make sure to escort my mom to the massage chair with the swirling footbath because I am petrified that today could be the random day she falls down.

The owner invites me to pick out the colors for my mother, and I just assume bright red is the closest to the Revlon Red that she and all of her friends helped make popular in the '40s. I hope this will bring back some fond memories for her.

While I am seated in the chair next to her, enjoying my own pedicure, I can see the expression of the attendant behind her mask once she pulls my mother's feet from the bubbling footbath. She says something in her native language that I can only imagine would be "oy vey," or "ay Chihuahua," meaning she has got her work cut out for her. My mother is oblivious to this and smiles happily as if to offer as much encouragement as possible.

Her nails on her big toes are longer than they should be, and my mother is prompted to warn the woman, "Be careful not to cut down to the quick." All her nail technician can do is nod and smile with the eyes of a person who feels punished to have gotten this customer instead of the sixteen-year-old cheerleader type who walked in behind us. The loveliest part about today's experience is that a second attendant does my mother's manicure simultaneously, and this really makes her feel special.

The thick lotion, the hand massage, the careful filing, and the vibrating chair all make my mother feel like she is queen for the day, and that is priceless. When we are done an hour later, she has a hard time walking in the paper flip-flops, so she opts to walk out the door barefoot and is probably safer for it. Finally, the last item on my to-do list is checked off for today. I am literally exhausted, but I have to teach tomorrow, and I must drive to my own house tonight. I stop to pick up something from the dinner bar at the grocery store next to the nail salon, and we head home.

Over dinner we make plans for what still needs to be done in the remaining five weeks until school lets out for me. We absolutely need to see the carpet guy on Saturday, and I absolutely need to attack the mail situation, uncover any that has gone into hiding, and create a filing system so I know accounts are not slipping through the cracks. It gets harder to say good-bye when I have to leave her in this big house alone, but I will be back on Friday night, and we will get a lot accomplished next weekend.

# CHAPTER 11

# A Good Filing System

Throughout my week at work, I help to calm the nerves of my seventh-grade students about the state test they will be taking within the next two weeks. I have the best group of students this year, and they still don't know that when they pop in to visit me next year, I won't be here. I always try to steel myself against tears at the end of the school year, but I am usually the first one to crack when the children I have looked forward to seeing every day for 188 days begin to say good-bye.

I try not to gush, but these tender moments come despite my efforts to keep cool. The kids know how much they mean to me, and I know how much our year together means to them. I've got great parents this year too; they are tremendously supportive, which makes me feel doubly lucky. My students have worked so hard this year, and naturally I have a lot of confidence that they will perform well in the coming weeks.

However, the impromptu essay the seventh graders are given to assess their skills in critical thinking through writing is still ahead. We never know what the state will assign as a topic, so we train hard all year. Even though I get results year after year, I never take it for granted. Juggling the move back home to care for my elderly mother while tackling the end of the school year craziness is all that is filling my planning calendar. Sticky notes are saturating the sidebar column, and highlighters in different colors keep my school obligations separate from arrangements that need to be made before I leave behind my life here.

School being beyond busy, knowing I have to empty out my classroom and lug everything home to my mother's house, and still not knowing where I will be working in the fall is all beginning to weigh heavily on my shoulders. It's a good thing I am organized and that I regularly purge throughout the school year because thankfully I will not have the typical trucks full of materials to cart with me that most teachers have acquired over the years. Yet synchronizing a clear out of my entire classroom, my current home, and my mother's home so it can be re-carpeted in a few weeks is becoming quite daunting even to a taskmaster.

After making it through a treacherous week at work, I make the two-hour trek to my mom's and realize this is why I rarely come down on Friday nights: traffic. I am stuck in long stretches going nowhere for the majority of the first hour. I could be halfway there, but I am really only twenty minutes from home. I am so tired, I decide to scrap it. I call my mom and let her know I just need to sleep. I will be there early in the morning, and then we can go carpet shopping. She is disappointed not to see me tonight but mostly worried that I need my rest.

I go home and climb into bed with my dog, Daisy, who is always overjoyed to see me. I let her lick my face for extra long just to make sure she knows how much I appreciate her displays of affection. She is well taken care of in my absence, but I miss her on these weekends away. I can't believe I am leaving in little over a month. How am I going to get everything packed up in time?

After my morning routine, I get myself out the door by seven o'clock feeling a lot more refreshed and raring to tick off the last of my priorities at my mother's house. Things are coming along, and getting new carpet will make the biggest difference. There is no traffic this morning, and the two-hour trek feels like it takes only forty-five minutes.

I absolutely love driving through the ravine that separates the country people who prefer cowboy boots and have land to plant crops from Silicon Valley, where the hustle and bustle of technology startups are dotted all along freeway exits lining the path home. I regularly spot a herd of cows in its green pastures on rolling hills, and the giant windmills placed every hundred yards remind me of Don Quixote and his adventures. This is the land between cities where natural power is working, but I don't know if the land belongs to farmers or to the power company. I keep the music playing, and I am wide-eyed. Pretty soon my weekends spent driving in will have to stop because I need to pack up my house and my classroom, and start working on my résumé so I can line up interviews in June.

*Ding, ding, ding* sounds the doorbell enthusiastically with my multiple pushes of the button.

"Who is it?" As if my mom doesn't know, but I am glad she is willing to take precautions.

"It's me," I say, thinking this is obvious enough.

"Who's me?" The charade continues.

"It's Steffie," I say, feeling almost exasperated and wondering if she is having fun with me.

"Well, hello d'ere." I am welcomed with her favorite expression.

After our exchange of "hellos" and "how did you sleeps," nothing sounds better to us than grabbing some coffee and heading to the carpet store, which should be opening in half an hour. We are both really excited to see what is new in the carpet world, and the idea of finally being able to replace the grungy, grey carpet that she has lived with for three decades is beyond imaginable to her.

The carpet she laid so long ago wasn't even pretty when it was new. It looked much different from what she intended, and what stuck with her all this time was the surly remark I made as a teen about it looking like gravel. It really did though, and not even cute pea gravel. A light-grey concrete hue with dots of brown mixed into the weave made it look very industrial, and thank goodness it has worn well enough to defend our floors from kids running amok and animals using it as their litter box.

I have never needed to go into a carpet store before today, but we both know how to navigate our way through a fabric store, and this is no different. We meander with Malcolm, the friend of Brother One, until we feel comfortable to spend some time on our own sifting through the more modestly priced samples. We love color but avoid it for now because we specifically came for something stately and elegant that will wear well. There are a number of beige patterns, but we quickly decide we are not beige people, and we do not want the new carpet to begin looking worn within the next ten years, so we look for chocolate palettes.

There are many different kinds, some of which remind me of apartment carpeting because of their very thin weave and low pile. Other chocolates fall into the bronze category, which does not look stately at all but reminds me more of an '80s bachelor pad with bulky, black leather furniture.

Then we see it—the one we think could possibly work. It is darker than sable brown but nowhere near black. It is plush to the touch and has a sophisticated pattern of miniature squares woven into the center of a square larger than the size of my palm. It is definitely elegant but still masculine enough to ground some of the furniture that is more feminine. It is the perfect color to bring some balance to our home, and with a sample in hand and a date set for Malcolm to come out and measure the house, we are off to a late breakfast of pancakes—what else?

When we return home, I feel energized. With the rest of Saturday ahead of me and gorgeous weather streaming in through the wall of northern-exposed floor-to-ceiling windows, the family room is perfectly lit for me to tackle the mail and put a filing system into place. If I wait until evening, I will be relegated to sorting in a dimly lit house and torturing my eyes, which have already been ruined from grading the work of seventh graders in 1,200 essays a year.

The best way to start is to have a pad of sticky notes and a thick Sharpie marker before beginning the sorting. My goal is to create a separate pile for every business statement I come across and place the piles along the length of the hallway wall facing the family room's open floor plan. I retrieve the bankers box from the garage that I packed last weekend, the one I was sure to label "Action-Statements-Current Year," and I grab a brown grocery bag that will become my burn bag for discarding papers I won't need to keep but don't want to throw in the trash with their identifying account numbers.

If you don't have a fireplace, you can shred financial documents either the slow way, by doing it yourself in a shredding machine with a motor that will likely burn up within six months of heavy usage or become jammed when you are only halfway through your job, or you can call the Shred-It company, which will bring a truck to your house, take your bags and bankers boxes full of highly sensitive documents, and shred them into itty-bitty pieces in front of you within seconds—and charge you a mere $10 per box. The benefit of experience has taught me that it is well worth it to trust the Shred-It people, especially if you have no fireplace of your own.

Because the popularity of this method is on the rise, there are other competitors providing the same services. Some may not drive to your house, but you might find their stores are conveniently located near your local shopping mall, so it is worth stopping in to see how they operate. Be sure you can witness the shredding activity yourself if you are new to the process because it will bring you peace of mind. A reputable document-shredding center will provide you with a certificate of proof that the shredding took place if you are unable to stay; however, I trust in what my eyes can see.

Armed with a box weighed down with a year's worth of mail, I begin. For every new company name found on a statement's heading, I create a Post-it tag and stick it to the wall several inches up from the floor. I have already had to fix a couple of piles whose sticky signs were positioned too low and became hidden from view, which made it harder to sort quickly, especially when two piles toppled into each other with the intent to merge into one.

For statements from Bank of America, I write "BofA" on a sticky and put it toward the left of the wall since I anticipate there won't be many more accounts ahead of the letter B. I am wrong because I discover several accounts I am unfamiliar with—stock and dividend statements from companies that begin with the letter A. I scoot my "B" piles to the right a smidge and hope I have enough room on the length of my hallway wall.

I continue pulling from the magic box as if a rabbit might appear next or a goldfish in a baggie. I never know what is coming, and this is such an illuminating way to learn about the business I will be doing on my parent's behalf. Once I have thirty accounts lined up in the hallway and wrapping around into the family room, propped up against the wall and balancing atop couch shoulders, I have a very good idea of how many files I need to create.

The problem is we do not have a good filing cabinet that can sit in this family room, next to the secretary's desk where I anticipate I will be opening mail, paying bills, and filing the statements I have reconciled. So, off to the office supply store again, and on the ten-minute drive it takes me to get there, I am filled with gratitude that so much of my running can be done within the vicinity. In the town where I currently live, I drive an hour round trip to the bank once a month because I am petrified to bank online for fear of a security breach. My closest friends think I'm nuts, but I am a creature of habit, and it is hard to get comfortable when hackers are more tech savvy than I am. My point really is the office supply store nearest to me here is also next to the bank.

The first office supply store has more than what I hoped for: the short, two-drawer filing cabinet I find is made of the exact same wood as the secretary's desk and will blend nicely with the family room. I pick up three dozen canary-yellow hanging files and skip the manila folders because I have found they only duplicate the labeling process. Why do I need to label the manila folder, insert it into the canary file, and label the canary file as well? I learned a long time ago that it is much easier to retrieve what you are looking for if you can just drop your statements into the hanging folder.

I also gave up using the system where you write the title of a file on a tiny slip of paper, fold it, and stuff it into a stiff, plastic tab. Now I prefer the convenience of using miniature-sized sticky notes because I can quickly change them out if I decide to rename the contents. Plus I can color code them, which you cannot do easily when the canary-yellow files come with canary-yellow tab dividers.

Heading home, I pick up dinner from the usual dinner bar at the nearby grocery store and decide on meat loaf again since it's been a few weeks, and it is still one of my mom's favorites. Until I can get into those cupboards in that kitchen, I can't start cooking. There are pots and pans covered in cobwebs, and some of those pans date back to more than fifty years ago when the only thing my mother wanted for her wedding gift was a cast-iron frying pan. My thoughtful father bought her a Griswold set of three.

Finally home and back in the family room, the lighting has not changed enough to dim my work area, so I plug away and have fun writing in my best block print the titles of all of the accounts I have located.

Before I pack each account into its new rightful hanging file, I sort through the piles once more to organize papers in reverse chronological order so the most recently dated is on top and the oldest document is at the bottom. Then I peruse the history to see what activities have transpired from the start.

I find that most bills have been paid on time. Most have been paid with checks written by hand. But some accounts are on an automatic payment deduction that Brother One set up online. All of this means that in order to prevent against something getting marked for insufficient funds, I really need to know the daily balance of my mother's checking account. I also need to determine the amounts that were paid for checks that were written from her account but not recorded with anything but the check numbers in the register. Based on necessity, I will become a convert to online banking sooner rather than later.

During this time I realize there is probably a deeper paper trail in the garage, and I want to sort through the box marked "Archive-Statements-Prior Years 1-5." I decide to give myself just an hour to see how much I can get accomplished. Halfway through this box, I can tell I need to double my time because it is slow-going. I have mounds and mounds of multiple years' worth of envelopes stuffed with statements that need to be added to the piles I have scattered around the family room.

But it's a good thing I am taking the time to go through this process because I find other accounts that are not currently active, and this leads me to discover something I never would have uncovered otherwise. In the first year of my arrival, I will stumble upon records that confirm to me that our home insurance policy was forcibly terminated two years ago after failure to pay. This saga leads to so much change for my mother and me that I can't address it this early in the book. It's a good story, and I'm sorry to leave you hanging, but it needs to be covered in another chapter where it can be thoroughly appreciated in the midst of all the other chaotic events. Just know that when you get to the part called "Pip Saves the House," you have gotten to the part worth waiting for—I promise. The moral for now is to keep digging. Do not toss any paperwork unless you have a good understanding of how it pertains to the status of your parent's financial health.

I finally have file folders nearly an inch thick with papers from the past that I am not confident enough to shred. I want to spend more time than I have today to absorb the past and really know which investments changed hands under different company names. I need to track where the money is because the reference list I found in my father's desk of assets held under differently named companies does not correspond to the corporate names my mother is doing business with today.

I create additional sticky labels for the new accounts I have unearthed and begin the process of putting everything into the filing drawer in alphabetical order. This takes me the better part of three hours, and it would take a lot longer if I stop to read through everything. I can do that at a later time. At least I have a lay of the land, and this is all I need for today because it puts me in a better position to evaluate how much more time I will need to spend on dissecting finances in the future. The answer appears to be "a lot."

I know the first person I need to schedule an appointment with when I move home is the family accountant, who has handled our income tax business, but not any investment business, for decades and is a trusted friend of both of my parents. At least I will be able to have some sort of intelligible conversation with him when he fills me in on the direction I should take to consolidate and manage my mother's finances. From what I have gleaned from the files, I can now begin to formulate my questions.

This is the best approach to take when figuring out what your parent's financial situation is. You must look at the statements. Make sure they are in a central location, and make sure you have the most recent ones; if you don't, start calling the phone numbers listed on the fronts of the statements and request that they send copies.

Just know that in order for you to have any legal communication on behalf of your parent, the company representative will request to speak with your parent personally to verify his or her name, date of birth, and Social Security number and to gain permission to speak to you specifically. All of this will be documented in the phone conversation and kept on file, but the process will need to be repeated step by step for any future calls you make.

Don't even think of pretending to pose as your parent—companies have ways of knowing when people do this. I didn't attempt this myself, but it was suggested to me by a sneaky sibling, and I can tell you that sheer nerves alone would give me away in a nanosecond if I were ever so brazen.

So no, don't try to be sneaky. It will catch up to you somehow, and somewhere along the line you will lose your credibility. There is, however, nothing against supplying your aged parent with information he or she may have forgotten or cannot read if it is on a card in front of him or her. Even if the operator is listening in, I have found that representatives are compassionate people and can tell when a daughter is genuinely trying to help.

Dinner is overdue, and my mom and I have a night of catching up ahead. I spend the next day vacuuming with her feeble tug-and-tow model that follows me like an obedient dog but hardly picks up any dirt with its whisper-like suction power. So, I add to the list of things this house needs a new vacuum cleaner, preferably one made in the twenty-first century. The weeks ahead will be spent on me and all that I need to do to clear out my life in order to make this move a smooth one.

The carpet selection is agreed upon and won't be put in until June. The date for measuring is set for Mother's Day weekend, which is when I will next return, and then in the middle of June I will drive up in a moving truck, and my entire life, and my mother's life, will be changed forever as we merge together and forge ahead.

# PART 4

# DAMAGE CONTROL

## REALITY 4
### *Managing Health—Both Medical and Financial—Is a Second Full-Time Job*

# CHAPTER 12

# The Pill Tray

Mother's Day weekend comes all too soon, but I am not yet having any trepidation about my decision to go live with my mom. We have had some delightful weekends despite some near emergencies and are relaxing into our old friendly routine of twice-daily phone calls during the week with lots of generous support from one old teacher to a younger one. My mom always tells me I work too hard. But I know when she was a teacher she had only one class of elementary students, which is a lot different from middle school, and it was in the 1950s, when standards were not in place, and performance accountability was not measured every year by a single standardized test. Nor did she have to teach essay writing to five classes a day with more than thirty-five students in each class some years.

So, she is probably right, I do work hard. But I haven't figured out how to do less without cheating the students out of the education they rightfully deserve, which I am fully capable of providing. Fortunately my hard work has built a reputation for me among administrators, parents, and students as a highly regarded teacher, so that, in and of itself, is my reward. The only daunting part of this move is knowing I will have to build my reputation all over again in a new district with new parents who will pass the word as fast as wildfire can spread as to whether I am any good or not.

Since this will be the first Mother's Day we have had together in many years, I shop for something special that will be meaningful to my mom as we start our new life together. My favorite boutique in town is a small drugstore that pays homage to the old-fashioned days, where you can have a cherry soda or a shake at the fountain, see Dolly at the post office window in the back corner to send your parcels, and visit the pharmacist, who recognizes your face. The store's line of birthday cards is the funniest I've found, and it carries everything Mary Engelbreit from stationery to cookware. I love it there for the Andy Griffith's Mayberry feeling I get. These are friendly people, proud of their multigenerational roots, who have propagated many vineyards outside of Napa Valley boasting some not-so-small labels. Ever hear of Woodbridge?

I find exactly what I want: the perfect casserole dish to hold a generous single portion of pasta, painted in shades of Mediterranean blue, with butter-yellow scalloped edges, made in Italy. Undeterred by its $27 price tag, I buy two so we can match.

I also find a beautiful, gold strand necklace with tiny chain links, long enough to hover below her bosom, beaded with a turquoise stone every three inches. This aqua color has always been good on my mother, offsetting her nearly white hair and her signature ruby lipstick that makes her alabaster skin glow. Today I ask for it to be gift wrapped, and I am willing to pay the extra $7 and wait the thirty minutes it will take for Mrs. Hammond to carefully select the bird and flower paper and cut the ribbons just right after she toils at length twisting them by hand around her knotted fingers.

When I arrive at her house, my mother is full of anticipation for another slumber party weekend complete with a little bit of pampering. The only real priority we have for today is to wait for the carpet measuring guy so Malcolm will know how much to order of that gorgeous brown sable we are dying to walk in barefooted. Today we go to lunch at a little tea house that used to be one of our favorite jaunts before we would go fabric shopping across the street. The restaurant is filled with other lady combinations of mothers and daughters who also have the same idea of trying to beat the brunch crowd by celebrating a day early, but to no avail.

After waiting for a half hour, we are finally seated by the corner window, with the sun streaming in and the air conditioning on full blast. It is the best seat in the house. We are cozy and purring like kittens coiled up for a nap in the warmth of sun sprayed on the sides of our bare arms. We laugh a lot and indulge in the finger sandwich tower for two that is served on a multi-tiered tray displaying cucumber with salmon, egg salad, and tomato and cheese, all without crusts, on tiny, triangular pieces of bread. We have our own tea cozies, and today is one of the best days ever.

The next day is the officially observed Mother's Day, and jovially, Brother One comes a-calling. He doesn't have flowers in a beautiful spray, or even in a modest bouquet. He doesn't have his children or wife in tow. He comes alone with a card to wish his mother a Happy Mother's Day. After finally catching the score on TV, and during the next commercial break from the game, he casually goes about multitasking his weekly routine of dispensing my mother's prescriptions into her med tray while carrying on a robust conversation with me about all that is happening for him in his career. I marvel at the assortment of pill bottles that are stored in a brown grocery bag in the china hutch.

I nervously watch as he rambles on and on about all the personalities at his work and the promotional opportunities in his future; all the while I am wondering if he knows what he is doing. I am reminded of that scene from the Jimmy Stewart movie *It's a Wonderful Life* when the elderly pharmacist, in a drunken stupor over telegram news that his son has just died, mistakenly puts poison in the pills and insists that young Jimmy gets it to the neighbor right away. When Jimmy gently suggests that maybe the stressful news made him get the prescription mixed up, the pharmacist becomes indignant and angry, slapping Jimmy so hard across the face his ear begins to bleed, but then the pharmacist realizes his error in the nick of time. I can't take it anymore, and ask Brother One to focus for a minute just on the pill arranging because it looks like such a confusing job, I wouldn't want to be the reason for distracting him.

"Oh, believe me, I have done this so much, it takes me no time at all to get everything sorted. Never fear." And he gives me his reassuring chuckle as if to say, "Silly girl, this is child's play."

"I could never do this part of the job. You will have to keep managing the pill tray even when I move back because it looks way too complicated, and I would be sick if I messed it all up," I am genuine in my remarks as I watch him take a blade cutter to chop some pills in half.

"Don't worry so much. I'll teach you. There's really nothing to it."

I have a hard time accepting this at face value. There are at least eleven pill bottles in front of us, some identical in color and shape, with unpronounceable names on their labels and different due dates for renewals. This does not seem streamlined to me, and I do not understand how he can be so calm about keeping track of it all when it wouldn't take much to give an accidental overdose, which my mother almost did to herself because she couldn't read the labels to see what she was swallowing.

I am scared to death to assume this as part of my responsibility. So every time he comes over in the future, I sit with him and listen to him talk incessantly about his life while he barely watches what his fingers are doing because he has this drilled down to the five-minute routine it takes. The pillbox is almost as wide as a hardcover novel, with slats dividing the multi-tiered tray into days of the week across the top, then into time zones of the day down the side, labeled "morning," "lunch," "dinner," and "bedtime." This is why that emergency room nurse insisted I get organized and create a list of meds being taken along with their prescription strengths. Your chart is critical because doctors need to customize the mix of meds since, all together, they can wreak havoc on your blood pressure.

Throughout the next two years, the looming question of which med was making my mother fall erratically was always a point of conversation at the visits to her primary-care physician's office. Was it that she was taking too much Coreg? Was it that some of the generic brands were tweaked slightly differently, making enough of a difference to her chemical reactions? Was a return of her diabetes making her little toe so lazy she couldn't feel the loops in the rug edges and kept falling? Did diabetes ever really go away? I did not know what I didn't know. I could only begin with questions from my observations.

As Brother One was leaving on Mother's Day, it had been

previously arranged that Brother Two would be dropping by with his soon-to-be wife to bring his mother flowers. The Brothers do not get along and avoid each other at all costs. There is contention between them stemming back to their adolescence, when Brother One was horrible and cruel, and Brother Two has not forgiven. From what I know of it, he has good reasons. So, this is the way our family manages, peacefully avoiding further dissention by people taking turns with their mother. It's like kids from divorce who spread themselves thin by going between parents' houses on weekends except that our parents stayed intact for fifty-four years while we children became divorced from each other.

My mother is overjoyed to see her second son and his girlfriend, who still won't set the date. I have never met her before, but at first appearance she looks like she could be his identical twin. He was the most beautiful baby I have ever seen, and I hope they will have equally lovely children. This is the first time in years that I get a chance to visit with Brother Two, who has learned of the news of my impending move home without saying anything more than to confirm our mother really can't manage on her own in this big house. He's glad she won't be alone and asks if I need any help while they are both here for the hour.

I put them to work with the chore of ripping the covers off of all the magazines she has kept because on the reverse side, my mother has printed all of her identifying information, including her full name, address, and telephone number, so that should they ever be lost, these rodent-infested copies will be returned to her home. I am not one to be paranoid, depending on who you ask, however I am one to take full precautions in order to keep my mother safeguarded in her home, and passing out her contact information does not seem prudent to me. While Brother Two and his woman, as my mom refers to her, are busy tearing off covers for the burn bags and recycling issues in the bins, I am making them lasagna for lunch.

We have a lot of catching up to do, but neither of us really cares to get into anything more than just polite conversation. I learn about my brother's girlfriend's family and her family's business, which they both work for, and I begin to connect the dots. Through her his future is secure. Before I know it, they are out the door, and he makes sure to remind my mother that she will hear from him on the Fourth of July, and maybe he will come up to watch the fireworks celebration that happens to take place directly across from our house.

This is our last weekend together. It will be only a few short weeks before school is out and the moving van will cart away my personal belongings. I am getting rid of more than I am bringing with me, and I would actually look like the true minimalist I aspire to be if it weren't for having to haul an entire classroom of curriculum to boot. As much as I desperately want my entire life to fit into ten boxes, school alone will end up consuming more than half of my moving van.

## CHAPTER 13

# Heat Wave

From March to June, I am so consumed by the business of dismantling two households that I keep telling my boyfriend, "I'm fine. I'm fine. We'll be fine, everything will be okay" until I catch myself at the kitchen sink the afternoon before the moving van is scheduled to arrive, when all my well wishes stop dry in my throat. I am not fine after all.

I do not know how it starts, but I am clinging to the center of the sink counter, holding myself up while I am wailing pitifully amid heaving sobs. I do not want to go. I am not ready to leave. I do not want my mom to be alone, but I do not want to give up my comfortable life. I do not want to go backward to a house that is a wreck and to a brother I do not respect. I do not want to leave my boyfriend, and I do not want to leave my job in a district where I am highly regarded by parents who see to it that their children are in my class, where I have worked long enough to have taught four siblings from the same family.

Between each statement I come up from the floor, where I have sunk unwittingly because the pressure of holding myself up is too much. I do not know how I am going to muddle through this. I do not want to leave tomorrow. I do not want to change my life. I do not want my mom to be alone. I do not want it to be me. All my boyfriend can do is hold me until my sobs subside in an hour. He vows that he will come out to visit at least every other weekend and that I can count on him. And in the morning, he helps me load the moving van, and I begin my new life with my mother.

Thank goodness my boyfriend is here to help me unload and to make sure Daisy and I are set up. I feel very much like I am going away to college again. I know there will always be a support system in place for me two hours away if I need him, but I am looking ahead at the new experiences I have to carve out for myself alone. Promises to see each other and dates set make saying good-bye less traumatic. But the fade-out of our relationship is evident to us both. It isn't that we left each other; life just pulled us apart.

Once my mother and I are settled in together on the absolutely hottest day in decades, I can't shake the feeling that I have just upended my entire life and all the security that went with it. I have no friends left in my old hometown. People moved away decades ago to find housing that was more affordable for young families outside of the San Francisco Peninsula. The person I was closest to in my family is not here, but all of his possessions surround me to remind me of his presence. Even the smell of his musty den and his open book marked with his pen don't bring me the comfort I would surely feel from being able to see my dad again.

I have multiple interviews set up for Monday, and I am nervous about what the future holds. I am forty years old, and my mom keeps telling me how wonderful it will be for us to have each other in our dotage. I don't know what the word means, but I have a feeling it has to do with being a spinster, so I look it up. Merriam-Webster defines it as "the period of life in which a person is old and weak; the state of having the intellect impaired, especially through old age; senility." I am sure this is what my life will come to because there is no way I am going to meet anybody new while living at home with my mother.

I unpack as much as I can before I need to think about dinner. I leave all of my school boxes outside by the pool, huddled under the cabana just in case we catch a break from this heat spell with an unlikely rain shower. Daisy is busy exploring her new house, and her bowl of water and food dish are set up in the bathroom, devoid of any competition the cats might feel with their own setup in the kitchen. Daisy loves the space to roam and has found that she can really get her stride on running the circumference of the property if I leave a couple of pass-through gates open. She is having a ball despite working herself into a lather.

"Mom, this scorching heat is abysmal. Never has it ever been this hot, not even when we were growing up. How often is it like this now?" I am profusely sweating even with my hair up in a ponytail and shorts still on from the hundred-degree heat I just left in the valley.

"Oh, it comes and it goes, and it doesn't stay hot for more than three or four days," she says as her cheeks begin to flush.

"Mom, it's got to be a hundred degrees in this house. Are you hot? You look like you're hot." I start to wonder if she can take this kind of heat without getting a stroke. "Let's get you cooled off in the bath."

"No, I don't want to take a bath now. I want to have a nap." This is a tone I heard many times when I babysat neighborhood kids thirty years ago.

"I have an idea. Let's go sit in the pool. I'll help you wade into the shallow end," I say with as much enthusiasm as I can muster while wondering which box has my bathing suits.

"I don't want to go swimming either. I want to have my nap."

I can see there is going to be an hour of negotiation ahead of me.

"How about you sit on the first step in the shallow end just until I can see that your body temperature is lowered, and then I will leave you to a nap, and you can spend the rest of the afternoon in bed until I get us some dinner," I say, rummaging through her drawers, trying to find the one good swimming suit I know she still owns.

"Oh, I suppose."

I leave her to change, hoping she has not gotten back under the covers instead. I listen for the sound of elastic snapping as she harrumphs around the room until I am satisfied that she is actually squirming into her suit.

I stick my toe in the water of our unheated pool, and I must say, it is refreshing. On a day over ninety degrees, our pool can feel delicious as the water that used to be prickly to the touch envelops you slowly with a tepid temperature you can swim laps in all day.

Here she comes, all dolled up in her navy-blue suit with white daisies. "How am I going to get into the pool?"

I am wondering the same thing because there are no handrails for the shallow end.

"Well, hang on to my arm, and we will go in together." I am remembering the nightmare that was the bathtub experiment, when she decided to sit on me instead of squatting into the tub.

After a lot of coaxing and laying down couch cushions and

pillows on the concrete around the shallow end, we decide we have a foolproof plan to get this unsteady eighty-five-year-old into the water where she can cool herself before she suffers a heat stroke.

Mission accomplished. She is safe and securely seated on the second step in the baby end of the pool with water up to her chest; her knees gently bob against the rhythm of the undertow. Thank goodness she is comfortable. I swim a few laps, and Daisy barks incessantly while running to keep pace with me because she thinks I'm drowning.

When we finally get out, I make sure my mom has a cool cloth to keep the pulse points behind her neck from over-heating, and I make sure she is dry and comfortable enough for her nap. On my way out of her room, I spot the thermostat poking through its cutaway in her bookcase, and would you believe that thing is set at ninety degrees? The lever has been manually pushed all the way to the right to the highest tem-perature it will go. No wonder it feels like an oven in here. It *is* an oven in here.

The first night sleeping in my old house, with Daisy at my side, knowing that I am not leaving here ever again is very disorienting. I cannot believe I have accomplished so much in my life and gone so far only to end up back at home where my mom thinks I am fifteen again. She certainly knows I am older, but she can't shake the fact that I have grown up and has me trapped in a time warp. Some days this is charming, but mostly it is unsettling because I don't want to be a teenager again.

The even scarier part of sleeping on this first night back at home is the thunderous pounding of what sounds like booted men urgently stampeding across our tar-and-gravel roof. My heart is racing, and Daisy is bracing herself for an intrusion with a low growl and a protective stance. I think it is robbers, and I try to peek out the bathroom window, where the moon is shining brightly enough for me to see into the dark dog-run alley that divides our house from the neighbor's.

There, sitting atop the fence, are two heavyset raccoons staring straight into my gaze with nothing but a feeble window and its old screen to separate us. It's as if they are making their own plans for how to perpetrate something against me and our house. While they are stalking me with their menacing eyes, I am distracted by sounds behind me coming from the other bedroom window, which I left open to get a breeze blowing.

I dart into my old room to peek out from behind the shutters, with Daisy running ahead, chasing the sounds, and spy a family of raccoons rummaging through the mountain of Hefty sacks I have started in the courtyard for Pip's next haul away. The problem is that I also included some garbage, like the box from the pizza we had for dinner since it was too hot to cook tonight. Now that I see what I have to look forward to in the morning, I drag myself back to bed knowing there is nothing I can do tonight because I am not brave enough to go head to head with a raccoon. The most I can do is try to intimidate them by shining flashlights in their eyes through the window to scare them away, but they just seem to be more appreciative of my gesture as it provides them with the extra light needed to find any items they may have missed on the first go-round.

What I don't count on finding in the morning is the damage they have done to my boxes of school materials that I stored out by the pool. Once they sniffed out the little decorative one that I allow my students to take a dip in ever so rarely when someone has earned a special treat or a homework pass, those raccoons anticipated all of my boxes must have had something equally tasty in them, which they didn't. There are torn papers scattered around the pool and candy wrappers shredded up and down the length of the patio. All that made it into the pool is easy enough to scoop out, but that which has been dragged by a gypsy family of rodents up and down and all around our back yard will take me hours to pick up. And, of course, now there are ants to deal with again.

I never suspected I would have this problem today, and there is an even greater crisis to deal with because my résumé packets are destroyed. I don't have my printer connected to anything yet, and all I need is to retrieve one good copy from this mess so the print shop can make some more. This is exactly what I do not need to be doing today.

The next morning begins with my marathon of interviews. I have four schools that I would love to work for that are also ready to take a serious look at me and what I can offer them. The first one is the sentimental favorite—close to home and a school I attended. It starts with the entire interview panel keeping me waiting for a half hour while they all mosey in late from getting coffee at Starbucks. I only wish they had thought to bring me one too. I will need to make my other three inter-views today more of a priority.

The next interview is the one my mom and I get a good chuckle over for months to come. The superintendent sits me down in a formal conference room with everyone looking prim and seeming on edge. There is a vibe similar to a roomful of rocking chairs with a long-tailed cat stuck inside. Am I the cat? I don't feel nervous. But when the superintendent, coiffed and polished, begins to speak, I can only smile, secretly won-dering if this is really how their district does business.

In an affected, regal tone, she opens with, "Now, today is your interview. We will begin by asking you one question, and then you may respond. It will be most helpful if your comments are brief and to the point. We will continue around the table with each of us asking you a different question, for which you will direct your answer to the panel member. At the end of this process, we will ask if you have any questions before we excuse you. We hope to let all our candidates know our decision prior to the end of the week."

It seems so elementary to me. I teach interview skills for one of my electives, so I am dumbfounded that someone would need to explain this process in such mind-numbing steps. When I relay this to my mom, all she says is, "Let's go home and make some tea. First I'm going to fill a pot with water, then I'm going to put it on the stove until it boils. After that I'll pour the hot water into a cup, and finally insert a tea bag."

Oh, I laugh so hard. And it never gets old. Whenever we have a lull in conversation, my mom will burst out with, "First you take a pot of water," and I will still laugh just as hard as I did the first time I heard her say it. My mom's sense of humor is unexpected, and when it comes out, she really shines. I wish I were as quick-witted as I am discovering she is. My dad always said she was funny, but I just never saw it while I was growing up.

I see two more panels in the afternoon. One is filled with a highly spirited and buttoned-up group of people whom I like immediately. When they ask me one of my favorite questions, which is to name three adjectives that describe me, I reel off, "Dynamic, delightful, and driven" with lots of zeal and radiant smiling, and wholeheartedly meaning it. They love it. They always do. The other site I interview for has all the tantalizing elements the right environment can produce but comes with a job description I am less enthusiastic about.

By the time I get home, there is already a voicemail waiting for me from the school that loved my three adjectives and more. They said they made up their minds within the first ten minutes after I left, and they are holding a spot for me at one of their top schools, and to please call back as soon as possible. It is the perfect fit for me, and I do not delay. The other two schools call well into the evening with equally good offers, but I am so happy I chose the school I did. It turns out to be full of good people, great students, and parents who, thankfully, cement my reputation as the teacher you want to have for your child.

# CHAPTER 14

# Health, Safety, Style

It was a good Monday. Tuesday smacks me in the face like a two-by-four when I decide I need to get my father's den ready for the carpet installers next week. I have done every room except for this one. I am daunted. Looking from corner to corner at the wall-to-wall furniture amidst filing cabinets and folders buried beneath more folders from my mother's rifling, and more stacks of financial paperwork sitting on the little daveno, and a built-in, floor-to-ceiling cupboard filled with hundreds of books about investing, inventors, stamp collecting, and corporate leaders, I am finally reduced to tears. It is a lifetime's worth of stuff that I cannot possibly unearth by myself within the week I have left before the carpet installers arrive.

The fireproof, steel-grade filing cabinets are so heavy I cannot budge them even an inch. There are nooks and crannies of storage drawers throughout my father's desk that are stuffed with papers that were important to him, so they should mean something to me, but I don't know how to interpret them. There is a closet full of shelves storing more memorabilia from victories in his company division and plaques and awards for his career achievements. There is the projection camera and family film reels from the '60s. There is just so much more compacted into this one room than all I have lugged out of the house in the past three months.

The hardest part about this room is that I know it will need to be inventoried, and I know there will likely be information I come across that I will need in order to help my mother. But, surveying this scene today, and starting a new school year in a couple of months, I cry a bit harder knowing I will have to work from sunup to bedtime every day in order to at least organize it into some sensible system.

Brother One shows up unannounced as usual, a regularity I am not getting comfortable with yet, and sees the conundrum I am fretting over. When I ask if he can help me, he offers what he can: the suggestion that I call Pip to see if he would be willing to make some extra money by clearing out a bedroom and doing some manual labor aside from hauling. Thank goodness Pip and his crew are so willing and compassionate. They spend several days moving furniture and the boxes I have already labeled, identifying their contents from the drawers of filing cabinets and desks. They help me clean out corners of the garage where only dark, creepy things have roamed, evidenced by the residue they have left behind. I buy these guys lunch every day, and I feel like they have saved me because the carpet installation date is met without a hitch. Unless you call rolling up with the wrong brown carpet a hitch.

Fortunately for us I had just come home from doing paperwork at my new district office to find that the carpet was not the same one my mother and I had ordered. Somehow there was a mix-up, and Brother One graciously went to the store for me in my absence to reconfirm which color brown it should be. To him all brown looks alike, and he and Malcolm selected their best guess and went with the cruddy, cheap carpet that is probably most popular for high-turnover rentals with frugal landlords. It is a problem we are spared from having, though, once I show Malcolm my paperwork. After postponing our installation date for one more week while we wait for the replacement, the carpet layers show up ready to go to work.

Fernando and Armando get a lay of the land to determine how much they can get done in one day. They begin with the living room, and I go about my business in the back of the house. The grunting I hear from all the way down the hallway has me curious enough to investigate the progress they have made in their first hour. It appears that with the soiled carpet rolled and ready to be removed from the living room, the padding above the linoleum is the only piece left to come up. I surmise from the grimaces on their faces and the kerchiefs they have covering their noses and mouths that the going is not smooth.

"How bad is it?" I ask.

"We do a lot of these jobs, a lot of people with the animals that makes the mess, but even after the twenty-three years we been doing these work, it no look like these ever," Fernando explains as carefully as he can, removing his bandana so I can understand him more clearly.

"How many pets you keep?" Armando asks.

"Well, we only have three cats right now. But my mom has had cats my whole life, and we have had this carpet here since I was in middle school." I try to empathize.

"These is probably the worst job I seen. I'm saying these is a lot of animals. We find stains all over." Armando points to all the yellowed spots that have soaked through to the under pad while Fernando is showing me places where seepage has ruined the linoleum beneath.

"I am just so sorry," I say, feeling so mortified that outsiders should have to see our filth. "This is why we're getting new carpet," I continue, feeling so exposed even though it's not my dirt because I haven't lived here in decades. "You're doing a good job, though, thank you so much."

I want to bow out of the room because I can tell they are judging, and I begin to feel resentful because it is their job after all to lay carpet, and what do they expect? Does everyone replace perfectly good carpet with newer carpet? But I feel horrible because I believe it when they tell me this is the worst job they have ever seen.

After two days of buying the workers lunches and trying to ignore the criticism I am certain must be filling their heads about the kind of house we have kept, I finally have this place in working order. At least phase one is complete with one kids' bathroom, three bedrooms, the kitchen, and the dining room set up not to be embarrassments if anyone stops by unexpectedly. I call Pip again for another haul away, and while he is here I finagle his and Marley's help to rearrange my bedroom furniture. I have discovered there just isn't enough floor space for me even to consider trying yoga with my double bed hogging the center of the room. He is getting to be a regular fixture around here every month, and it is really nice to have someone who is willing to help whenever I need it.

Something peculiar happens a few days later when I happen to be washing my hair. I see the shadow of a man walking past the windows in back of the house, striding right by the bathroom, which luckily has linen café curtains to block direct views. Stunned, I run to the north of the house, where my mother's bedroom faces the pool, to warn her there is a stranger on the property before I am about to call the police. We both sit very still, listening to him rustling by the side gate as he hoists himself onto our embankment then jumps over our six-foot fence. He continues swiftly toward the pool's end, where the heater sits beneath the cabana, next to all of my boxes.

He is whistling, so I am thinking he must not be worried about being detected. I can also see he has on a uniform shirt. I ask my mom who this guy is, and she says she thinks he might be the one who comes to maintain the pool, but she doesn't know his name, even though she offers him a Dr. Pepper from her stash every time he shows up.

"Why is he jumping fences to get onto our property?" I ask because it seems like a legitimate question to me.

"I suppose that's how he gets into his houses."

I slip out through the family room slider to meet him squarely. "Hi," I begin to introduce myself, "I am living here with my mother now. Who are you?" I say with my hair wrapped in a towel.

"Oh hi there. I'm Rob. Your brother hired me to do the maintenance work on the pool, and I installed the entire gas pipeline and new heater. The old one was a dinosaur." He seems harmless enough.

I explain to Rob that I prefer him not to jump fences to circle around the private areas of the house where the bedrooms and bathrooms are located, especially when my mother is least expecting him, implying that I am sure he can understand why I would want to keep the property secure, and I ask if he could please ring the doorbell. Rob seems a little put off. He says he will oblige even though he is no longer smiling.

After a couple more times of Rob not obliging, I decide to

put a lock on the first gate off the driveway. I figure this will be a sure way to send the hint that we happen to be homeowners who prefer workers to ring the doorbell before they are allowed on the premises. I start to anticipate his regularly scheduled arrivals every week and will coincidentally meet him out front, where I happen to be watering the flowerbed while drinking a cup of herbal tea.

This works pretty well for a couple of weeks. We develop a rapport, and I am able to get his ideas on how to safeguard our pool so I can help my mother into the water more easily on those hot, hot days. He says our pool should absolutely have handrails leading into the steps, and he knows a good cement guy who can help with the work required to dig up the concrete and pour new cement to securely fit his specially made handrails.

"If you ever plan to sell this house, you will regret not having handrails with a pool," Rob tells me.

I know he is right. And I know that someday in the far distant future, we will need to sell this house. I know that on hot days, my mother needs a place to cool down so she doesn't have a heat stroke. I also know that couch cushions won't always make the best sense. So we forge ahead to modernize the pool. The tradeoff for saving some of the cost is that we will need to do the heavy lifting by carting away the quarry-size pieces of broken concrete that are jackhammered out before the fresh cement can be poured.

This is the deal that Brother One brokered, and I am happy for his involvement because there is something unsettling about Rob. He is a good-looking guy about my age, married I think, but there seems to be something disingenuous simmering beneath that smile, and after the next time I catch him traipsing across our backyard without having been invited in, I fire him on the spot, but not before we have all of the pool needs handled.

When Brother One comes to see what we are left with now that the demolition crew has completed their part, I am at a loss for what comes next.

"Stef," he says, "go get the wheelbarrow so all this concrete can get moved to the courtyard for Pip to haul out of here."

Trying to help where I can, I dart to the courtyard and retrieve that handy wheelbarrow right from where I left it months earlier when I was moving out broken clay pots by the dozens.

"Now," Brother One continues, "start loading these pieces so I can wheel them over to Pip's pile, because I've got a bad back."

I am thinking to myself that this doesn't sound like a job for a girl, and I've got a lot of stuff to do inside the house still, but I don't want to seem delicate, so I try to heave a piece into the barrow. There is no wriggling this block of cement. I simply don't have the strength. And when I begin to tell him so, something else snaps.

He decides to lambaste me for multiple issues he seems to be having with my reentry into his picture. Where is that bottle of car-wash product he has always kept in the garage to wash his truck? When I tell him I threw it out because I thought it was left over from the days when mom still had a car a decade ago, he begins to curse a blue streak, accusing me of coming in and taking over our mother's house like it belongs to me.

I try to diffuse the situation. I apologize for my oversight in tossing that bottle and ask how much it will cost to replace his special car-wash solution. When he tells me it is $2.99, I know right then and there that this is not an argument over replacing something that costs less than a few dollars but more about feeling threatened because his escapism from his life at his own home has been forever altered.

The unleashing does not stop here. For the next couple of weeks, there are sporadic moments when he will come over, temper flaring out of control. It becomes more and more alarming as he rails on me about his perceived notion that I am meddling in his marriage when, over dinner with his wife, I asked if she knew about the funny time when he was a little boy and jumped off the roof into our pool. It seems like an innocent enough story to share, but the words somehow cut him to the core because he interprets it as me showing how he has kept secrets from her, and how dare I bring up any subjects about him from his past? I am not following his logic but promise to keep future topics limited to the weather. He is still seething even after my apology for misspeaking, and what happens next is what becomes a deal breaker for me.

Brother One gets in my mother's face and starts haranguing her about what she is going to do about my meddling, and why am I not paying any rent, and why am I eating here for free, and why am I here acting like this is my house, and why am I taking advantage of her? He is full-on screaming in her face to the extent that she has to bury her head in her hands as if she can wish it away, shrink into her lap, and become invisible under a protective shield. I have seen him in this state before, and it always ended badly, with someone getting hurt. He was a child then. He is a responsible adult now, so I am expecting better.

I run to my room with my dog to think of what to do next and how to protect myself, hoping my absence will calm him down and he will leave our mother alone. It doesn't work. He has her alone now, and there is no talking any sense into him. I go back out there and tell him that he is upsetting her.

"Look at what you are doing to Mom," I say as she begins silently rocking herself in a seated fetal position. I am sick with fear, and I think about calling the police, but I don't want the entire neighborhood to be poking around in our affairs. I tell him to leave until he can collect himself. Something finally makes him go even though I don't think he ever heard a word I said.

With his truck out of sight, I hold on to my mom and tell her that the way he screamed at us is not okay. That there is no excuse for verbally abusing her or me, and that I had no idea a friendly childhood memory shared over dinner would have brought on such a tirade. I tell her how sorry I am that I didn't just get her out of the situation and take her into her room. I feel like I was at such a loss to protect us both. I am reminded of a history filled with pain, and all that I have escaped from him is now in front of me again, all because I chose to come back and help our mother.

All my mom can say is, "I stick up for him, sometimes he gets a little excited, but he's a very good son," and then she wants to lie down for a nap.

I can't believe it. After his thirty-minute rant, she sticks up for him? Is this the classic response victims of abuse utter because their greater fear is that they will be abused again if they do not acquiesce? While she shuffles into her room down the hall, I sit alone on the couch in the living room and stare blankly into the fireplace, wondering what I have gotten myself into. This is not the kind of relationship I want to have in my life. This is not going to be healthy for me. With a complete feeling of engulfing doom, I hang my head and sob. I am very afraid for what I have just done to upend my life. I am facing the reality that I have an unstable brother who sees my presence as a direct threat to him and all that he has been finagling for himself while the work still in front of me to get the rest of the house in order seems insurmountable.

The idea that I would take advantage of my mother in any way is beyond hurtful. My mother specifically outlined that her invitation included for me to live here rent free, since the house is already paid for, if I can take care of her, and she is happy to help with groceries if I do the cooking. The monthly maintenance bills are something she already affords easily with my father's pension checks, Social Security, and stock dividends. Anything above this I happily agree to pay for, and down the road there will be plenty of expenses I will cover.

Sadly, this is how several people view my return home— that it is more she who is taking me in instead of the other way around. This is the downside of helping your elderly parent to remain in her home as she wishes. There will always be someone suspicious of your good intentions. This is why transparency will be your friend when it comes to bookkeeping and recording wishes in legal documents. And this is why the words my mother told me within the first weeks of my arriving home—"it will be your privilege to care for me"—are replaying in my head. I am as stupefied now as I was then because it all seems to be more than I ever bargained for. A lot more.

I decide to look for a new place to live. I need to be safe, and I need to keep my dog safe. I do not feel that Brother One will ever change. Just as I find a darling, affordable cottage nestled on the back of a wooded estate and make an appointment to meet the owners, Brother One shows up late one night. He slips through the side gate next to the pool, careful to not let its familiar squeak alert me that someone is trying to get in undetected. He quietly slides the glass door to the living room across its tracks and appears out of nowhere as a shadowy figure in the dimly lit kitchen off the family room where my mother and I are enjoying another episode of *The Mary Tyler Moore Show*. When I catch sight of him out of the corner of my eye, I go into full intruder alert, my posture rigid, feet planted at the ready in case I need to run for help out the back door. This time I have a plan in place.

He sees that I am on edge, and he stands in his tracks at the kitchen counter as he begins his speech. "I messed up the other day. I shouldn't have lost my temper. They say in AA that it is important to ask forgiveness, so I am asking yours for the wrong I did here. I know you are only here to help Mom, and I don't want you to worry about me making things difficult for you. I wish I could do more for her, but I have done a lot with getting her to medical appointments, and I am still happy to help with that if you need it." His smile looks warm and relaxed. "What do you say, can you forgive me?"

It is a question I have had to answer a lot in my life. What can I say? The purpose of my being here is to care for my mom, and if he fully wants to support that, then I should not stand in the way of my mom getting her wish fulfilled to remain in her home and to be given the care I know she needs and I know how to give. So, I ignore the burning rush of feelings coursing through my intestines and offer a faint attempt at accepting his apology, though it is clear to us both that it is under duress and I am skeptical at best. My mother is overjoyed that he has taken such initiative and practically casts him in a glowing light with his halo fully tilted upright.

# CHAPTER 15

# The Doctor Is In

Slowly things get back on track, and my trepidation eases with each passing week. By the start of the new school year, I am feeling more relaxed. This summer has brought long days of waking at sunrise and working until bedtime to square away financial accounts and to follow instructions from my first overview meeting with our family accountant.

The hour with Mr. Nolan was spent guiding me on the top five priorities I have ahead. First I am to consolidate the many little accounts that are hanging out there. Second I am to track down whatever other financial assets we do not yet know about. Third I am also to be sure the house is named in the trust. This is very critical, he explained. One of the last five directives includes me getting to the attorney he has referred to draw up the legal docs we still foolishly do not have in place. By the time a person is living within the ninetieth percentile of life expectancy, you are taking a great risk if you are operating without the four documents you will need to have before you can manage someone's incapacitation or death. Don't worry, vital papers will be covered in much greater detail in Part 8, Chapter 39: Legal Documents Binder.

His advice plagues me. There is so much to be done immediately that my front burners are becoming overcrowded. I have just started teaching in a new district, and the days are hot in my upstairs classroom that has no air conditioning. I am working long hours because there is a lot to be done when you are trying to make a good first impression. I am also still in the midst of tweaking my curriculum, aligning to standards, and regaining the momentum that made me a star in my last district.

In order to concentrate on work, I need to know that my mom is settled and functioning during the school day. My first concern is how she will eat lunch. Some of the teachers I am befriending have suggestions ranging from Meals on Wheels to restaurants that deliver. I decide to use the former service because I have heard good things about their reliability. I am relegated to taking the knobs off the stove before I leave every morning because of what happened this summer.

One day when I was out running errands, I came home to find that my new favorite kettle had melted all over the burner because my mother wanted a spot of tea, but took a nap instead while waiting for its whistle, which she never heard. The coating on that pot got so hot, its red paint slid right off and stuck to the burner in a gooey puddle the way expensive pots never should. Perhaps I could let this one time slide if it had not been a lifelong habit.

After searching high and low for an identical replacement to my cute little kettle, which carried sentimental value because it was a special gift, I came home another time to find that it too had suffered the same senseless death, abandoned and melted all over the stove. I could not believe my eyes. Knobs off. It is the only way to prevent the house from burning down in my absence while I am at school. And now we are down to two good burners I can use to cook upon.

My other concern is about my mother's erratic falling. There seems to be no indication of what will spur it on, and it doesn't necessarily need to involve her tripping. The first weekend I escort her to church to reunite with people I remember fondly, and some not so fondly, we are congregating in the hall when she slides down the wall that is meant to be holding her up and instead collapses onto the floor. I have not seen her fall since my first weekend home in March. Now, a few months later, this is the first time her unsteadiness has led to such a scene.

The brethren are trying to get her to her feet, but I am so upset by her vulnerability and what I can only imagine is the beginning of the end that I slip from the crowd of people around her and into the classroom behind me to cry alone for two hard minutes. I have never seen her this way in my entire life. It's time to sit with the doctor, like I did with our accountant, to assess what we do know and speculate on what we don't.

When our appointment time comes, there are quite a few more scenes I can paint for Dr. Goodcare, who is beginning to imagine what the picture at the end of this story will look like. I bring Brother One to our first meeting so the doctor can see we are working together toward a clear passing of the torch. Brother One has a lot of complimentary things to say in my presence about how I have cleaned up the whole house and paid particular attention to my mom's personal needs, and that I make a healthy dinner every night since his wife helped me to finally unload all the contents within the cupboards so the kitchen could be set up for cooking.

I chime in with the change in my mom's diet from

spoon-feeding herself a jar of Ragu several times a week, to the fall at church, to the outright disinterest in Meals on Wheels; she told the man who delivered her third frozen meal to stop bringing her this crap right before she threw it back in his face and slammed the door. I continue with the time I came home from school to find her giving out the beginning sequence of her Social Security number, with her checkbook already open on her lap. I grabbed the phone and told the solicitor on the other end never to call here again just as Brother One coincidentally walked through the door and lowered the boom on them in the way that only he can. I had to change her phone number after that, and I had to hold on to her checkbook so she wouldn't be caught in a vulnerable position again.

I recall for the doctor the melting teapot episodes, and I include the ditty about hiding my first paycheck under her mattress because she thought it would be safer there, which inspired me to open a post office box for all future mailings. Once the district office assured me it had been mailed to the correct address, the idea to turn her room upside down during the two weeks I was searching everywhere else in the house had simply never occurred to me. And then I saw her. In the midst of turning over drawers and shaking out pillowcases in the other rooms, I noticed she was sitting staunchly on her bed, her eyes fixed on the wall in front of her, while she slyly stuffed her fingers in between the box springs, where I was sure she was hiding salami or candy again. This was how I found my paycheck.

The doctor is listening while simultaneously perusing my mother's file, which must be two inches thick. I know how much she adores him, but I find him to be gruff. Dr. Goodcare is a portly little man whose personalized service reminds me of what was probably standard in post-war decades. It is he who places calls to our house at nine o'clock in the evening with results from tests or requests for appointments, not a nurse or assistant. It is he who answers my call in the middle of a Sunday afternoon to confirm if my suspicions are correct. It is also he who reels off diagnostic information that he expects me to remember in the blink of sixty seconds. When I tell him I need to write it down and ask him to repeat it slowly, and to give me more clarification behind the medical mumbo jumbo that I cannot be expected to understand, he is not condescending, just struck by the oddity that medical terms might need to be further defined for the layman.

By now I have become an expert at things I never thought I could do in my lifetime. I learned how to drive a stick shift. I learned how to put contact lenses in my eyes. With the same stick-to-itiveness and laser-sharp focus, in the span of a week I have now also learned how to prepare my mom's med tray. I created a streamlined process that started with relabeling all of the categories on the med box so I can use the slots more efficiently to fill the tray with not one but two weeks' worth of meds at a time.

I move the pill supply from its jumbled grocery bag to a decorative shoebox. I organize the prescriptions alphabetically in rows. My preference is to arrange them on their backs, lying faceup so I can easily read their labels as well as see the amount of pills remaining, but there are too many bottles to fit tidily, so I have to stand them in lines like soldiers. I use a Sharpie to mark the lids with the due dates for refills. It's a start.

I became familiar with the shapes and distinct etchings of each pill so I can distinguish all the white ones from each other in the event that they ever spill onto the floor—again. I also added a column to my prescriptions chart that shows when medications are due to be renewed and assemble all of the R$_x$ numbers at hand to provide the pharmacist so renewals can be called in within just a couple minutes. All of this comes by way of anxiety-inducing trial and error when realizing too late that a prescription has run out and requires a doctor's approval to renew. This is not a discovery you want to make when you are doling out dinner meds and the doctor's office has already closed for the day.

To celebrate my mom's eighty-sixth birthday in the fall, the two of us dine at one of her favorite restaurants, where she can feed the ducks. Is it still referred to as "dining" if you are eating your dinner before the five o'clock news? Brother One has promised to stop by later, and Brother Two has already sent his card. The phone has been ringing today with birthday wishes from the few friends near and far who are still living and still mindful. Only Sister Two, who is trying to manage her own life two hours away, remembers to call. Another year passes without a word from Sister Three, a deliberate oversight not lost on my mom.

We have settled into a quiet routine, with the days getting shorter and darker. She is already looking forward to Halloween, her favorite holiday. She loves to see kids dressed up and waits for them by the front door for the quarters she has been giving out since I was a child, when a quarter could buy a few things at the five-and-dime. I suggest we give out candy too this year, just to change things up, and while she is at first aghast at the idea of ruining her tradition, she finally relents, and fortunately the five kids who do show up are able to leave with a fun-size candy bar each along with a shiny coin. Lucky them.

Our streak of quiet weeks stops with an all-night vomiting episode and starts me on the path to emergency preparedness. I have never seen my mom sick in my lifetime, not with a temperature, not with a broken arm, not with a hospital visit— not ever, with the exception of the time I took her myself six months ago. To find her barfing in her bed in the middle of the night scares me to death, especially when I see that it is coming up red. I know bleeding internally is a serious sign and requires urgent care, but I don't want to leave her side. I tell her I need to call 911, and she can only nod approvingly because she is heaving her guts out. Her gurgling noises scare me so much, I become frantic before the operator comes on the line. I am already crying too hard to get my words out clearly, but she understands there is an emergency and assures me help is on the way.

When the paramedics show up three minutes later, the lead captain assesses my mom with a lot of fancy equipment in many different portable boxes. It looks exactly like fishing tackle for medical roadies. They hook my mom up to IVs and get her stabilized. And then one of the paramedics brings in a tiny gurney, smaller than my ironing board. Up to this point, I have still been crying inconsolably because I have never been in this situation before.

The captain is a gorgeous girl who I imagine is the youngest of six with all older, tougher brothers who probably told her crying is for sissies, because she has little sympathy for my sniveling. She asks me why I am still crying when my mother is going to be just fine. But all of those wires attached to my mom tell my brain something else. I look at the captain, and she sees my perplexed expression as to what that stretcher is supposed to be used for. She tells me they had to listen to my

911 call several times to prepare for the scene, but all they could make out was "six-month-old baby." I have to laugh now because what I had tried to convey through my inaudible tones and inability to catch my breath due to heaving sobs of hysteria was "eighty-six-year-old lady."

It turns out that my mom had gotten up in the middle of the night for a drink of cranberry juice, and instead of having a polite, eight-ounce cup she guzzled the entire sixty-four-ounce jug. A former diabetic cannot do this. That was why her vomit was red. I sincerely hope there won't be a next time. But the future holds a different plan.

# CHAPTER 16

# Apple, Penny, Chair

When I touch base with Dr. Goodcare to fill him in on the paramedic visit, he wants to see my mom again just for a routine visit. Something in the conversation he has with her leads him to ask if she knows what year it is, who the current president of the United States is, and what the date today is. She does great with all three. When he asks her who the president before this one was, she makes some funny jokes about why should she pay any attention but answers correctly, although I can tell she is feeling like she is on the hot seat.

The doctor is on a roll. When he asks who the president was before that one, she is rusty. I can't say I blame her. Why should an eighty-six-year-old be expected to recall twelve years of politics? She has other more important things to think about. Dr. Goodcare doesn't take his job lightly, however, and he refers her to a specialist: a neurologist I will come to call Dr. Dementia. And just because Dr. Dementia wears a bowtie, it does not mean he is harmless. He asks a lot of ridiculous questions that torment my mother for days before each of her subsequent appointments until she is sure she has committed the predictable answers to memory.

The first visit is "getting to know you" propaganda. Again, what year are we in? Good. When is your birthday? Good. Who is our current president? Fine. Who was the president before him? Good. What about before him? That's okay. Take your time. We had rehearsed this in case it came up again because I don't think it's fair to judge an elderly person on their faulty memory about a subject most people even my age don't pay much attention to. The exam continues with a test of memory.

"I am going to give you three words to remember, and in a few minutes I will ask you to repeat them back to me. How does that sound?" he asks pleasantly.

"Well, if I can do it, I will certainly try," my mother says with a mix of hope and anxiety.

"The words are *apple, penny,* and *chair.* Do you think you can remember these in a few minutes?"

"Apple, penny, chair, apple, penny, chair," she repeats under her breath with her eyes tightly shut as if she is praying the words won't slip away. "Apple, penny, chair."

Oh, this is torture for me to watch. Why must we test her mental strength? She is just trying to get along in life doing the best she can without bringing any harm to anyone else. This reminds me of exactly how I felt when my dad would come home from the stress tests his cardiologist used to make him take by walking at a very fast pace for minutes on end on a treadmill. My dad wasn't a runner or a sprinter, and he had just had angioplasty surgery; did he really need to be put through the agony of these Jack LaLanne machines? My dad tried to explain to me that the doctors were just trying to build up his heart muscles so he could be his strongest and live for a longer time. Still, it bothers me a lot to see my parents tested beyond their limits.

"Apple, penny, chair," she is still whispering to herself, willing it to memory.

"Let's try something new now. I want you to think of all the kinds of animals you know. Don't tell them to me yet. I am going to give you one minute to name as many as you can while I write them all down." The doctor is just about ready to start his timer when I stop to check for understanding, as any good teacher would and certainly every doctor should.

"Mom, do you know what the doctor wants you to do here?"

"I am going to name animals." She looks at me with her pale-blue eyes, hoping she has the right answer.

"That's right, Mom. I don't even think you need to give the names of our pets, I just think you are listing the kinds of animals you might find in a zoo or in a house." I am hoping this isn't too obvious of a hint to give her a good head start.

"Okay, and begin."

"Dromedary."

Oh, good God, she has failed. I don't know what is wrong with my mother. She seems like she is mentally fit to me. I know there might be some slippage. Everyone knows there might be some slippage. Even the CPA said that when my mom first came in after my father passed away, all she did was dump the old briefcase onto his desk and tell him to sort through the mound of papers that amounted to junk mail and rubber-banded statements. But now she is making up animals that don't even exist. Why couldn't she start with *cat*? She's had enough of them. Or *dog*? She and Daisy practically wrestle for the spot on my mom's bed since Daisy jumps into it eagerly every time my mom goes to the kitchen for a snack. Certainly *dog* should be at the front of her mind.

"Aardvark. Crustacean. Scorpion. Armadillo. Chimpanzee. Giraffe." She pauses to think with precious seconds ticking away.

"Time is up. Good. You got seven," he says with a faint smile to encourage her for the next exercise.

"I wasn't sure if you counted *dromedary*." I hope he gives her a bonus point for creativity.

"Oh, a dromedary is a very fine animal. They are the one-humped camel." He smiles broadly at my mother, who sits up straighter and relaxes her shoulders knowing she has impressed him with her knowledge of Middle Eastern animals.

"Thank goodness, Mom. I thought you were making up a new animal." I let out a sigh of relief because I was worried for nothing.

"All right now. Do you remember the three words I gave you a few minutes ago?" the doctor asks.

"I think so." She looks to me again with a worried expression, and all I can do is nod and smile widely with all the robust encouragement my teacher's eyes can offer.

"I will write them down as you give them to me. They don't have to be in any particular order. Whenever you are ready." He is poised to record.

"Apple."

This one comes easily. All I can think to myself is, *Good job, Mom.*

"Hmmmm. Penny, is that right?" She is hesitant, but this too comes pretty quickly.

"You're doing a great job, Mom." I am so proud of her. She has remembered two words.

"Hmmm. Let me see. Apple. Penny. Hmmm." She is staring at the floor as if there might be a cue card there to give her the answer, if indeed she could read at that distance. She has not given up, but it just won't come. She wants to know this word so badly, but it is not retrievable before the doctor finally tells her the answer.

"Chair. That's right. I knew it." She is so disgusted with herself for forgetting. I hold her hand in mine and stroke her tiny fingers gently. I want her to know that I am very proud of the hard work she put into today's session.

The doctor tells her what a good job she did and that he'd like to see her again in three months, just for a follow-up. He just wanted to get a baseline of where her brain was today since Dr. Goodcare is concerned about her falling potentially causing trauma to her head. It sounds reasonable enough to us both, and we are on our way.

We laugh all the way home because I thought dromedary was a made up name, and my mom is feeling smarter by the second that it was the first animal she thought of. I tell her we will practice some of those tests at home together, and we can try to double the number of animals she can name within sixty seconds before we go in for our second visit. Preparation is the only way I know how to approach test taking. And I am willing to rehearse as much as possible if it means I can stave off a report of onset dementia.

Lying in bed, watching TV in the guest room for a change of pace while my mother watches some opera on PBS in the front room while enjoying her oversized, wraparound couch we bought this summer, I happen to notice a streak of ants trailing up the wall in a single file. I cannot believe we have ants in the back of the house, especially since I never eat in bed. I am trying to find their starting and ending points, but all I can see is their path to the roofline, where they are trying to cross the beam as if it is their bridge to salvation. It's not.

I still have ant spray and I use it generously. I am sick and tired of ants trying to take over this house and pleased with my progress at quickly displacing them. I am feeling so lucky right now that I don't need to sleep in this guest room anymore and doubly relieved that I did not have to be awakened in the middle of the night by a streak of ants across my face. That would be horrid.

The next morning my pride completely evaporates when I see before me in the bathroom a swarm of ants all over Daisy's food dish. I follow their black mass up the linen closet wall to the ceiling, where they are toiling with the idea of penetrating the roof from the beam they have become so attached to. I have never seen so many ants congregating in one place. This is way bigger than the traumatic episode I experienced as a kid when my feet dangled over an ant pile clamoring at an old hot dog bun left beneath our patio picnic table. And when I discovered streaks of ants in the kitchen mess I cleaned up months and months ago, this is even worse.

Swarms of ants are converging in the way you would expect on an anthill or a jelly sandwich sitting in the sun next to the aluminum garbage can in the park. This is beyond what I can annihilate with the last can of spray I have in the garage. The good dousing I give clears out only twenty percent, and I know there are professionals to take care of a problem this size. So I call Terminix. They guarantee me that someone would be here within the half hour and that they will do a full-scale investigation to root out the source of the problem, and yes, that will include going onto the roof. But when Tomás arrives, he is committed to doing everything except for going on top of the roof due to his union regulations. The problem is the ants don't want to be down, they want to be up. They aren't swarming the floors; they are scaling the walls to the ceiling. Logic dictates that someone should look at what is on the roof.

Tomás is in the middle of giving me several good reasons why he is forbidden to go onto the roof. I am listening intently while I am moving in and out of the garage, carting my short, aluminum ladder awkwardly under my arm. He follows me to the embankment on the backside of our house, where he watches me plant its wobbly legs in the mud and gravel as he continues to reel off legitimate reasons why he cannot go up on the roof. As I ask him to hold the base of the ladder that I have already climbed up halfway so I can hang on the roofline to see for myself what's happening up there, he can't take it anymore and convinces me to come down so he can take a look for himself.

Would you believe what he found? There is a black pool— literally a pool as wide as the roof—of ants on top of ants, all clamoring to burrow in through the ceiling to get at whatever it is they seem to want. These ants have met their match in Tomás. He goes to his truck to get the big guns. These are the weapons they taught him to use, but he has never had an occasion to rely on them until now. Tomás gets excited, and he gets his own big-boy ladder because he does not want to fall from the overhang as he suspected I was about to do.

Within another forty minutes, Tomás has sprayed every single living ant in that massive ant pool, plus the ones inside the bathroom that I thought I already killed, plus the perimeter of the house and the garage and kitchen just to be on the safe side. I am left to clean up two thousand dead ants in the bathroom, and if you don't know what fun that is, you don't know what you're missing.

Paper towels upon paper towels soaked in water are used to wash the walls, the floors, and the insides of the linen closet. The guest baskets all need to be emptied to be sure there has been no infiltration of ant troops. I wipe down the entire bathroom floor on my hands and knees like Cinderella and continue the scraping of wet ants stuck in place along the ceiling and the beams. All the while I keep checking to see if dead ants have fallen into my hair even though I took preventive measures by tying a kerchief around my head. This job is beyond anything I have ever taken on. It is hard and disgusting, and as time goes by I will discover it is only going to get worse.

# CHAPTER 17

# Call 911

The next medical appointment we have set for this week is with the eye doctor, who likes to check my mom's vision every two to three months to make sure her macular degeneration isn't progressing too quickly. She loves this young doctor and flatters him every chance she gets. I feel like I am a third wheel when I sit in the dark room for her routine exam because they prattle on about all that has been occurring in their lives since her last checkup. I think I am invisible, and the prospect of meeting a doctor to date is quickly diminished because my radar tells me this one is already partnered up. I am too busy to date anyway, but it would be nice to have someone to talk to besides my mom.

After he concludes everything looks normal, and we schedule our follow-up appointment for two months from now, I decide that what I need is a little break. Some me time at the ocean sounds divine, and Brother One promises he will take care of my mom and Daisy, and yes, he will spend the night. My greatest worry is that my mom will fall and no one will be there for her. So I leave for two nights to a lovely hotel where I can hear the rolling waves, read a good book, and kick back with absolutely no obligations. I call home at bedtime to see how things are going, and my mom tells me that Brother One has run to his house, and he'll be back soon. Fine.

An hour later, at ten o'clock, I phone a second time, and still Brother One is not there. I call him at his house, and he assures me he is on his way up to my mom's, and since he only lives five minutes away, I am expecting this should only take five minutes. Not to seem like I don't trust him to take care of my mother the way we agreed, I decide it prudent not to call again.

Instead I do a drive-by to look for his car on our street. It is now midnight, and there is no sign of him in sight. All the house lights are off, so I use my key to go inside, half hoping that his wife dropped him off and kept his car for some reason. Daisy needs to be pottied, and as I let her out, my mom meets me in the hall where she is in the midst of doing her walking exercises.

"Oh, you surprised me. I thought you were enjoying yourself on the coast," she says nonchalantly.

"Well, I wanted to see if Brother One is here, and I can tell he's not," I say, sounding a bit miffed.

"Oh, I'm fine. He was here until about eight o'clock, and he'll be back first thing in the morning," she says assuredly.

"The thing is, Mom, this was not the deal, and I can't relax if you are not being looked after. How would it be if you fell here by yourself and he didn't find you until the morning? Or what if you decide to guzzle more cranberry juice and start upchucking again?"

"Well, I can't do that because you don't buy it for me anymore." She thinks she's so smart.

"Let's go to bed. I can pick up my stuff from the hotel in the morning. I won't be able to sleep there anyway knowing that you are here alone." And this solution seems to soothe us both.

When morning comes Brother One knows what he will be walking into because my car is in the driveway. All I can say to him is that I am very disappointed that I couldn't trust him to follow through with our agreement, and that I am the one who has had to call 911 and take our mom to the emergency room, so I know the kind of constant care she requires.

I remind him of the trip they took together to Santa Fe, when she decided to take a midnight shower after he was asleep and slipped and fell in the tub. I tell him he should know better and that I think his decision making is reckless and puts her at risk because if she falls, how is she supposed to get to a phone?

Her ninety-two-year-old friend Magda just fell inside her marble entryway, breaking her collarbone and shoulder so she couldn't even crawl to the phone three feet away. She waited all day before her neighbor found her, and now her home has been sold and she lives with her son and his wife three hours away from everyone she has known for the last sixty years.

He agrees and apologizes profusely, and I have to repeat this same scenario only three or four more times before I am fully convinced that I cannot count on him to follow through with what he promises because he is too busy managing his own life with a wife who wants him at home. He doesn't want to say "no" to his mother or to his wife, so he tries to straddle two households to the best of his ability, but it's not enough. I get it. He's stuck. But it cannot work this way.

The doctor appointment we have scheduled for this week is to see the same doctor we just saw, except he has a different title. What I learn after lots of confusion is that Dr. Reuben

Klein, the optometrist we saw last week, is different from Dr. Reuben V. Klein, the ophthalmologist who performed my mother's cataract surgery and has requested today's follow-up appointment. To make matters worse, I discover this error only after I have already dragged my mother unwittingly to the optometrist we already saw, whose assistant explains the difference between the two doctors whose names would be identical if it weren't for the distinguishing middle initial used by the ophthalmologist, and I now need to cart my mother across the street to the building where her appointment is starting in five minutes.

Do people not know how much work there is behind the scenes to get an eighty-six-year-old dressed and out the door to be on time for an appointment? It takes a lot of advance planning for me to get out of afternoon yard duty or a meeting so I can race home in time to pick up my mother, who has done a half decent job getting herself pulled together but still needs help with a few items like hooking a bra, which I insist she must go back inside to put on. Then I need to make sure her medical card is where it should be because sometimes she likes to play with the contents of her wallet to amuse herself, and on afternoons like this I do not find it amusing at all to be on the hunt for insurance information that was tucked safely away last night.

We now have five minutes to get back in the car, for which I already scored a sweet parking spot outside her medical building so she wouldn't have to walk too far, in order to drive across the street, where we will end up parking in the far back of the building because all of the handicap spots are currently taken up by people who are on time for their appointments. We will have to scurry across a long parking lot as fast as two people locking arms using a cane can scurry, which is about at the pace of a tortoise, before taking the elevator up to the sixth floor. We'll make it, all right. In about twenty minutes. It's not like she can run with me.

I found out her days of jetting around the city were numbered when I took her to see *Jersey Boys* in San Francisco over the summer. I still had it in my mind that she could rush across Union Square in order to make curtain call at the clip she used to keep when she would dash up stairs two at a time, in heels, to get to her next college class. It never occurred to me that she would have slowed down. Getting into our seats at that performance, and getting out of the city's traffic after that matinee, were enough to put her into a comatose nap for the rest of the weekend—and finally to admit out loud that she simply can't keep up the pace she once used to.

Inside the ophthalmologist's office, we spend only the few short minutes Dr. Reuben V. Klein needs to look into her eyes with a laser beam to determine there is no further loss of vision beyond the last measurement. I ask about the growth of the tumor behind her eye that she told me was the reason she would eventually go blind, and he looks at me puzzled.

"There is no tumor behind your mother's eye."

"I thought you had to perform her surgery to prevent the tumor from getting bigger, but you couldn't get it all, so that's why she will only be able to see vistas before she goes blind," I say, trying to jog his memory.

"There is no tumor. I don't know where you got that idea."

We both look at my mother.

Here's what I have always known about my mother: she has a flare for the dramatic. Although it has been infrequent, I have heard her mention a couple of times now how much she wanted to be an actress in her lifetime. Not that the prospect of this ever presented itself, but she did believe her rendition of Ebenezer Scrooge as an eighth grader in her school play was the best that her town had ever seen, back in the 1930s. From this one laurel, she gleaned so many accolades that she became semi-sure a call to acting was a missed opportunity for her.

So, in order to make up for the drama of the theater, she created drama in her life. A simple cataract surgery would not be enough to draw sympathy from her audience; she would add in the tumor. The time she says there were three fat, beastly raccoons sitting on the kitchen counter one dark night that only she could threaten enough in her robust stage voice to scare back outside is hard to imagine. Even the stories she told of the first few times she fell in her home were met with suspicion by family members because she has always enjoyed a reputation as the little girl who cried wolf. At least now I know the doctor's version of her health report, and it doesn't sound like she is going blind anytime soon.

Our days are filled with frenzied mornings of me trying to get out of the house in time for school after I have given her the morning meds, made her a hot breakfast, made her some hot coffee because she won't be allowed to use the stove when I am at school, and made sure that her lunch options of yogurt, an already peeled hard-boiled egg, or cottage cheese are on her lunch tray so she doesn't have to dig through the refrigerator to figure out what there is to eat. Sometimes she gets overwhelmed by all the contents in the fridge and will just resort to the ice cream in the freezer, which I have been forced to buy in Dixie-cup sizes for $2 a pop, with no more than three in the house at a time lest she has a craving that throws off her blood sugar levels.

Once I am ready to walk out the door, she is tucked back in bed for her morning nap, and before she closes her eyes she insists that I show her my outfit.

"Oh, that's a beautiful skirt. Now turn around so I can see how it hangs in the back. Oh, you have such a nice figure. The kids are going to love seeing you today." She is my best fashion critic because the routine is the same every day, and I always leave the house feeling like I can touch the moon.

"Ta-ta, Mom, I'll see you after school." I give her a kiss as I rush out the door. "Have fun with Daisy," I toss over my shoulder as I see Daisy already trying to nestle up to my mom like in the story of the camel in the tent. The camel and his master are in a desert storm when the camel begs to warm his nose inside the tent if his kind master will allow it. The master is suspicious of the camel's intentions, and as the story continues, the camel worms his way into warming his two front legs, his humps, and finally his tail before he runs away with the tent completely. My mother knows that as soon as she heads to the kitchen to toast some sourdough bread to have with her stick of butter, Daisy will be warming herself in the spot my mother just left.

"Ta-ta, dear. I'll be waiting for you. I want to hear all about the kids," she yells down the hall enthusiastically. Her teacher's heart has never left the classroom even after fifty years of being out of education.

Our evenings are spent with me doing chores while dinner is in the oven, and she is tuned in to the evening news on BBC. She has a hearty appetite for my double-stuffed pork chops, or salmon, or homemade macaroni and cheese with seasoned croutons I make from scratch. We are down to a regular bath routine every other night, and thankfully one of my new colleagues at school has already been through this experience so she gives me the bath chair she used for her own mother, and what a godsend it is. It fits perfectly into the dimensions of the tub and is safe and secure with rubber feet. The venting holes in the seat allow the water to rush through after a thorough cleansing of all my mother's hard to reach parts, and we are both relieved that I can now get her sudsed up and out of the bath within about four minutes. Grace even brings me a copy of the catalogue she used religiously to find products for seniors she couldn't find anywhere else. It is called Dr. Leonard's Catalogue of Senior Aids, and it gives me tons of ideas about what a senior might need in the future if my mother's life takes a turn for the worse, which I doubt will ever happen.

On a rainy night when neither of us has the energy to do anything but watch an old-fashioned black-and-white movie I have rented, we decide to order pizza and have it delivered. There is something wonderful about food coming to you without your having to lift a finger. There is a gourmet pizzeria very nearby that's known for stacking heaping mounds of cheese onto a crust that can never support the weight of all the goodies on top of it. Whenever we watch the rotund man in the window twirling the dough in the air, we wonder who could possibly eat the monstrosities he is heralded for creating…as we lick our lips, ready to take on the challenge.

After our night of indulging in one large slice each, we finish our movie and tuck ourselves into bed. Even though I installed a French door in the hallway to separate the back half of the house from her master bedroom and the rest of the house, its windowpanes are not thick enough to drown out the choking noises I hear in my sleep. Once again she is barfing with the urgency of someone who is losing precious fluids rapidly. I run to get the yellow plastic bowl from the kitchen cupboard and get it beneath her chin to catch the hurling contents that are hitting the spittoon, forcing splashes up the sidewall like an ocean tide hitting its container wall before the hurricane ramps up to a category 5.

"Oh Mom, you look awful."

She can barely see me through her tearing eyes as she hugs the bowl closer. "Call 911," she says dramatically, which has become her answer to everything.

The last time we had the paramedic team here, the thrill of several doting young men for the better part of an hour made her feel remarkably well again, and she began sizing them up individually and saying out loud, "Oh, I like this one here in his uniform." It is embarrassing when your mother can flirt shamelessly while discarding the fact that she is still in her nightclothes, and it makes her look less like she needs an ambulance and more like she needs a date. Furthermore, I resent the fact that I didn't think of it first.

Again her attention-getting mechanism kicks in, and she wants to gain an audience, which is why I always hesitated about ordering a Life Alert bracelet for her because the last thing I want is for my mother to have access to 911 so someone can come to the house to make her a snack or to keep her company. So I am on to her, and an ambulance is against my better judgment at this point. I only hope it isn't the wrong decision.

"Mom, you know the rule. Unless there is blood or you are unconscious, we are not calling the ambulance," I say lovingly but firmly.

"I had too much of that rotten pizza," she says as she gurgles out another few mouthfuls of spit.

"Oh, I am sorry you feel so badly." I dab her forehead with a cool cloth and tuck her hair behind her ears. "But you will feel better in a few minutes once you get it all out of your system."

"You're wonderful, Steffie," she says with pure tenderness in her heart. I am lucky because she tells me this often, and I get a sense she is very grateful that she doesn't have to weather feeling crummy all by herself.

Once she is done with her bowl, and I have her cooled down, cleaned up, and changed into new clothes, I bring her ginger ale and a couple saltine crackers. Her color is returning to normal, and I feel like we are out of the woods. We both decide that pizza is not worth the risk and that we will never order from that place again.

As the school year winds down, marking my first-year anniversary at home with my mom, I think back on what I have accomplished. I have managed to get most of the house in proper condition. A neighbor, Mrs. Hoover, who used to take my mother grocery shopping when she first lost her privilege to drive, popped in within the first month of my return just to stick her nose in and see if my mom was being well looked after. Her very first comment was to ask if I got rid of all the cats, to which I replied no, I just cleaned the house. She was quite impressed by such a positive transformation in a relatively short period of time. And she was very relieved to see my mother, who appeared from her room, newly shorn, clean, and dressed in something other than her tattered, blue robe. I finally coerced my mom to let me cut off the right sleeve completely where the elbow had worn straight through to show a big, gaping hole. Believe me, the two different sleeve lengths on that robe she will not give up are a great improvement.

Then Mrs. Hoover told me what I have suspected all along: "Your mother missed you so much in the years you were away.

She was hoping so desperately that she could get you to agree to come home to help her. You were her only choice. I'm glad you did it, Steffie. You are doing a good job here. As her friend, I thank you." And she gave me an unexpected hug and told me if I needed anything just to call.

For the job I thought neighbors and other relatives should have been doing for my mother all along, I now realize there is no way other people could have undertaken fixing what I have seen in this first year. The disrepair of her home, the personal care she needed, the meals that weren't being prepared, the ants that needed to be managed, and the animals that needed better care were all beyond the scope of what a neighbor or a holiday brother or another brother busy with his own family to look after could possibly manage.

I get it now. This is not a job for the faint of heart or the casual observer. It takes commitment and patience and constant planning. I am so grateful that my teaching year has been an easy one to slide into; anything less might have put me over the edge. Thank goodness for Pip's being so available and reliable and earnest. And the story I promised you earlier, the one where Pip saves the house, is finally ready to be told.

# PART 5

# WARNING SIGNS

## REALITY 5
### *When Your Home and Your Parent Begin Falling Apart, Get Prepared*

# CHAPTER 18

# A Sinking Feeling

Before Pip plays his pivotal role in saving our house, I need to set the scene. The house is falling apart. It seems as though I have entered the money pit from the first day I set foot on the property. I do not ever remember my father having as many bad breaks with this house as I seem to be having in my first year. While repairs are part of what's to be expected for home-owners of any age, I am especially uneasy about the costs of upkeep that are mounting for a senior on a fixed income. I will soon come to discover that the ants, the refurbishing of rooms, and the re-carpeting will amount to very little compared to the next misadventures, which will rear their ugly heads in succession.

With just a couple months left to go in the school year, I am aching for summer. I am exhausted but anxious to have some uninterrupted time to finally tackle my mother's room so we can update its outdated look. But the unpleasantness of major sewage problems interrupts my advance planning for future decorating. All of our toilets are backing up at once. Brother One has used his plumber friend in the past for under-the-table jobs conducted after hours at my mom's house, and I figure this is a good time to get that guy back here. None of us can determine why all three toilets are having the same problem, and while I am no plumber, I can only imagine one thing: this is going to be expensive.

There is wet toilet paper coming up from the pipes beneath the sewer grate located in our dog run. At first I think my mom has something to do with plugging up all the plumbing, but even after Nick, the nearly free plumber friend of Brother One, comes to take a look, it is obvious that he has neither the time nor the equipment required to snake a job this big. He recommends we find a specialized company to look under the house with a camera. I am forced to call in the experts, and they arrive the next day to investigate the pipes beneath the house.

My worst suspicions are confirmed when I see the look on the plumber's face. Apparently he has become accustomed to delivering very bad news like this to customers, enough to know how to sandwich the blows with a gentle bedside manner. First Al starts with a compliment.

"Well, ma'am, you did the smart thing by getting us out here right away. If you waited any longer, it would cost you thousands more." He smiles weakly because he can tell I am scared now—really scared. Why is he speaking of thousands more? How much are we up to already?

After this compliment comes the news that doctors usually deliver with a nun or a priest standing at their sides.

"You see we have this specialized tractor I like to call Little Al because he goes where I can't. He has a camera attached to his hood, and with his little lamp he can show us all the damage that has been done to your pipes over the years. We plug a long cable into his caboose and let him run his course, showing us what we can't get to ourselves."

He can tell I am a little suspicious. How can a toy-sized machine, one that looks a lot like the remote-control cars my nephews always begged me to buy when they would spend the night at my house, which included a Toys"R"Us trip as their treat, be this accurate?

Al continues, "You see, ma'am, we have this here video monitor that we watch as the camera is recording, and that's how we can see the problems and pinpoint the exact location of the pipe that has burst." He is about to go on when I jump ahead and begin to work myself into a frenzy over a pipe bursting.

I pepper him with questions like, "How did this happen, and how much is this going to cost, and how long will this take to fix?" All the while I am worried about the fixed amount we still have left in savings and how I did not anticipate this house would ever need anything more than the little sprucing up I could mostly do myself to save us money. This is sounding like it will rob us of all we have left in the bank. Al has nothing to offer me to assuage my fears.

"Ma'am, I'm sorry to have to tell you this, but it's worse than you think." He turns on the video monitor to show me what Little Al, the motorized car, ran into underground.

"You see this here tunnel of light? That's the car moving through the sewer pipe just fine until…you see this here dark mass?"

I am looking at a dark mass of something. I can only tell Little Al can't move any farther.

"We're stuck under your driveway. We make it all the way

from the back of your house, through the entire center of the house, and through the garage until we get stuck here. The cement in your driveway has been sinking over time, and it has finally crushed your pipes."

And this is where the nun would move in closer to hold my hand, or the priest would give me last rites. I must look this bad because even Al asks if I need a minute to digest this information.

He rewinds the tape and plays it again. He makes a copy of it for me to keep, which I will watch a few more times by myself. Part of me is fascinated that modern technology has come up with such a clever toy to help plumbers who can't crawl under houses built on concrete slabs. The other part of me feels lucky that we don't have to drill into the middle of the dining room, a point Al was sure to make as he completed his sandwich of blows with this last bit of positive news.

And another part of me is starting to worry about how many times we can afford to be surprised by big expenses before the last of the proverbial money trees growing in our backyard are completely hacked down. It's completely taste-less to talk about dollars, so to give you an idea, let's say if I started with twenty-five trees and the front landscaping took about six trees, and I have spent about two more trees' worth on the inside of the house, we are down to seventeen trees. I am expecting seventeen trees to be just the right amount to get my mom through the next several years comfortably if we keep frills to a minimum.

"Oh, this is not the news I was expecting. How much do you think this will cost?" I am trying to remain calm, trying very hard to not cry.

"Until we know how bad the pipes have been crushed, we

can't give you the exact cost. We don't even dig up the concrete. You'll have to find someone who can get the machines out here to dig up your driveway, and then we'll get our guys out here to take a look at what will be involved in fixing your pipes." Al smiles a little more broadly this time and again tries to leave me with a good feeling before we part ways.

"I know this isn't what you wanted to hear today, but just remember, we've done this kind of work for a long time, and we'll get it done right. It's a good thing you called when you did, and it's a good thing the problem is outside so we don't have to drill inside your house. We've had to do that before, and it's a huge disruption for the family." He shakes my hand and asks me to call him just as soon as we see pipe from the digging.

I can only sit and heave heavy sighs. We are still in the dark as to what this could cost, but it's not going to be cheap. I go into my mom's room to show her the tape and explain everything I have just learned.

"Oh boy," she lets out in a bellow of frustration and then resigns herself to my handling it. "You'll get it done" is her way of saying she trusts me, followed by, "How am I going to pay for it?" Which is her other way of saying, "I am worried, and I am glad you are here to help me through this."

I assure her that we are not going to run out of money because of this one thing, but it does mean we need to put other things on hold this year, like her room makeover, which we were both looking forward to doing together. We know we need the toilets to work, so we forge ahead, and I put Brother One in charge of finding a reputable place that can rip up our driveway and then pour it again for less than what I want to pay. Brother One knows someone in every field. He apparently has a friend he has helped in the past who works as a cement contractor and agrees to do this job for the discounted price of two trees.

Once the jackhammering has finished over the course of a day, the plumber tells us we can save even more money if we supply our own labor to dig out the five-foot trenches required to get to the pipes. Again Brother One has an idea for how to get cheap laborers, so he brings a crew of three men he does not know, who do not speak English, and leaves them and a few shovels with me so I can give them directions in my broken Spanish. I am not sure I love this idea, but it is the best solution at the present moment.

While the workers are digging a trench in the driveway hour after hour, I watch them from my bedroom window, peering from behind closed blinds to be sure they cannot see me. It is slow-going, and they talk a lot, but there is dirt being thrown over their shoulders in heaping mounds, so I imagine they are working to the best of what anyone can expect.

The next day I watch them again. The trench is beginning to look like there is some depth because they are now in it up to their knees. The more they talk, the more I know they are working because it seems to keep them in a rhythm. I offer them cold bottles of water and pop that I leave in an ice chest, and I buy sandwiches for them from a deli. The day after this, I give them a choice, and when I return with their burritos from the Mexican restaurant across the street from the deli, this really makes them happy. They continue to work long hours, talking and shoveling, talking, and shoveling.

On the third day, they start out just the same way as always. But today they have brought their own lunches and smile a lot, which I take to mean that while they appreciate my hospitality, they are able to provide for themselves. Good. I go about my work inside the house since I am on spring break from school, and it is not until hours later that I start to notice something different. It is suspiciously quiet outside. I hear no voices, and when I go to the bedroom window to peek out, I see no men. Are they shirking their responsibilities without having completed the job? I wonder to myself.

I am so maddened by the likelihood that they have gone off to a long lunch somewhere, and we are losing valuable time since I want the pipe guys to get here before the end of the week so this job can be finished already. I have worked myself into a dither by the time I round the back gates to go through the courtyard off the driveway to inspect how much work they still have left to complete.

Imagine my surprise when, teetering above the trench, I find that there, at the bottom of a six-foot drop, is Miguel standing fully erect, yet hidden by the driveway that towers over him at least several inches. He is still shoveling dirt as fast as ever, but instead of heaving it over his shoulders, he is building an enormous pile to his left. When Victor and Luis return from their short break, they will excavate the dirt from the hole.

This part of the project is only a few hours from completion and will definitely be done tonight. Miguel can already see pipe showing through beneath his boots. I am very grateful that they are trustworthy and hardworking. I call Al, who confirms he'll be there tomorrow, and we are on our way to getting this problem solved.

It turns out that the reason the driveway has been sinking for the better part of sixty years is that the builders in the '50s were rumored to have saved money by installing the rebar to pass inspection and removing it once the inspectors left. There is now no rebar under our concrete to hold the driveway in place. Therefore, over the course of decades and earth shifts, it was only a matter of time before the pipes would become crushed. Fortunately for us the damage is not beyond repair; it could have amounted to a lot more expense if the work required were more extensive. I cut down another tree.

# CHAPTER 19

# Waiting for Summer

Just as this little problem is taken care of, the doctor calls one evening. It is a few days following a visit that he requested for lab work, and now that the results are in from what I expected to be routine exams and blood work, Dr. Goodcare is sharing the simple news that my mother needs to be put on insulin for her diabetes. I need to go in with her to pick up the kit and receive my instructions on how to inject her daily. Nothing could petrify me more. I am not a fan of needles, and I am not looking forward to pricking my mother's finger to draw blood every morning and night. Nor do I wish to stick her with a syringe attached to a vial of powerful medicine. This is a lot of responsibility for someone who is not a trained nurse. These are the fears I share with him while he assures me I can do this and then proceeds to show me how.

Thank goodness my mom is not the least bit fazed by this news. She used to give herself the injections, but it would be nearly impossible for her now since her eyesight has become so poor. She is grateful I am here to help and decides to live with the news.

"That Dr. Goodcare is determined to keep me alive," she says enthusiastically.

It's a sentiment I will hear many more times in her future. She believes he is the very best that medical care has to offer, and sometimes I agree. I really like that he pays so much attention to being proactive about her tests. But I also don't like that he pays so much attention to being proactive about her tests because this results in more appointments for her. Every time we visit his office, he schedules tests at the hospital or refers us to another specialist.

After her fall at church, she had her bone density tested to see if she had weak bones that were making her fall. We still see the neurologist every three months, and I don't know why Dr. Dementia keeps asking her to memorize "apple, penny, chair," and mostly I am worried as to why she can't keep these three words in her head long enough to pass his exam. He keeps chronicling her onset dementia, and we keep leaving his office feeling slightly dejected.

There are additional meds to take and a jug for her to fill at home so the calcium levels in her urine can be monitored. We do her blood testing twice a day and still run back and forth to the two eye doctors with the nearly identical names. There is also the hearing doctor she sees once a year, and his appointment is on the horizon. It seems my mom is on every roster of the popular doctors who see all the other senior citizens, so it is very hard to get rescheduled if I cancel because of parent conferences, which I did.

Our new time has finally come today, and after checking in, we wait for our appointment. It takes an hour in the waiting room for my mother to be seen. She is nearly asleep because this is during her afternoon naptime. I am nearly asleep too because I have been teaching all day. I wish Brother One could share more of these appointments, but his schedule has changed, and he is not as flexible as he once was.

My mom's hearing is not great, but at eighty-six years old, this is to be expected. Her tiny ear canals collect more wax than a bee's hive, and while she is not being fitted for a hearing aid this year, there are more scheduled appointments in her future for regular cleanings.

Between the medical appointments and the house throwing me surprise after surprise, I am still hearing the words of our trusted financial accountant: "Get your financial papers in order." I cannot sleep for many reasons, and this is one of them. Finally I am able to schedule some time with the attorney he referred, and when I arrive at the law offices of Carol Durham, I feel immediately relieved that I have gotten this ball rolling. She is warm and engaging and quite good with seniors. I explain that my mom cannot hear that well, so Carol makes sure to speak up.

While we all meet together for the first half hour, it is behind closed doors for the rest of the meeting time that Carol ascertains my mother's private wishes for her estate or any changes to it. I am not privy. Thank goodness we already have the trust and the will securely in place. It is the matter of the two powers of attorney we need to square away today, one for managing my mother's financial matters should she become incapacitated and the other for health-related decisions, known commonly as the advance health-care directive.

This is how the summer ahead will be spent: full of meetings with Carol wherein I will escort my mother inside and then flip through lengthy magazine articles while I wait in the lobby for the hour they meet together. It takes a series of conversations to make sure a senior is of sound mind and can articulate the care she would like to have when it comes to her end of life. I am just so thankful I did not delay getting her vital papers in place. More about the details of these legal documents will be shared in Part 8: Estate Management.

All I need is a weekend away. I am about to collapse under the constant running at home and the pressure to help my students at school perform to their level best. I will be administering the state test at this school site for my first time. I know my principal is anxious to see how my kids will perform since he knows about the successes I had in the past. He is counting on me to help raise the performance index for his school. This is a year that matters.

In two weeks my students will take this test, and we won't know the results until after we return from summer break. I want to go away for the weekend after testing is finished, so I begin scouting places that will provide me with a trustworthy caregiver who can look after my mom and Daisy and the cats while I am gone. I see a lot of commercials for different services that make it sound so easy to find care for my mother.

The first agency sends a fifty-year-old woman to be interviewed. My mom and I decide that if I like the person well enough after prescreening, I can wake her from her nap so she can get acquainted with the candidate. I really like this lady a lot. She is congenial, smart, and friendly, and obviously very, very caring. We talk about my mom's routine, and I go into detail about when she likes to eat her meals and when she has her naps, and entertainment she might like in the evening.

I begin to go through the med routine when the woman interrupts me to make sure I know the only way she can dispense meds is if they are already prearranged in separate cups with labels indicating date and time, and then my mom would have to be the one to take the cup, and this woman would only be there to supervise. If I am comfortable with this, then we will be in compliance with her guidelines. Fine enough. I can easily pull the pills from the pillbox and set them up according to what she specified. I am so looking forward to getting away.

I continue to explain the routine for insulin injections when she stops me completely right there. She has no clearance for administering injections of any kind. Unless my mom is capable of doing this herself and the woman is there merely to oversee that it is done, this will not be a fit for her agency. How sad. I was *this* close to getting a break. I can't see any way around their worry about a potential negligence suit, so I can only thank her for coming, and I sit down alone to think about who else I can find.

A name is passed to me from someone who knows someone else. She is a young girl who is finishing her nursing program and used to take care of her grandmother before she died. I like her immediately on the phone and am happy to discover she is even better in person. Her name is Summer. How glorious. She is a breath of fresh air, lovely looking with chestnut hair and fair skin and golden-brown eyes that twinkle when she talks to my mom. They hit it off right away, and I let them do most of the talking. I ask Summer if she is familiar with giving insulin injections, and coincidentally enough she used to help her grandmother with this, and she doesn't balk at the idea of doing it for my mom.

Summer loves all animals and lets Daisy lick her face beyond the length of time I know it takes when someone is just being polite. Summer is organized and takes good notes. She is newly single and brokenhearted to the point that her eyes mist over when she says it is really for the best because they are young and just want different things. I can see a whole summer in front of me with Summer here to help. A nursing student needs money. I need a break. I would love to pay her to come one weekend a month so I can go stick my toes in the sand and heal my soul at the edge of the earth, my favorite place to be. I feel lighter already, and we schedule this Saturday as the first dry run for a few hours, so she and my mom can get comfortable. If this goes well, then I can make reservations for my Memorial weekend away.

On Friday I call Summer to confirm the time she will be there in the morning, but I am sent to her voicemail. I still don't hear from her by dinner, so I call again. To be polite I figure maybe she is out on a date, and she will call me in the morning to say she is on her way over. I don't sleep soundly. Would someone who really wants a job leave me to wonder all night if she is really going to show up, date or no date?

Saturday morning comes. I run to Starbucks to pick up my mother's favorite mocha, which has become her ritual now twice a week since we also treat ourselves on library night every Wednesday. Even though I am back before Summer arrives, I feel I should call to make sure she got my other two messages. Voicemail again. It doesn't take me beyond lunchtime to figure out that Summer is a no-show. I never hear from that girl again. I will always wonder what happened to her. Maybe she was daunted by all the responsibility she would be taking on in the course of one weekend. Try living here.

Several weeks later my mom and I have a date to celebrate school's finally being over. We go out to a matinee, and when we return after having a dinner of matzo ball soup at one of our favorite restaurants, we climb into bed early for once. I can hardly keep my eyes open. The end of the year has caught up to me, and I feel like it has been a thousand years since I left my old life. I consider opening a book but decide just to shut off the lamp and watch television quietly for a little while.

I am coming to detest this guest room because I hear noises again. It sounds like there is sawing coming from within the wall I am leaning my head against. Patterns of scratching in a rhythmic pace, surging between urgent and quiet, urgent then quiet, are nearly enough to lull me to sleep. But then my mind starts to conjure images culled from scary movies I used to watch as a teen. I cannot figure out what is trying to get inside the wall. I dart out of bed, deciding there must be something in the closet—the greatest fear I had when my sister would torment me with this idea when we shared a room as children. I half expect to find a burglar hiding in there with some kind of a hook hand that he has been scraping across the wall, so I bring my perfume bottle to spray it in his eyes. I quickly slide the door across its tracks…and find nothing. The noise has suspended.

I go back to bed and mute the TV, and in just a couple minutes, the scratching starts again. I remember there is a shed on the other side of this bedroom wall, but it hasn't been used or opened since the years when my dad was still here to mow the lawn. Now we use the gardener I borrowed from the neighbor across the street, who apparently always complained to him about how wretched my mother's front yard looked. I wonder why she never did anything to help her elderly neighbor when it was obvious my mom could not do anything to help herself. Did she expect my mother to lug a lawnmower around the property?

I start to get a sickening feeling that I know what could

be hiding in the darkness of that old shed, and I don't like the way my wild imagination has these varmints burrowing their way through the wall tonight to make their nest in my hair. I run into my own bedroom, where Daisy is patiently waiting for me, and I decide I will need to call Pip in the morning. He will investigate this problem for me. When I do call, he says he will drop by in the afternoon to take a peek, and just as we both suspected, there are rodents building nests in the shed out of batting and stuffing that fills the whole place from top to bottom.

Obviously this is going to require another clear out, and I put Pip in charge. I tell him whatever he needs to do to get it all entirely emptied and hauled away as fast as possible is fine by me so long as I don't have to come out and look at it. He agrees to come back over the weekend when he can get his crew together. There is more peanut stuffing in this shed than one could ever use in a lifetime, and how it got there in the first place remains a mystery.

I have been waiting for these uninterrupted months to go back to the paperwork that has yet to be squared away. I remember finding insurance papers for the house policy that showed it was canceled for failure to pay two years ago. This means we are living in a house that is uninsured. I find the box marked "Archive-Statements-Prior Years 1-5" and the insurance papers I need are right on top, just where I left them. I call the number for the local office, and all I am told by the agent is that we can no longer renew our policy with the firm that has carried our house for thirty-five years. If the insurance was canceled due to failure to pay, the only way to get a new policy is to go to a different company. What a crying shame. I ask if there is any possible way they could have any leniency since my mom is a senior citizen who had more on her plate to manage than she could handle. And here is what the guy tells me:

"I am looking back in the notes, and I see your brother had conversations with our agent two years ago when he was trying to reinstate this policy. The notes say that Brother One was aggressive and belligerent and cursed at our agent. This is not how we do business even if we were in a position to renew your mother's policy."

Mortified but not surprised, I can only offer my sincerest apologies. "I am so sorry. I am sure those notes are correct. I have a lot to manage here for my mom now that I am living here to help her. Where do I go to get new insurance?"

And fortunately he offers me some good names of competitors he is friendly with. These things happen from time to time, he says, and I feel better when hanging up from my call with him.

## CHAPTER 20

# Pip Saves the House

I make calls the next day to see which agents have the best rates. In the midst of my research, Pip shows up to take care of the infestation waiting for him in the shed. I don't even want to know what he finds. When I return to my telephoning, every agent tells me the same thing: "The only way you can be considered for insurance is if you have a current roof inspection," which I do not, therefore, "You need to hire a roofer, and if the house is in old condition, you should expect to put on a new roof before we can insure you."

You have got to be kidding me. This seems like highway robbery. A little old lady who is just scraping by, hoping that her money holds out for the next ten years, is now supposed to spend her savings to replace a roof that doesn't even leak just to be eligible for home insurance?

When I check on Pip's progress, I see he and Marley and their dad are all wearing masks like hospital attendants. They are unloading enough material to build a kingdom of nests. Yuck. Pip makes the mistake of asking how I am. While today is unusually hot, it's not the heat that has me steaming. I cannot believe we are in this position. If only the policy had never lapsed, we wouldn't be worrying about this mess. And now I need to have the roof inspected to get insurance. I am saying as much to Pip when he gets a glimmer in his eye.

"I know a guy. I know a real nice guy. He is a roofer and works at a good company. I'll call him so you can talk to him. He probably can help you—"

I cut him off in midstream. "Pip, I don't want to know a guy. I don't want to have a roofer here. I don't want to put a new roof on this old house. I just ripped up the driveway to fix the crushing pipes. I am not made of money. I am not going to get insurance, that's my solution. It's been fine for two years. Do you want something to drink? I've got cold water or lemonade." And I turn to head into the kitchen.

When I return to the garage with three glasses I am juggling coolly with my college waitressing skills still intact, Pip is standing there with that white, toothy grin, holding his phone to my face.

"Here, talk to him. He's a really nice guy. He'll help you with the roof."

I just look at Pip like I can't believe he called this guy when I explicitly said I didn't want to do anything about the house. So, just to be polite, I trade my three lemonade glasses for his phone, and in my most snarly voice I say, "Hello."

"Hello, Ms. Shaffer?"

What heaven-sent dreamboat is this on the other line? I wonder, grinning broadly to myself. He has a smooth, velvety, baritone greeting that melts my ears.

"Yes, this is she." I can hear my voice going high and tinny. Must come down, must breathe. I remember the last time I judged a man by the sound of his voice and agreed to a blind date. Worst mistake ever. He had a great British accent, which I totally fell for—and the long, snaggly British teeth to go with it, unfortunately.

"I understand you might need some help with a roof," he continues with his engaging voice.

"I am pretty sure I don't need a new roof. We just need a roof inspection, which I am not even convinced I want to pursue," I say, still sounding miffed at the insurance company.

"Well, Pip and I go back a long way, and he thought I could be of some help. It won't cost a thing for me to do a roof inspection, and at least you would have the information you need to make a decision," he says casually. "If you do decide you want to get this done today or tomorrow, I have a couple of openings."

I don't really even know what he is saying to me because I am just listening to the sound of his voice. Yet I remind myself about Snaggletooth.

"I suppose it would be fine for you to inspect the roof. Just know that I really don't think we need a new one because nothing leaks." I do not want to give him the impression that this is going to turn into a sale.

We set the appointment for tomorrow afternoon when, coincidentally enough, Pip is coming by to finish the last of the clear out in the shed. I don't hang around the house in sweats because I feel more productive when I am dressed for the day. So it doesn't strike my mother as odd that I am in black tailored shorts, an aquamarine fitted blouse that wraps at the waist, and my high wedge sandals—plus mascara, which I normally don't wear in the summer. My hair is up in a high ponytail because we are still enjoying hot weather.

As I'm taking one last peek in the mirror, the doorbell rings. This is always Daisy's signal to start rushing the person on the other side of the door with her loud barking, making her sound half frantic at the prospect of danger and half eager at the prospect of a new face to wash. I cannot hear anything over her and do not want her to charge the roof inspector, so I open the door a crack, slide my leg out, and back away from Daisy, greeting Greg Stacy with my caboose first.

Oh my. He is more delicious-looking than his voice led me to imagine. I immediately go into my all-business mode because I do not want to come off like some schoolgirl, but he is probably the best-looking man I have ever laid eyes on, and I am beginning to feel stupid for gazing at him directly because it makes me self-conscious. He might even be prettier than I am.

"Hello, Ms. Shaffer, I'm Greg." He shakes my hand firmly, not like some other men I've done business with who grasped my fingertips and gave them a little half squeeze. Greg Stacy has the kind of handshake that says he's earnest, personable, confident, and ready to do business.

While in his grip, I glance over his shoulder at Pip, who is tinkering with something in his truck and unable to mask the grin that keeps sliding between his ears. I look at him like, *I see what you did here.*

"Hey Pip, come over here and say hi to your friend Greg," I call, and while they are walking toward each other with hands extended, ready to shake enthusiastically, I hear Pip greet him very warmly.

"Hello, my brother, how you been?"

There are good vibrations all around. I watch them interact for a minute before I show Greg where the ladder is, but then I realize he has brought his own. With Pip now gone and Greg up on the roof, I am trying to work in my new office, which was my dad's old den space, but my concentration is broken with every one of his footsteps overhead. There is no way a good-looking guy like that is single. And even if he is, he probably has a lot of baggage, which is what I have been finding with the few dinner dates I have had recently.

What I didn't count on was the way an old college flame slowly convinced me that maybe I could give him a serious look. That maybe he wasn't the conceited person I knew decades ago. He was very sympathetic to my plight with my mom and knew I would never abandon her. He became the kind of guy I would drive to see in the city through an hour of traffic in the pouring rain whenever he was in town. I remember asking my friend why I was going to so much trouble for a man I didn't even love when I could have been at home in my pajamas watching *Mary Tyler Moore* with my mom on the couch. I should have paid more attention to those feelings.

But once he snared my mind, getting me to think about him day and night, his game was over, and he left me with one last phone call in which he told me he was seriously involved with someone in Los Angeles whom he had been dating for years. It just never occurred to me that I was not his primary focus since everything he seemed to say and do was to the contrary. Just as well—my mom's needs are central to my life right now. But it did sting to realize that he was the same player he had been in college, and in my diary entry last night I wrote him off after shedding only a couple of tears.

Greg Stacy climbs down the ladder and rings the bell again. I don't invite strangers inside, so I sit with him on the bench on our front porch.

"How does it look?" I ask, feeling completely vulnerable that I am in this position.

"Well, the first half of the roof looks newer, which is good news to an insurance company," he says. He pauses but keeps his eyes locked on mine. "The other half of the roof is not up to code and needs to be completely reroofed, which is not the news I know you are wanting to hear." His eyes are filled with sincerity and green flecks that make them appear more hazel than brown.

"I don't know why we need the insurance anyway. We haven't had it for two years, and nothing has happened." I feel so taken advantage of by the insurance company. "How much would the new roof cost? Do you have an idea?"

He gives me a staggering figure that amounts to eight more trees.

"I don't want to have to cut down the last of the money trees growing in my orchard to pay for a roof that doesn't even leak just to satisfy the insurance company." I think my voice is quavering because I can't fix this situation, and eight trees is a lot of money. My mom still has years ahead when those trees will be needed. We have only fourteen trees left. This roof will leave us with six. I think Greg can tell I am distressed.

"I want to ask you a question," I say. "Tell me honestly: do we really need home insurance?" I study his face, which is smooth and tan, as he puts his clipboard down to look at me squarely.

"Well, Ms. Shaffer, you could go without insurance if your mom's house is already paid for. Most people get insurance to protect their assets from being robbed, but if you're not so worried about that, then you could decide just to live without it. But then, you have to ask yourself what you would do if there were ever a fire. You would lose everything."

He is really thinking through his advice here and wants to make sure I know he is on the level. "The other thing is, remember that big storm we had in January? And you see how close your big pine tree there is to the roofline? Well, it wouldn't take too many more storms like that one for a branch to break off and tear down parts of the garage roofing with it." Something in his demeanor tells me he is not trying to make a sale, so I continue to listen.

"And your mom is elderly. I noticed the cracks you have in the cement coming up your walkway. If any of her elderly friends come to visit her, those are easy enough for someone to trip on, and if they become injured, it is always the responsibility of the property owner to pay for their medical bills, which is what people rely on insurance for."

He is gently producing scenario after scenario, which gets me thinking that we are at a greater risk going without insurance. Especially since I remember the new pool guy's telling me about the liabilities I assume as a pool owner—even for a teen who hops the fence to swim in our pool illegally and drowns while he is trespassing on our private property.

All I know is Greg Stacy has me thinking. I was so sure we could avoid being lured into an insurance ploy. But I know my mom's elderly friends are feeble, and even I have tripped on that walkway once or twice, especially in the dark. I also know Greg Stacy has one of those faces I need to stare into for more than the five minutes I get today.

After a good, hard think and talking it over with my mom, and the sudden appearance of a quarterly dividend check equal to one tree, we decide it is prudent to put on the new roof. I tell Greg Stacy that I am also looking at other bids, and when he asks if he should drop his by the house, I know this will be my chance to get a better assessment of the man behind the roofer.

When I hear his truck pull up and then the doorbell ring, I happen to be on the phone. I am able to get to the door before my mom and quickly tell Greg that I need a couple minutes to finish up a business call. I ask if he can please wait for me.

Suddenly I hear the truck door slam hard, and I figure Greg Stacy has decided to leave. I hurry off the phone and sprint down the hall. But I open the door with a casual cool lest Greg Stacy think I am chasing after him. He is standing at the truck's back fender, talking on the phone as if he has all the time in the world for the girl inside. When he sees me approaching with Daisy in tow, he hustles up to meet me at the fence line.

"Sorry that took me a bit longer than I expected. Thanks for your patience," I say, shaking his hand while the sun bounces off his chestnut hair, which has turned gray around the temples in the same way Richard Gere made salt and pepper cool.

"Waiting for you is no problem, Ms. Shaffer." And I wonder if there is some hidden meaning in that.

While we are reviewing his bid, he walks me around the driveway, pointing out which parts of the roof will need the work and filling me in on the details of the job. Somehow we get to talking about what I do for a living, and it turns out he knows my principal and several of the teachers I work with. It also comes up that he just got out of a long-term relationship—his first since losing his wife ten years ago.

My ears prick up. "When a door closes, a window opens," I say, and after he repeats my line with a big smile, it feels like there is nothing more that needs to be said today.

Out of all the bids I review and pass along to Brother One to put in his two cents, I honestly feel like Greg Stacy's plan is the most comprehensive one we have to consider. I call to say I've signed the proposal and ask if I should mail it back or if he needs to pick it up in person. We decide to meet at Starbucks before my dance class. We never talk about the bid, but we do talk about a lot of other things we have in common. I never make it to dance class that night or on any other Thursday night. He is interesting and, I think, interested.

Greg Stacy is a huge dog person, and I explain Daisy is my first. He tells me he's got three boys all out of high school and finding their ways into their first careers. Throughout this first hour, I keep thinking, *This is a really nice guy*. Pip was right. But then I remind myself that even most jerks come off well in the first hour. Soon enough he invites me to have lunch at the beach. So with our date set for Sunday, Saturday night takes me by surprise. I am working away in my den on a conference speech I have to give in a few weeks, one I am a bit nervous about because there will be a few hundred teachers there to impress, when my phone rings.

"Ms. Shaffer, it's Greg Stacy. I was just thinking about how nice it was to talk with you the other day, and I'm looking forward to lunch tomorrow."

I am so glad to hear this because for a minute I thought he might be canceling.

"And I was wondering," he continues, "if you have some time now, do you want to grab a coffee?" His voice is like ear candy and has me in a haze.

"Right now?" I am wondering how fast I can comb my hair and put on some make-up and look like a presentable date even though our real date isn't until tomorrow. What a horrible thing to do to a girl on a Saturday night when she is obviously planning on staying in with her mother.

"Sure, I'd love to if you don't mind the girl-next-door look."

"Oh, Ms. Shaffer, I think you look great all the time. See you in ten minutes."

I dash down the hall to tell my mom I'm heading out for coffee, which she considers an opportunity to place her mocha order.

It isn't very often that I can get away without any make-up and still feel confident. My sweats are black yoga pants that make every girl look five pounds trimmer than she really is and help me look put together even with just a black T-shirt. When I walk in to the Starbucks where Greg Stacy and I agreed to meet, I find a card waiting for me. I don't even remember mentioning that my birthday passed a few weeks ago. He listens intently to everything I say and makes me laugh often. He is as funny as I imagine Tom Hanks probably is every day. He buys my coffee along with the one I'm bringing home for my mom and tells me he's looking forward to seeing me for lunch.

The next day is when I can see we have less to talk about. I start with random trivia questions about his favorite things and places he would like to vacation. By the time we sit for lunch, I ask him to name three things he would bring to a deserted island.

He promptly responds, "You, a loaf of bread, and a bottle of wine" without even thinking twice. While the waitress is watching this all unfold and awaiting my response, I can feel a flush come over my face. I am so embarrassed and flattered, and wondering if I just fell for one of the oldest lines in the book. It was so smooth, and sounded so sincere that I really wanted to believe he meant it.

Our second date will be on Friday night; he is taking me to a steak house in the city where reservations are hard to come by, and an opportunity to wear a dress is presented. When I greet him at the door, he is all gussied and polished like I have never seen him before, and I can only breathe in his intoxicating cologne, which is so subtly placed I want to follow him around like a dog to get a better whiff.

What I told him to expect for this, our first official dinner date, was to be properly interviewed as I had never done to any previous prospects. I know interviewing is my strength and want to sort my suitors more thoroughly since my faith in mankind needs restoring. Greg's instructions were to come to dinner with three great questions for me to answer as well. He was game for my game.

I am absolutely impressed and taken aback by the depth of the first two questions he presents and engaged and bemused by the third. He has serious and funny mixed together, and combined with my questions they lead to such interesting dinner conversation that when I look up for the second time this evening, there is no one left in the restaurant.

Thus begins our "getting to know you" phase. We are two weeks in and one week away from the roof being done, and my greatest worry is mixing business with pleasure. I do not want anything to go awry before the roof gets finished and the insurance policy gets put into place. But something besides Greg Stacy grabs my attention for the pressing moment.

While I am blow-drying my hair in the bathroom one morning, I am besieged by wasps that belong to a nest I find burrowed inside the muddy bank outside the back door. Through the window I see about fifty wasps buzzing intently as they try to get back inside our house.

I have never met a bee up close that I liked, so I make a beeline for the yellow pages and find a guy who removes live bees, transferring their hive to his property where he milks the honey and sells it. After he jerry-rigs a wedge to unearth a massive, twelve-pound hive nestled in the retaining wall, he carefully carts it to his truck. As he is leaving, he reassures me the problem is taken care of and says those yellow jackets have been building for years. It is one of the biggest hives he has ever removed. Of course it is. This is the money pit after all, where any problem suddenly occurring is now the biggest problem professionals have ever faced.

During the week that our house is getting roofed, my mother and I decide to stay in Carmel, one of our favorite places to be. My mom has become a dog person after all. She pets Daisy, and naps with Daisy, and talks to Daisy like she's a human little girl. She scolds Daisy when her snack food disappears from her plate but does it lovingly because she knows it's her own darn fault for turning her head.

It is debate season with a presidential election only three months away. I have my favorite candidate, and my mom has hers, and Greg Stacy has his. So we have lots of political dialogue to engage in with high-stake hopes for which candidate will be the one famous for turning the country around. Greg calls to give me a progress update on the roof, and my mom eavesdrops while we talk for a long time about the debates we are watching simultaneously.

There's not much that gets by my mom. But I am able to keep this budding romance under the radar for several weeks while I determine the potential of its integrity and longevity. By the time my mother's eighty-seventh birthday rolls around in the fall, Greg Stacy and I have taken a good, hard look at one another and found a real kinship in each other. We have had three months of interview questions in my "getting to know you" game, which has turned out to be more illuminating than I could have hoped. In my answers to his questions, I have been assertive in stating what are the absolutes about me and my beliefs and my hopes and dreams for my future. There is no mistaking where we stand, and, fortunately for us, we have a lot of common ground.

There is more to him than meets the eye, and he makes sure to let me know that I am someone he is seriously pursuing. Flattering, yes. However, the only long-term commitment I have made is to my mother, the one who is planning our spinsterhood together, and I expect her to be around for at least another ten years because longevity runs in her family. So, while I am twitterpated, I cannot imagine reneging on my promise to care for my mother. It was the whole purpose of my coming here: for her. And I stick by my word.

With a party to mark my mother's celebration, she is excited to be at the center of attention with old and new friends. It is at once her birthday party and a "getting to know your relatives" party. Greg's family comes, including his parents, and so do our dear neighbors and Brother One with his family. Everyone has brought thoughtful gifts for my mother, and she is quite endearing even to Greg's nearly grown boys. I bake a triple-high chocolate cake and frost it in a pastel pink, topping it with long, elegant white candles. I have made my famous lasagna for dinner, and the evening has been lovely.

In eight months' time, Greg Stacy and I are married. My mom absolutely adores him, and she and I spend a lot of time beforehand talking about the prospect of how much he likes me. She would say, "It's obvious he more than likes you, dear. What are you going to do if he proposes?" And her mouth would widen in anticipation of my answer.

I would tell her, "Mom, I came home to take care of you, and I am not going to leave you. I know you want to stay in your own home, and I am committed to staying here with you so you don't have to be alone." I could see relief wash over her face—and, at the same time, excitement about what the future may hold.

After Greg Stacy and I got engaged in Carmel, which was a surprise to me but one I had hoped would come, we went home to see my mother. He explained to her how much he loved me and how much he admired me for wanting to come home to care for her. Sitting snug up against her on the couch, he continued with the sentiments that he would like to take part in caring for her and that as he takes on me as his wife, he also commits to taking her on as his second mother, and that together we will all live in a happy home.

He finally ends with asking for her permission to marry me, and she welcomes him to the family with one gesture. She puts her right hand in the center of our tiny football huddle, I join mine on top of hers, and Greg Stacy, my fiancé, layers his on top of ours, and we stack the rest of our free hands on top, and in this grand moment of all three of us coming together we become, tearfully and gratefully, as tight as the three musketeers. My mom feels doubly blessed. I feel special. And Greg Stacy has tears in his eyes on our wedding day, when the two of us elope to Carmel to be married in the sand without the worry of my mother falling.

And this concludes the story of how Pip saved the house. Pip was instrumental in altering the lives of three people. There is no amount of money that can pay an eternal debt of gratitude, but Greg and I gave him one heck of a gift for Christmas this year along with a loving note expressing how lucky we feel to have found each other, with thanks to him for putting us together.

# CHAPTER 21

# Mom on the Move

The support of a man around the house is tremendously helpful to me. Greg makes time to get my mother to hearing and eye doctor appointments. He loves to cook and takes over menu planning, grocery shopping, and making dinner. I stick to baking, and we all three enjoy our time to talk and talk as I listen to Greg engage my mom in ways that bring out her flirtatious nature. At dinner she will regularly say to him, "We are so lucky. You just fell from the sky through our roof, and if you ever try to run away, I will chase after you down the hill with my cane to catch you in its crook." She roars with laughter, and he comes back with something funny and flattering, like how would he ever think of running away from the girl who bakes and the nice lady who feeds him salami from her stash?

Greg will take my mother on dinner dates every now and then just so I can have some quiet time for myself. He knows I hear a lot of noise and commotion all day in the classroom, and he knows how much my mom loves my companionship. I have missed my me time, and I am grateful when I get it. Greg is a magnificent son-in-law. In fact my mother calls him her "son-in-love" because she adores him so very much. He goes on mocha runs for her, he sits and talks with her when he gets home before I do, and we have a very warmhearted, congenial home for the most part. It should have become apparent to me that there were warning signs of my mother's deteriorating health, but isolated events don't mean much except for when they are added together. I just didn't know how to do the math.

Warning one: Very early in our marriage, I heard footsteps before dawn ambling down the long hallway where we were tucked away sleeping behind the privacy of the French door that closes off the back of the house. In a very purposeful tiptoe, my mother came into our room to tuck Greg into bed. The covers were disheveled, and I am sure his hindquarters were hanging out when she pulled the blankets down around his bare hip as if he were her baby. She then silently retreated from the room and went back to her own bed.

When she was out of earshot, he turned to look at me with only one eye open. "Did your mother just tuck me in?"

"Yes, I'm afraid she did, and I know what you're thinking." I hardly knew what to say next.

"I am a grown man. I am sure I don't need my mother-in-law creeping down the hall to be moving my blankets around me when I'm nude under the covers," he says plainly and firmly.

"I know, I know. I am so sorry. This is so embarrassing. I don't know what she is thinking." And when I think this conversation can be done and forgotten, he tells me I need to talk to her.

This is really making a mountain out of a molehill. I have no idea how to broach the subject without hurting her feelings somehow. But I do it as delicately as I can manage. However, there will need to be a few more conversations like this in our future because she just wants to be on our side of the house.

In the meantime Greg's sons are enjoying bachelorhood in the home their dad still pays for, allowing them some time to slip into the realities of the world gradually. While they are building their skills and finding their ways, we celebrate birthdays and holidays at their house because, while the boys are in their early twenties, we don't want to rip the sense of familiarity from them that they enjoyed with celebrations around the Christmas tree in their own living room. Greg and I manage to do separate celebrations with his boys, combined celebrations with his parents, and combined celebrations with Brothers One and Two but separately at their appointed times with my mother, until we are all thoroughly and completely worn out of the holiday spirit.

My mom and I introduce Greg to our weekly rituals. Wednesdays are our library nights. We go to the same library she took me to when I was a child learning to read, only it's grander now that it has been remodeled. Since she can only see headlines and pictures, I usually pull from stacks of *Architectural Digest* and other home magazines that might entice her with their pictures.

We now go to the beach, all three of us, just to watch the sunset. It is a chore to get out of the car anymore with the safety issues surrounding my mom's falls, so we sit and talk while the sun goes down and then head to one of our favorite spots for dinner along the coast. My mom's best friend in the neighborhood, Constance Kirkpatrick, has been around since I was a child. She has been a loyal friend to my mom through the decades and is one of the few who is still living. Together they have enjoyed more lunches on the coast—and secrets, as my mom likes to brag—than I will ever know.

Warning two: During a particularly busy weekend of housecleaning and shoring up closets to make certain they are not becoming overstuffed again, I finally make it to the hall closet, which has been my nemesis from day one. It is still filled with coats that belonged to my father in the '50s and first-aid kits filled with unlikely things I would never need, like caster oil. There are a slew of jackets left unclaimed by family who forgot them in their haste to get out the door and visitors who never came back. Perhaps everyone is just becoming more forgetful. I decide that anything worthy will go into the donation pile, and most of it looks like it could be of good use to someone else.

I spend hours on this closet. I dig out boxes of old Christmas cards that were kept way in the back of a hidden storage cupboard built into the rafters. These are not new cards for sending; they are old cards saved from those who thought of our family back in the '60s and '70s. Why my parents wanted to keep these is beyond me. I do find the remaining pieces of the china pattern that belonged to my mother's mother. I even find the silver tea service my mother was sure had been lost, stolen, or accidentally thrown away. Why do people feel the need to fill every crevice of space with their unused possessions? It makes me claustrophobic anymore to find drawers and cupboards filled to the brim. I am surrounded by so much, even after all I have done to clear our space, I am still canvassing corners of closets to create order and function from the chaotic stuffing of vagabonds.

So, it is with tremendous displeasure that, when I am finally finished with this closet, my last big project outside of the garage, I come home from school the next day to find all of the remaining coats that belong to my mother and Greg and me strewn about the entryway as if a tornado has touched down. I ask my mother what happened. Was she looking for something she had trouble finding? I am sure the answer will be "no" because I left that closet neat and tidy, with jackets hanging according to color and sectioned off according to hers, hers, and his.

"No, I just thought I needed to do a little spring cleaning of my own." And she turns over to continue her nap.

"But Mom, you know I spent hours on that closet just yesterday, to get it in order and de-clutter the last part of the house," I say, holding my tone evenly, all the while hearing the voice of Mommie Dearest ringing in my head with "no more wire hangers!"

"Why did you throw everything on the floor?" I ask, sincerely trying to understand her rationale for making this new mess that spans the entire walkway from the front door, past the living room, and to the kitchen.

"I really don't have much to say about it, but you've got some work to do to get it cleaned up," she says so matter-of-fact, so disinterested and detached.

I have no idea what got into her. Maybe she was feeling territorial. Maybe I have finally stepped on some toes unwittingly. She has done such a great job of turning a blind eye for the past two years that it never occurred to me she might want to be more involved in the discarding of old clothes. I am trying to come up with as many explanations as I can, but I still can't seem to find one that justifies creating such a mess for no purpose.

I decide to wait for Greg to get home before I pick up anything. I want him to see what she has done and maybe get his help to put it all back together. Is my tidiness beginning to bother her? Is it my color coordination that has her unnerved? For the life of me, I am at a loss. When Greg does finally walk through the door, he uses some humor to diffuse the whole situation and decides to take us all out to dinner where my mom can feed the ducks, which always seems to lift her spirits.

As we head into year three of my being at home with my mother and almost six months of my being married, I am given an opportunity to follow my administrator to a new school in a new district where she has been made the principal. It is a district I very much like, but I do not like so much the idea of having to earn my reputation all over once more. But the advantages far outweigh the disadvantages, and I like her so much I am willing to put in my resignation the week after I am given tenure in a ceremony at my current district. Talk about bad timing.

What this really means is I have a hefty summer ahead of emptying one classroom and setting up another, and also carving out time this year to finally give my mother's bedroom the makeover we have been putting off. Once the school site shift has been made, my mother and I decide to dedicate the month of August to recreating a lively, buoyant bedroom with some frill and plenty of color for the years ahead when she might be relegated to her bed.

We go carpet shopping again, and with the budget of some newfound money from a CD we did not know existed—we only discovered it when closing up a safe deposit box—we can afford to buy her first-choice quality carpeting. This time we are not being conservative. No sable brown for this room. A complete departure from the stained, beige carpet that was once a dark peach is definitely in order for my mother. I want her to relish her cheerful surroundings every morning, and I want the room to feel bright even when it's raining outside. We accomplish this with cherry-colored carpeting. It is not red, nor is it violet. It is really a rich ruby that seems elegant, like in a king's cape of velvet trimmed with white fur. We love it right away.

When we go home, I draw a sketch for her of what I imagine her room to look like finished. This is her favorite part: the re-imagination. She loved to draw when she was in college and took design courses as part of her home economics major. Her art skills continued into my childhood with patterns she would draw by hand and begin sewing once she saw I was so enthused by the pretty dresses she sketched before my eyes.

The design for her room includes a poppy theme on the curtains and the master bedspread, which we already own but haven't pulled out since it was tucked away in my great-grandfather's cedar chest in the '90s because it was not part of the dusty-rose everything collection she had in mind. This bedspread is a vibrant lemon yellow with colorful tulips and gerbera daisies painted throughout the pattern. I draw long, white curtains with sparse clusters of poppies in orange and ruby, with a sable-brown valance above.

There will be a coordinating sable-brown bed skirt to match, which will tie in nicely with the wingback chair in an ivory, and—wait for it—the ottoman in a leopard slipcover. It may not sound good to you, but it turns out gorgeous, especially on bright, sunny days when the light streams in. Her entire room feels welcoming and vibrant but not in a loud, tasteless way. Her things are in reach, and her space is inviting for visitors.

Warning three: On a sunny Sunday morning, I arise to start getting my mother ready for church as Greg and I have committed to taking her weekly so she can still enjoy her familiar routine and keep those things in her life that are precious. She has been part of this congregation for more than forty years and remains one of the last in her generation of friends. While Greg is not especially religious, he insists we not skip meetings, and whenever he gets dolled up in a suit, my mother can hardly stop herself from salivating. I must say the first time we picked him up at his house, he came to the car in his dark suit and tie, and we both just looked at each other the way celebrity stalkers do when they finally get up close to George Clooney. And I am sure Greg Stacy found it funny that we both wore expressions of *Aren't I the luckiest girl in the world?*

As I amble down the hallway to see if my mother is up yet, I see a huddled mass on her bedroom floor, and from a distance without my glasses, I wonder if she has gotten hot in the middle of the night and thrown off her blankets. As I get closer, I scream for Greg, who immediately comes rushing down the hall.

"Mom, are you okay? What are you doing on the floor?" I shout. The poor thing is in her nightgown, shivering only two feet from her bed.

"I…I'm…c-c-cold," she stammers.

I bother her with a slew of urgent questions, asking her if she fell, how long she has been lying like this, why didn't she call me, does she feel sick, are her legs working—to which she only replies, "I…I'm…c-c-cold."

Greg and I get her up and into bed. I find the heating pad in my emergency box and start warming blankets in the dryer. Layer after layer I pile onto her, and still she is very cold. I make her hot tea. I make her hot cereal. She is just not feeling like herself. So I call Dr. Goodcare's office even though it's a Sunday, expecting his service can reach him. To my surprise he picks up directly, which is why, despite his gruffness, I am so happy my mom is in his care. After I explain her symptoms, he wants me to get her seen at urgent care. The doctor on call is so gentle and loving, she makes us all feel that my mother is getting exceptional care. I keep her number so I can pursue getting myself onto her roster in the future.

My mom isn't urgently sick, and there is no direct indication of what might have caused her to end up on the floor. She tells me only that she decided it would be better to wait for me until I got up and that I would find her eventually, so she didn't want to bother getting into bed by herself. Was this for attention? I did not know, but I have to wonder.

Warning four: In the middle of the night, Greg and I listen to what has become the familiar pattern of kitchen cupboards opening and closing with frantic urgency night after night in the hours before dawn. I know it's my mother looking for sugar, but there is none to be found because the days of stashing Hershey bars and ice cream are long gone. I have even taken to inventorying her bathrobe pockets when she sits on the dining room chair she has pushed to the front door so she can hand out candy on Halloween. Her policy is "one for them, five for me," and she knows if she doesn't eat that candy fast enough, I will find it on her. I have to tune in to her with my teacher ears from the other room just to listen for the crinkling of foil unwrapping from a tiny, bite-size Reese's peanut butter cup because I will have only about six seconds to run from the family room to the front door to retrieve it before it goes into her mouth.

Since there is nothing for her to find in the kitchen, we just go back to sleep night after night. I think we are safe, but when I decide to bake cookies one rainy evening, I realize we have underestimated my mother's determination to obtain sugar. It has never occurred to me that she is getting into my baking supply stored in Tupperware. I open the canister holding flour to find a claw mark of cocoa dragged through it, which confuses me, and I think, *How could Daisy have gotten into my baking cupboard?* Then I open my raw sugar canister, and there were more cocoa claw marks like a critter has just left its paw print. And then, in my raw cocoa Tupperware, there is a space carved out of the middle the size of a child's fist or two adult fingers. Thankfully my husband is handy and installs childproof locks on the baking cabinet to thwart this habit.

Warning five: A few months later, after my mom's eighty-eighth birthday, Greg and I go out to dinner, which we enjoy doing once a month. I will make dinner for my mom, and he will keep her company while she eats so I can finish getting ready for our date. Very often it is the three of us that go out together, but we are newlyweds who still need some time to be alone, and she is always very supportive of this. She has PBS programming to look forward to, and by now Greg has bought us a coffee pot that can automatically brew coffee and keep it hot for two hours. He will make her just enough to keep her happy and not too much to keep her caffeinated.

When we get home sometime after eleven, having had a wonderful evening out, I call to my mom from the front door, announcing that we are home in case she is indisposed or indecent. We hang up our coats, and I head down the hall to check on her, but she is not in her bed. She is not in her bathroom, nor is she in her walk-in closet. I think perhaps she is lying down in the guest room for some reason, so I call out again as I charge toward the back of the house. Not there. Not in the kids' bathroom either.

Greg can hear the urgency in my voice becoming frantic

as my mind shifts to panic; I'm thinking she has finally collapsed in the pool, and I begin to run toward the glass slider off
the family room. Greg is checking the garage and the outside
property on the front of the house while I head to the back. I
am nearly in hysterical tears because I can't find her, and there
were no plans in place for her to be going out tonight.

As I reach for the slider to the patio, from the corner of my
eye I see a figure sitting very still in the wingback chair in the
living room opposite the kitchen between us. I tilt my head to
see if it is really what I think, and sure enough it is. I dash to
my mother, who is sitting there coyly watching as Greg and
I charge around the house, screaming for her at full volume
because I am thinking she has finally gone deaf.

"Mom, there you are. I am sure you heard me calling you.
Why didn't you say anything?" I am practically choking back
tears because this is the most fearful I have been in a long time,
and I am wrestling with the rising anger boiling in the back of
my throat for her torturing me this way.

"I just wanted to see what you would do," she says, and she
has no intention of moving out of her chair, her throne.

Greg enters through the back door after being outside
looking for his mother-in-love. He is calling my name down
the hall, asking if I have found her yet, when he comes upon
us, sensing a stand-off.

"Lolly, where were you? Didn't you hear Steffie calling your
name all over the house?" He is seriously perplexed as to why
she would just sit there.

"I knew you would find me sooner or later, so I just sat
very still."

By now Greg is disgusted with her. This is how people get
hurt.

"That's a dangerous game to play, Lolly," he says. "Have you ever heard of the little boy who cried wolf? When he really needed something, no one would believe him." And he looks at me as I finally start to cry because I am equally so frustrated that she would intentionally scare me like this, and completely relieved that nothing has happened to her.

"Look at Steffie," Greg goes on. "She is crying now because she was worried sick and was just about to check to see if you had drowned in the pool. Lolly, she's very upset. I think you owe her an apology," he says in a gentle but scolding tone, the way a four-year-old needs to be reminded why it is so important not to run into the street chasing her bouncy ball.

"I'm sorry, Steffie. I'm sorry Greg." My mom is full of humbleness and asks how our dinner was, and what did we have to eat, and we try to recapture the night as if nothing out of the ordinary has happened. But Greg and I will remember this occasion for a long time to come, and fortunately an episode like this is never repeated again. However, there will be stranger ones to worry us in the future.

# CHAPTER 22

# Man around the House

Our one-year anniversary approaches on Valentine's Day, and I have talked Brother Two into staying for the weekend so Greg and I can get away. This was no easy task, but Brother Two relented when he figured he could bring with him all of his oversized electronic toy boats to run in the pool, and helicopters to fly with his fancy remote control, and video games that I am surprised a grown man has time enough to play.

I guess too much money and time, and not enough heart for charity work, plus a girlfriend with an endless supply of patience can produce a witless teen at any age. So, Brother Two unloads his truck of all his toys before I sit him down to explain the maintenance that goes into taking care of our mom. He has no idea what he is in for, and, just as I suspected, when Greg and I return from a weekend away with Daisy, Brother Two is finished with his volunteer service at our home.

"It's just too much. You have my permission to put her in a home," he says, devoid of any compassion. "I think you're doing a great job, but if you ever need to take a break again, I can't do it." And he simply starts packing his toys into the back of his truck.

When I ask if something happened, if anything went wrong, he just goes on to tell me how difficult it is to engage Mom in conversation and how she just sits there staring at a television that she prefers has no sound, and how dirty she is with her greasy hair, as we decided it might be too awkward for him to try bathing her while I was away, and his list of complaints continues.

The news that Brother Two will not be available in the future as we have previously discussed for my week off during spring break is disheartening, to say the least. Greg sees how discouraged I am and offers to stay alone with my mom while I go on vacation by myself. That's not the point. The point is why can't these siblings chip in more to help? Why can't they all be more willing? While Brothers One and Two lack the capacity, Sister Three simply won't, and Sister Two can't even begin to take care of herself. My shoulders are feeling heavy, and I am so tired of worrying about my mom and when the next fall will be and if she is safe and if she is happy.

Then I am sidelined by another distraction altogether. The neighbors have sprung a leak in their garden, which I discover one night at 2:00 a.m. When I open the back door, I see that the entire alley is flooded, with water seeping down from underneath their fence. When I wake up Greg, who investigates with his flashlight and rain boots, he figures a pipe has burst. The entire wall holding up our embankment collapses, pushing mountains of dirt onto our flooded pathway and ruining our dilapidated fence. It is beyond repair.

It is a daunting mess the owners feel no obligation to help fix. So I get down on my knees once again to give thanks for sending Greg Stacy into our lives, because not only is he hand-some and smart and funny, he's super handy with tools, and problem solving is his specialty. I did not know this when we first met, when he inadvertently ripped off a hook I had stuck to the pocket door of my bathroom so my robe and towel could have a place to hang. When the plastic hook came up, taking with it a piece of the white paint peeled from the wood door, I bit my tongue and mastered the art of pretending not to care.

Greg Stacy assured me he could fix it, and I refrained from my kneejerk reaction to want to ask twenty more questions about how it would look when it was done, if the paint would match exactly, if it would hold. I should have trusted a man who has his own assortment of electric tools.

After the flood, he tackled that bank by measuring the curve in the wall with string and precision. When it was fitted, nailed, painted, and pristine, it looked so much better than the rest of the bank that he decided to update the entire wall thirty feet to the left and twenty feet to the right just so the whole thing would match. And he did it all within two weeks.

Soon there were more projects that needed Greg's atten-tion. Once my mom figured out his skill was just like my father's, she had him building new thigh-high planter boxes to line the front and back yards. Greg Stacy went to work. He had excellent craftsmanship and high standards. So when the perfectionist in him invited me to help him paint, I knew he was really beginning to trust me even though we had already been married for a year and a half of the three years I had been caring for my mom.

When a stormy night literally blows the doors off of our shed, I am very glad that we have the home insurance finally in place. This open view into our double-wide shed that runs the length of the guest bedroom wall on the opposite side is a sight for all passersby to behold. Thank goodness it is not the rat trap it once was.

With my design, Greg Stacy builds me the carriage doors of my dreams to add so much curb appeal that neighbors actually come up to the front door to ask who made them. My dad would have loved to know Greg. They would have worked side by side and laughed at each other's little jokes or funny ways of telling stories. It would have been the kind of relationship my father deserved to have: a son who is a friend. My mother approves wholeheartedly of the doors and walks the perimeter just to admire all of the work that Greg has done on our home.

I can tell when she is coming down the hall to head out the back door so she can admire those doors because her metal cane hits the ground with a rhythmic thumping in time to the beat of her left foot leaving its imprint. In a way I am glad she has resorted to using her cane regularly within the house and not just when we are outside, because its signal always gives me fair warning that she is on the move. It helps me to keep track of her when she is headed to the kitchen and I have to wonder what sweet items I may have left out inadvertently. When that cane stops, I start paying attention.

Warning six: My mom cannot find sweets in the usual places because I hide everything inside cabinets with child-proof locks. I am trying to keep her healthy, and a diabetic should not have sugar the way she would like to have sugar. But one Saturday afternoon while we are all home, I become curious about the rim of dark blue that has formed around her lips. At first I think she is ill. But she is acting fine and talking to me nonchalantly about some item in the newspaper and walking around the dining room to admire all the plants I have arranged on tiers in front of wall mirrors that allow the spray of sun from the skylights above to dance around the room. I look at her and ask what she has been eating, to which her reply is the usual, "Nothing."

"Mom, why are your lips dark blue?"

"Oh, I don't know." But something about her demeanor tells me clearly she does.

"Stick out your tongue."

And she does, the same way a pouty little child who doesn't want to play with you anymore would. It too is completely darkened with long smears of dark blue. I immediately begin to wonder if she has been sucking on the wrong end of a pen that has leaked into her mouth and if maybe we should call poison control.

Greg comes into the room as he could hear the situation unraveling from down the hall where he was working, and he begins to comb through the kitchen for clues. Nothing. Then he does a full search of her room. She must have found some hard-shelled candy someplace, and the blue coating melted in her mouth from her sucking. Nothing again. No wrappers, no evidence, and her breath does not smell anything like food.

I am about to call the doctor when Greg comes to me with the evidence held inside his closed palm. When he opens his hand, I think that pointed, little blue rubber cap should be familiar, but I can't immediately place it.

"It's the top from the food coloring. She got into that old junk drawer at the end of the kitchen. You've got food coloring in red, yellow, green, and blue." He is giving me a thorough inventory of products that need to be removed.

"That food coloring box is left over from the time I made her pink frosting for her birthday cake two years ago. I can't believe that would interest her. It's got to taste gross just by itself." I smile at Greg as if to say, "What next?" Taking care of my mother is like managing rough-and-tumble toddler boy triplets. I have to keep a constant watch over her because I never know what can happen next. One thing I've learned: when you least expect it, expect it.

Warning seven: My mom and Greg and I are all very comfortable in our routine and very much enjoy each other's company. The door in the hallway certainly helps with privacy on both sides of it. Everything is amicable, and everyone has space to be alone when we don't want to be together. But one day, when Greg happens to come home at his usual time, something unusual catches him off guard. He is in the habit of announcing his presence as soon as he comes through the door just in case my mom is indecent or indisposed, so she will have plenty of time to pull herself together for the few well-constructed minutes he will linger in the kitchen for a snack or a drink.

On this day my mom is already in the kitchen to greet him. She asks how his day was and if he can make her some fresh coffee in the percolator since she has never learned how to do it herself. She asks him what is on the menu for dinner because she loves to have something to look forward to before she takes her late afternoon nap, and then she proceeds to amble down the hall to lie down. All of this is conducted while she is dressed from only the waist up, and without her wearing any underpants. Poor Greg Stacy. He is in shock and trying to erase the visual from his mind when he relays this story to me an hour later. At his urging I know I need to talk to her, but I am not sure if she was completely unaware that she was in a state of undress or if she was somehow flirting with him.

I do not know how she could be oblivious to the fact, so I approach her gently and ask, "Now, you may not have known that your pants were missing, but can we have a new rule that says if anyone wants to run free in the house, they need to do it in their own room since we have a man living with us now?"

"Oh, I think that's a good rule. I would hate to see Greg running around here with no clothes on." Is she missing my point? Was I too delicate?

"No, I don't want you to see that either, nor do I want you to be undressed in the house when Greg could be coming home at any given time since he lives here now too." I am having such a hard time being more blunt than this, so I hope our little talk is enough and I can just chalk this up to a once-in-a-lifetime incident.

But it does not end here. There will be a few more times that happen sporadically, not just when Greg is home but when I walk through the door, there she is like Daffy Duck, just walking around with her top and no knickers. Not even a top long enough to cover her bare bottom. I cannot figure out why this is happening.

Warning eight: With the warmth of the season change, the cats are outside playing more, and the little cat named Sis is a real huntress. She catches a bird at one point and brings it into the house, where it hides under the couch until I can finally shoo it out. Another time she carries a rodent equal to her size and drops it into the pool just to see if it will bob up and down so she can bat it around. My mom thinks this is so cute, which is why one of her favorite books to look through is a photographer's musing on all things cat, particularly showcasing their moods at play and sometimes capturing images of tortured play. My mother's favorite page in that book is a kitten holding a mouse in its teeth.

Sissy even shows off a mouse she proudly brings into the house one night that is stunned but still breathing. Greg is able to trap it in a bowl and get it back outside where it can run, run like the wind far away from Sissy, the dominatrix kitten. So why, on a warm day when my mother's room is attracting flies, does it not immediately alert me that something dead might be in there? I figure it is from leaving the slider screen open for too long. By day three the flies amount to more than I can swat or paralyze with hair spray that I hope will stick to their wings, allowing them to drop so I can just vacuum them up. There have to be at least fifty to sixty flies that I keep smashing against the window and Windexing off every half hour. I scour my mom's room looking for a present Sissy hid under the bed, under the ottoman, under the chairs, or behind the dresser, but I find nothing.

The next day my mom puts an empty laundry basket on the dining room table. When I grab it thinking I can put it away, I find the culprit at the bottom, dead and stiff.

"Mommmmm! Why did you put a dead mouse in this laundry basket?" I say excitedly because I don't like to scream, but I very much do not like rodents of any kind.

"I figured it was as good a place as any so you would see it." She is short and sweet and thinks it makes logical sense.

"You knew I was looking for something like this yesterday. Why didn't you tell me where it was?"

She shrugs her shoulders and just says, "He's here now."

I don't get it. Things that seem common sense to me aren't responded to with common sense. Maybe it is just too much effort for her. Besides her telling me a couple of years ago that she was slowing down, I can see that she is sleeping a lot more than she used to. Her regular routine consists of three daily naps for at least an hour or two. She has always been a night owl, but even this pattern seems to be more than what I have seen in the past.

# CHAPTER 23

# Winding Down

Warning nine: When I first moved home, it seemed prudent that my mom should have a little job to do in the kitchen so she could feel productive and useful in her own home. She wanted that too, but I also knew that chores like laundry or vacuuming were much beyond her capability. So we agreed she would be a tremendous help in the kitchen if she could be in charge of unloading the dishwasher. We did get a system in place, and despite a couple mishaps that were totally my fault when she unloaded dishes into cupboards without my having run the dishwasher yet, it was a job she did well. I finally got smart and made a sign indicating when the dishes were clean.

Her way to unload the dishwasher was painstaking at best, but I wasn't going to say anything because I was grateful for her help with my least favorite chore. First she would take every item out of the dishwasher and stack it according to theme on the counter. All of the spoons went together. All of the plates were sorted by size. All of the forks were lined up next to the spoons. When she finally had the entire kitchen sitting on the counters, she would then start putting things away.

Lately this process has become exhausting to her. Sometimes she will get tired after putting the last of the contents onto the counter and will bring over a chair from the dining room table that she can shuffle in front of her. This way she can sit down in front of the cutlery drawer, which is right next to the dishwasher, while she puts all of the spoons, knives, and forks away. It's not like we are using a service for twenty every night. There are only three of us to accumulate a handful of forks and knives and a few spoons from cereal every couple of days. But this task is taking its toll on my mother, whom I speculate at first to be faking so she can get out of doing it.

"Mom, why don't you just move the dishes from the dishwasher right into the cabinet? It would be so much easier than the multiple steps of laying them all out on the counter, don't you think?"

"I am doing it the best way I know how." And something in her tone sends a message to my brain that I won't receive until a few days later because I am not wired to recognize the obvious unless it hits me in the face with a two-by-four. My forté is solving the complex. This skill set is both good and bad at once. My mom is really winding down. She is frustrated that she can't do things the way she used to. She is tired—very, very tired.

It's a couple of days later when I see the same exercise in futility. I have come home from school to find her sitting on the chair in the kitchen while she painfully sorts spoons and forks, doing her level best to fit all of the coffee cups on the counter within the space that is left.

I come give her a squeeze and kiss her on the cheek and say, "Mom, you have done such a good job on this chore for the past four years. What do you say we give you a break now?

How about a vacation from doing any more chores in the house? I think you've earned it."

She looks up at me with an expression I can only read as a mix of appreciation for my having compassion for her and sadness that she cannot be of any real use anymore.

"Thank you. You're wonderful, Steffie." She looks up at me from her chair with a warm smile and glistening, blue eyes and says she'd like to lie down for her nap.

"I love you, Mom. You are precious to me." It's something I say regularly, and I am so lucky because she shows gratitude for my being here with her every single day. Whenever I bathe her, she thanks me even though she pretends to hate every moment of it because deep down she is the same feline her cats are, and they all hate to be wet. Whenever I take her to get her nails done, she feels special and purrs beside me, nuzzling up to my chin to tell me how much she loves spending time with me as she puts her newly polished hand into mine. Whenever I cut her hair, she seems to age backward, and I am reminded that the reason I love her pageboy haircut so much is it was the one she wore as a little girl of four.

She tells me stories about her youth when I blow her hair dry, and she makes sure I know how grateful she is for all of the pampering I bestow upon her. I am lucky. There are many people who never hear the words "thank you," "I love you," or "you're wonderful," and I savor all her sentiments. They linger in my mind, and her voice is attached to them. I never get tired of hearing her praise, her compliments on my outfits, and her words to my husband: "You're perfect." She says it to me too, but that is a word that I feel is too hard to live up to, so I always be sure to remind her that I will settle for "pretty darn good" instead.

Warning ten: In the fall of my mom's eighty-ninth year, Greg Stacy and I go out to dinner to celebrate my test scores coming in so high from the kids I taught in the spring. While this has been the case every year in my teaching career, I never want to take it for granted because you never know when you are going to have a year that doesn't produce the results you are accustomed to getting. So I humbly submit myself to a hundred new students every year in the hope that they will glom on to what I have been teaching and soak it all up like the little academic sponges I believe they are.

As I say goodnight to my mom before we head out the door, I notice a funny smell and ask if it is coming from her or her recent bathroom activities. She replies with great indignation that it is not her and that she cannot smell what that sniffer of mine can always seem to detect.

"Go and have a good time at dinner. I've got my cats here to keep me company," she says with good cheer, and she continues petting Nuisance, whom she renamed just that after his incessant meowing for food turned him into a kind of chunko whose belly grazes the floor when he walks.

The first time I met Nuisance, he took a swipe at Daisy's nose while perched on a dining room chair at eye level with her exploring snout. Daisy had never been introduced to a cat before, and my mom simply explained to us both—Daisy and me—that Nuisance thought he owned the house, and he'd be damned if he was going to be run out by a dog. I think we—Daisy and I—were both a little intimidated by Nuisance and his heft. The cat must have weighed about twenty-five pounds, and with his girth he never ran, so he had to rely on his formidable presence to keep others at a comfortable arm's distance.

Even Greg spent the first two years of our marriage trying

to coax Nuisance into letting Greg pick him up to pet him. Once he allowed Greg to hold him, there were time limits in place before Nuisance would begin scratching his way out of getting some love and affection. It took months for ten seconds to become thirty seconds. It took several months more for Nuisance to come sit next to Greg on the couch while we were all—Daisy and my mom and me—watching television.

We are just now beginning to see Nuisance being willing enough to sidle up next to Daisy on the couch in the midst of her doggy dreams, her eyelashes fluttering wildly, just to share some of her warmth. When Daisy awakens suddenly from Nuisance's heft against her, she merely looks at him as if to say, "Hey" and then goes back to her dream. Nuisance has become a part of the family and allows us all to live together peacefully.

When Greg and I return home from dinner hours later and come in to greet my mom and tell her what we had to eat and flutter around for a bit, tidying up her room and closing her drapes and shutting off lights before bed, I notice that smell once again. This time it seems more pungent, but I just can't place it.

"Mom, what have you been eating in bed? Do you have salami in your robe pockets again?" This is a habit I have tried to break her of, but I also know there are few things in life that make her happier, and why rob her of all of them when she is living quite well for a woman who would love me to serve her Challenge butter on a stick? When I reach under her mattress to slide my hands around in search of evidence, I find nothing, but I am closer to her bottom, and I can really smell a stench. I wonder if she has had an accident in her bed, which has never happened before, but lots of things have never happened before until they do.

"No, I haven't had an accident," she says, again with the indignation of the queen at my even having to suggest such a thing.

She continues petting Nuisance, who is cradled in her lap, but I need to move him so I can check under her covers just to be sure. He is pretty accommodating and doesn't put up a fuss the way any of her cats that are attached to her like Velcro usually do.

"Oh, Nuisance, you're a good cat. You know who's king around here," my mom says, and she continues stroking his fur while I shimmy him to the right to lift her covers.

She is clean. I cannot find the source of this vile smell.

I say "hello" to Nuisance and thank him for letting me move him around and tell him what a good kitty he is, and he listens and looks at me with his expression of boredom as usual, as if it is an effort to be such an accommodating prince. I pet him, and I can tell his fur is sticky and greasy again, but I refuse to let my mom try to cut out his mats like I caught her doing once before. It will be a long time in the future before Greg and I put two and two together that his fur was not naturally matted but became that way from Meat Mitts, as Greg lovingly nicknamed my mom behind her back, who would pet him with her greasy salami hands.

Nuisance was holding his pose and staring straight at me without so much as a nudge. Usually he would tilt his head as a signal that he wants his chin petted or his ears scratched.

"Greg," I call down the hall as he is changing from dinner. I don't want to alarm my mother, so I try to use sign language to indicate to him that Nuisance doesn't seem quite right coiled up in my mother's lap while she pets him.

And Greg confirms what my gut has already told me: Nuisance is the foul smell I have been detecting for hours.

"Mom, I am so sorry to tell you this, but Nuisy is not breathing anymore, so Greg is going to wrap him up and take him to the hospital."

My mom has very little reaction to this news. I think it is because she has had to say good-bye to so many animals in her lifetime, especially the calves she raised as pets and then watched go off to slaughter. Her childhood was very *Charlotte's Web*; since she grew up on a dairy farm, she is familiar with the circle of life. I, on the other hand, break into sobbing fits because I love that cat, and I have a hypersensitivity problem when it comes to animals in distress. I won't watch any of the sad animal commercials, and I change the channel every time I come across Animal Planet because there is always a show on featuring dogs who look like they need rescuing. The blanket Nuisance is lying on top of is wet with the liquid emitted when he expired. I let Greg wrap him in the covers, which we discard later.

I don't know how my mother didn't realize that Nuisance wasn't breathing when she was petting him all day. How long was she petting a dead cat? These seem like questions there should be obvious answers to. But the "apple, penny, chair" dementia doctor has only come up with news that yes, there is some slippage, which we knew going in.

Maybe I should be more worried about than puzzled by what has happened this summer. Last year I discovered a great way to catch a break for some quality me time by signing my mother up for some lectures and lunches at the beautiful senior center nearby. Transportation was not available in our area, and with my mother's sporadic falls, I didn't want to run the risk of having her get on and off a bus by herself. She was equally excited about the prospect of meeting new people and seeing the world through travel videos while relaxing in the center's cozy leather Barcaloungers, with popcorn to boot. The only thing she did not want was to hear other elderly people complaining about their ailments. My mom was a firm believer that what kept her healthy was her positive mental attitude. And I must say I agree because her lifelong intake of creamy butter sure hasn't given her a heart condition or even high cholesterol.

Since last summer went so well, I have really been looking forward to getting her signed up for more activities at the senior center on a regular basis so I can enjoy some of the summer for myself. There are still house projects to be done and always finances to review, but I have found the hardest part of taking care of an elderly parent is the time that goes into managing all of the same things for someone else that one manages for herself. It is double the time to balance checking accounts because there are now two people's accounts to manage. Anything I do for myself requires I do the same on behalf of my mother and her home. So it takes careful planning, but I have a rhythm, and if I can carve out the blocks of time I need, I can barrel through multiple items on a to-do list and feel like I am making progress.

We plan for two days a week at the senior center, where she wants to sign up for a writing class, since that has always been her passion, and current event lectures on another day, both followed by lunch. For three hours twice a week, I can have time to myself while Greg is working. Nothing sounds more delicious.

On the first day, I bring my mother to the center and make sure she is comfortable in the two rooms where she will be for the afternoon, and I find some elderly women who look like they are enthusiastic to be there for her to befriend. I explain to the registration ladies at the front desk that I will be back to pick up my mother at two o'clock, and they are gracious enough to put me at ease that she will be fine and is sure to have a good time.

When I return at a quarter to two since I don't want my mom to be the last one to be picked up, I find her already waiting for me in the lobby. I ask how class was, and she tells me fine and that she didn't know where to go so she just sat in the lobby. I was very alarmed by this and asked the lady at the desk why no one could help her get to her class. The registrar informed me that they reviewed the schedule with her, but she couldn't remember what class she wanted to attend and preferred to wait in the lobby.

This is a problem that is easy enough to remedy, I think. I make my mom a sign most kindergartners carry. It is on a four-by-six index card that we have folded into the pocket of her jacket. It has her schedule and my contact information as well as her name. It says that I am to be called the minute she decides she does not want to participate in an activity. So I feel confident that we have a good prevention in place, and she should be able to enjoy her day.

Thursday comes. I walk her to her first class, which is in what looks like a living room set up for armchair travel. I sit her down. I introduce her to the elderly folks on either side of her, and I ask her where her card is.

"It's in my pocket, daughter," she says with an assured confidence, as if it is such a ridiculous question. "Go and enjoy your afternoon. I'm fine." She is smiling and comfortable sitting and waiting for the picture to start.

Again I show up before pick-up time at two, and inside the lobby, I find my mother sitting on a bench looking disoriented.

There is no one at the desk today, so I ask my mother how her classes were.

"Fine," she says, but does not elaborate any more than this.

A lady shows up and says that she wanted to call me but didn't know how to get a hold of me. My mother has been sitting in the lobby for two hours.

"Mom, what happened? Didn't you show the lady your card?" I ask.

"I didn't know where it was, and I couldn't remember where I was supposed to go, and I knew you would come if I just sat here. So I've been waiting, and here you are, just like I knew you would be."

I have a flutter in my heart because I just narrowly escaped something that could have been so much worse, like her leaving the center and getting lost, and I am realizing I don't want her out of my sight.

"It's okay, Mom. Let's get you home for your nap. How does that sound?"

And she purrs.

I have a new problem on my hands: the flooding of the garage, which we never see coming. For all the years I lived here as a child, and for all the years I lived away as an adult, I never knew our house to flood. We are on high ground, and we don't live in storm country. Yet, this January, the fifth year I am here, the third year of my marriage, and the eighty-ninth year of my mother's life, our garage has taken on a foot of water from punishing rains.

Everything on the ground is getting soaked, and mostly what I am at greatest risk of losing is the inventory I have of my first book, which has just arrived in boxes for speaking engagement orders after going into its second printing. Greg is on his way home, but it won't be for another hour, so he recommends I call Brother One to see if he can help me lift these heavy boxes and carry them into the house. Brother One comes over right away but tells me it's my own fault the garage is flooding because this will teach me to check the rain gutters before a big storm.

I am flabbergasted by this kind of response when I am feeling we are in a bit of a dire emergency right now. I ask if he can help me move my boxes, which are too heavy for me to lift alone, and he tells me that will be another problem I need to solve alone because he has a bad back. I don't know why he bothered coming over at all. Fortunately I remember we have a dolly, so I scoot the boxes out of the garage one pallet at a time.

Everything else in the garage that is sitting in water is in plastic crates and in no way threatened to be damaged. This is another reason I highly recommend not storing pertinent items long-term in bankers boxes because the water will seep right through in a flood. For the archive statements that are still in paper boxes, I easily cart these away before the water reaches them. Disaster averted. Brother One can go home.

From this experience, though, I have a nagging feeling building in my mind that I need to be better prepared for an emergency. We have no power for two hours. If that can happen once, it can happen again. And if it can happen for two hours, it can happen for longer. It seems reckless not to have a plan in place when I am responsible for my elderly mother and three animals.

A thought keeps creeping into my sleep: *Get prepared. You are not ready for an emergency. Be prepared for what is coming.* It haunts me. The worst thing I can think of is to be facing a dangerous situation knowing that I had it in the back of my mind but I ignored all premonitions to guard against it. So I decide I need to follow the Girl Scout instincts I was trained with during my elementary school years, and I get prepared.

I go to a camping store and a sports store to buy the supplies I need to function and live for three days. I fill three different backpacks with identical kits so my mom and Greg and I each have our own emergency supply. I buy a crank radio. I buy jars of peanut butter so we won't starve to death. I buy toilet paper and stuff rolls into our packs. I have warm socks, underpants, and thermals so we won't freeze even though we live in sunny California. I buy medical supplies, flashlights, Sternos, and a camping stove, again so we won't starve to death. I buy cat food and dog food and insert doggy bags for picking up after Daisy. I have a gallon of water for each of us. And I spend $700 of my own money.

When I get home, I ask my mom to stand up so I can see if she can carry the weight of her pack so that when we need to walk to our meeting ground in case there is an earthquake and we need to get out of the house, she can handle hers. Yes, it is not too heavy for her, and she can walk three steps. I finally feel like I have done something to be proactive about warding off this disturbing feeling of doom that has been passing over me. I know I am well prepared for another natural disaster. I am certainly confident that I have thought of everything. What I don't realize then is that I have prepared for the wrong emergency.

# PART 6

# DEATH MARCH

## REALITY 6
### *A Birth Allows Us Nine Months to Prepare; Death Has No Timeline; Act with Urgency in All You Do*

# CHAPTER 24

# A Perfect Stranger

As a Christmas gift to my mom and Greg, I buy tickets to the opera for us to enjoy in early January. The local theater offers live streaming from the Met in New York, so I decide it will be wonderful for my mother to see *Carmen* on the big screen, and perhaps Greg will become an aficionado of something old that is new to him. This seems to make more sense than driving to the city, particularly since we have become accustomed to preplanning our outings with my mother by ordering a rented wheelchair. It lessens our worry about a fall in public and makes getting around so much speedier.

If wheelchairs were not such a threat to my mother's fierce independence, I would have invested in one a long time ago, when I discovered that a walker is not meant to be ridden. It was my first summer home, and my mom wanted to see the Fourth of July parade that my siblings and I participated in as children. It is one of our neighborhood traditions, and while the enthusiasm for it has faded as the clever themes and costume design have waned, there are still spectators who line the main drag hoping this year some family has thought of some spectacular new way to show off our spirit of independence.

Sister Two had mentioned that she had given my mom a walker fully outfitted with a cushioned seat and a storage basket beneath. I had zero experience using one of these, but it seemed quite logical to me that the cushioned seat was meant to provide comfort to an elderly person who was not yet ready for a wheelchair but needed help with going the distance when a cane could not suffice. Not so. A walker is built with a cushion only to assist the senior as an occasional respite. I did not know this until several months after the parade where we used the walker, which explains why my mother's feet dangled and kept getting twisted in the front wheels, and why, when I pushed her up the low-incline hills to get a better view of the parade, our balance was off and she would begin to roll backward. We made it safely back home, but I did think to myself that this rider could have been better constructed for seniors who are of average height. Some things you figure out the hard way when you are new on the job.

When the opera is over and our fun was had, and the crowded theater does not inhibit us from exiting safely, all my mom says about her adventure and the idea of repeating it in the future is, "Yes, we had a good time. But now we've done it."

I take that to mean she wasn't as excited about the opera as I thought she might be. She isn't excited about a lot of things anymore. Her eating habits have changed dramatically, and where in the past she easily put away second helpings of my double-stuffed pork chops or Greg's barbequed chicken, she now only nibbles at dinners. Menu ideas are not as interesting to her. She told me a long time ago that as we age, our taste buds change. I didn't think that would mean food would lose its appeal to her.

The only thing she remains interested in is Greg's and my company. It gets to be that our routine every night after dinner is to watch a bit of television together, choosing from a number of family shows that are still on the air. When she falls asleep on the couch and begins to snore, I suggest she goes to bed.

"I like your company" becomes her common response.

"But Mom, you are falling asleep." I look to Greg, thinking maybe this will be an opportunity for us to sit alone for a half hour. "Wouldn't you be more comfortable in your own bed?"

"I'll go when you go." It becomes her mantra. Greg and I are never left on our own, and while I can appreciate that she doesn't want to be alone, there are times when I feel like I am being chaperoned. So I ask my mom furtively if she wouldn't enjoy making it an early evening and retiring to bed just an hour before us twice a week so she can play cards or listen to the classical music I set up for her in her room. She is a hard sell, and an early-to-bed routine lasts only two weeks. She is happiest on the couch with us, with all the animals snuggled up against her. Before I know it, Greg is snoring too. This is our family time together.

The constant visits to doctors' offices for appointments on a rotating basis every two or three months keeps the calendar filled with weekly check-ups. Today we are getting her routine eye exam done, which goes well enough until the vertigo she is experiencing gives her the sensation she is going to fall in the office. I do not know if she does this so her handsome doctor will catch her as she swoons or if she is really this dizzy coincidentally whenever he escorts her out, signaling the appointment has ended. I cannot tell, and this is my biggest worry. Is she faking it for the attention?

While Dr. Reuben Klein holds her steady at the receptionist's counter long enough for me to put away my wallet after handing over her co-pay, I grab on to her arm tightly, sure that I can traverse the path to the elevator and maneuver across the street to the parking spot I found closest to the building. The swooning stops—sure enough as soon as we leave the office. But once we cross the street at the signal, something unsettling is happening to my mother. She intends to go, but her feet won't move. Thankfully I have a public garbage can to rest her up against while I assess the risk of moving her by myself the length of three cars to where we parked.

"Mom, are you okay?"

"I don't know." She grips the side of the garbage can's hood, which is conveniently almost as high as her elbow.

"Do you think you can make it to the car? It's right in front of us, only about three cars away." I am hanging on to her elbow tightly and gripping my purse firmly in my other hand while she hugs the receptacle.

"I don't know," she says. I can feel her beginning to sway, and her size is going to throw us off kilter, and she will surely have a head injury if she collapses onto this cement. I am trying to look brave, but we are vulnerable out in the open, and no one is pulling over to help us in what is quickly becoming an arduous situation.

In my desperation I spy a young man approaching us with the swagger of a hoodlum. His pants are sagging below his hips while his hems are bunched up all around his ankles. His tattoos are graphic designs symbolizing things I don't understand running the length of his entire left arm. He is not smiling at me, and he walks with a bounce although I hear no music. My mom is about to fall to the ground, and I decide it is worth the risk, so I scream for him to come.

"Please help me get my mother to the car before she falls,"

I say while thinking to myself, *And don't rob us of our purses.* Tears are welling up in my eyes, and he can see that he is my only hope of managing the danger my mother is in.

He rushes to her side and loops his arm securely around her right elbow, locking his elbow in place, and puts his free arm on her hand to help guide her while I do the same on her left. All I can think is, *Where is everybody else?* It's only four o'clock, but there is not another soul in sight. *Will he try to steal our car once we get there? Should I pay him for his help?*

It takes several minutes for us to navigate our way to the car, but we do it. I am so grateful to this kid who is easily in his twenties and may even have a kid of his own. I thank him profusely, and I have tears coming out of my eyes. In this moment somebody needs him. In this moment somebody trusts him. In this moment he is trustworthy. I don't know how he lives his life. It is easy to make assumptions by the story art he wears on his skin. But today he restores my faith in humanity and shows me that people in general are decent, and even if he is a young thug, he probably still has a grandmother who loves him dearly. I am so grateful to him because he came to our rescue when absolutely no one else was around.

I call Dr. Goodcare when we get home, and he doesn't like the sound of things and insists on a check-up at his office first thing in the morning. Greg plans to come with me, and I get a substitute to cover my class. I know there must be something to this whole business of my mom's being unstable on her feet; I just have no idea what it is. Maybe this appointment will be different from the others—maybe we will find out the reason and finally be able to fix it.

The routine exam begins with checking orifices and vision and hearing, and then stability by having her hold out her arms one at a time while her eyes are shut. It isn't going very well. She doesn't do well with her eyes closed. Finally Dr. Goodcare checks her blood pressure with the Velcro band that wraps tightly around her bicep. The numbers are alarming, with a reading of sixty over forty. It is the intent look that Dr. Goodcare sears into my brain that gives me every indication he means what he is about to say with great urgency.

"Go to the hospital now. I am calling to have your mother admitted to emergency. Her blood pressure is dangerously low."

You would think this would be enough information for me. But it does not fully compute in my head. Do we go to the waiting room first to be checked in? Do we need to call an ambulance? Which hospital should we go to? Will they know what to do with her when she gets there? Is she going to die?

He answers swiftly, "Get to Memorial Hospital now. An ambulance will take too long. I want her to be seen right away. Her BP is too low. Don't waste any time."

Marching orders like this are quite daunting. Greg and I borrow a wheelchair from the doctor's office and a nurse leads us to our car. My husband zips along the side streets, taking shortcuts he knows, speeding all the way, and planning to resist pulling over if a cop chases us, until we arrive at the emergency parking lot in mere minutes. There is no admittance beyond the general nurse at the front counter who must first check us in and, of course, she has not heard from Dr. Goodcare's office. I call Dr. Goodcare and explain the delay while he faxes his urgent request that my mother be admitted now for low blood pressure. I had no idea that this is a matter of life and death.

It is though. Blood pressure levels are not to be taken

lightly. As the team of doctors evaluates my mother behind the curtain of a non-private emergency room, I am there to hold her hand. After hours of tests and waiting for results, they feed her lunch. She really doesn't look any worse for wear, and it seems likely that she will be going home just as soon as the next round of doctors determines she is stable enough to be released. The shift change comes later in the afternoon, and by now she is quite tired. There has been a lot of excitement in anticipating if this low blood pressure is going to turn our little emergency into something extremely dire.

The news isn't great. Based on the tests results, the doctors want to keep her overnight for observation. Her blood pressure is erratic, and they want to monitor her closely. I send Greg home to get her a cashmere sweater to keep her warm and a few essentials she and I both need to be more comfortable for the next several hours until bedtime.

At this point I call Brother One, who says he will visit tonight when he gets off work, and Brother Two, who says he will call her later. I call Sister Two and tell her not to worry, and I ask her to call Sister Three, who should probably be told even though she apparently wants nothing to do with our family. I don't want to be an alarmist, so I clearly convey to the siblings that our mom is seemingly fine, but the doctor wants her low blood pressure checked, and the hospital tests indicate that the doctors here will feel more reassured if she is monitored overnight, and they should release her tomorrow. No big deal, really.

Here is what I discover: anytime an elderly parent goes into the hospital for any reason, it is a bigger deal than you realize. If you are like I am and have never heard the term *sundowning*, let me describe for you what it looks like.

My mother has no idea who I am when I show up the next morning to check on her after breakfast.

"Hi, Mom. How did you sleep?" I say cheerfully, pulling her sheets and blankets up to her chin and tucking her in.

"Be careful," she says in a low, husky voice I have never heard from her before. "There's a dead dawwwwg at the foot of the beeeed."

I snap my neck to the nurse behind me and ask what has happened to my mother.

"She is sundowning. This is very common in elderly patients who are away from their familiar environment," she says while busying herself with the clipboard that holds my mother's chart, avoiding direct eye contact with me.

"How long will this last?" I ask urgently. "Will it turn into Alzheimer's?" It is now just occurring to me that my mother's mother lost it in the end. That is how my mother always describes my grandmother's last few years of life: she was "losing it."

"Mom, I don't see a dead dog on your bed. There's just a blanket here I brought from home to keep you extra warm and toasty." I unfold it and pull it up around her shoulders, hoping its familiarity will snap her out of this state.

"Look! Do you see awllll of those caaaaats on the ledge? There must be a thousand caaaaats. How will we feed awlllll of those caaaats?" Her voice is raspy and hoarse, and she extends her syllables in an unusually long drawl.

"Mom, I don't see any cats out the window." Especially since we are on the eleventh floor, and there is only the rooftop of the wing next to our building to look at.

"Don'tchyou seeeeee? There's caaaaats. Look, there's one now! He's trying to get into the room. They're aawllll trying to climb in through the window. Do something!" She is frantic about the cats that do not exist. So I hope to calm her nerves by pretending to fix the situation.

"Here kitty, kitty," I say while reaching my hand through the imaginary window. In reality there is only a sheet of glass with no latches for fear that patients who are sundowning might jump to their death. "Oh, you want to be petted? Here, kitty."

My mother is watching me with intent eyes, and she wants to hold the cat.

"You want Lolly to pet you? Here you go," I say, and I hand over the fake cat. She takes him heartily to pet for a few strokes before launching into her worriment about the dead daww-wwwg at the foot of the bed.

My mother does not know her name, and, more frightening to me, she thinks I am a nurse. She does not know I am her daughter, and she does not know my name. When I step out of the room and burst into tears, it occurs to me that our entire lives might be about to change, and I don't know what Alzheimer's will mean to the care I am supposed to provide. Will I still be able to care for her? I have never known anyone with Alzheimer's before, and I am scared. I do not have enough of a support system to manage this myself, even with the help of a new husband.

I have been out of school for the whole week so I can be at the hospital with my mom. Today I take a breather from her bedside and walk to Starbucks across the street. Greg is at work. Brother One showed up the first night as promised and sat with my mother while he polished off her hospital dinner. He told me she wasn't very hungry, but what else would you expect her to say when she knows her son hasn't been home yet to have his own dinner? What a loaf. He can't even let his mother enjoy her own dinner on the first night of her hospital stay.

Sitting in the coffee shop, I begin to think about how the week took such a dismal turn. She was only supposed to be in the hospital for one night, but now they are worried about her mental state, and her blood pressure is still precarious. I know the longer one is in a hospital, the worse it must be. I can think of nothing else other than *I do not want to lose my mother.*

We are having such fun, and she adores Greg Stacy, and the three of us enjoy laughing together night after night. The two of them are hysterical together, and while I think I am quick at times, I am no match for their verbal repartee. I am not ready for her to go. I can't believe she doesn't know who I am. I cannot believe Sisters Two and Three can't get here to visit—it's a measly two-hour car ride. Even Brother Two doesn't visit her in the hospital. He stopped calling when she kept telling him about the dead dawwwwg. I begin to cry the way one does in a public place when you want to be inconspicuous but cannot stifle the tears that just keep rolling down your face.

Across from my sight line, a gentleman folds his newspaper, gets up from his spot, and sees me straightaway. He is Peter, one of my colleagues I teach with, enjoying a short break from his classroom on one of our rare, blessed teacher workdays when we don't have kids but do have trimester grades to enter.

"Stefania, how are you? I hear your mom is in the hospital. I hope things are going okay," he says sincerely, stopping by my table for what he intends to be a brief moment, I'm sure.

But the human connection makes me sob harder as I express to him, "My mother doesn't even know who I am, and she is seeing dead dogs." I try to collect myself because the last thing I want is for a colleague to see me cry.

"Oh, Stefania." He pulls up a chair. "I am so sorry." His words are genuine, and I will always appreciate how he is willing to sit in silence with me while he struggles for the right thing to say. His presence brings me solace and means more than any trite condolences ever could.

# CHAPTER 25

# Leg Therapy

Over the weekend my mom is released from her seven-day stay in the hospital. She is more like herself again, but I am quite suspicious about how sundowning can just come and go. The nurses reassure me it happens at night, when elderly patients are disoriented, agitated, and confused. Once my mother gets back to her own home, they tell me, she will be just fine.

After she has been out of the hospital for two weeks, I am still feeling like my mother has not quite bounced back. Greg and I skipped our second-anniversary celebration to be with my mom in the hospital for Valentine's Day, her favorite occasion to dictate a letter to her dear friends. But she isn't interested in sending cards right now. She is going through our routine as usual, but there is a lethargy to it, and I don't mean the naps that she likes to take multiple times a day. She is just listless and apathetic in general.

When Penny, the physical therapist appointed by the hospital, shows up to do leg exercises with my mother, hoping this is the root of the problem to her falling episodes, my mother just lies there in her comfy bed.

"Ma'am, you are going to have to wake up for this appointment. I am here to get you feeling stronger," Penny says with the tact of an army sergeant.

I coax my mom more pleadingly. "Mom, let's just do this for fifteen minutes and see how your legs feel, then you can go back to sleep." But it is like talking to a drugged person who can barely open their eyes and verbally wishes you away.

"Mom, we are going to do this today because your therapist is here and this is what the doctor and the hospital prescribed in order for you to improve. Don't you want that?"

"Oh, all right, I'll do it," she says in a cranky tone I rarely hear, and she pushes back the covers and lets the therapist manipulate her legs.

With every swing to the side and push to the chest, my mother asks if we are done yet. It's only been four minutes. Penny can tell that my mother is really not going to be any more cooperative today, so our session is over. She records in her notes that the patient was not responsive, and we look forward to trying again at our next appointment in two days. I promise a better response from my mother and apologize for the inconvenience surrounding today's disappointment.

I like this therapist. She is no-nonsense, but she also gives me a calm feeling that she knows what she is doing. She has taken charge of difficult patients in the past and feels confident that we will get better results in the next few sessions. After Penny leaves I ask my mother if she thinks she can do any better if we try it again. She gives me a loose commitment with her eyes completely closed and her shoulders tucked beneath the covers, which are pulled up to her ears. I know that trying to get any more conversation out of her at this point will be as useless as talking to an adolescent boy in the midst of blowing up things on his video game. So I let her sleep the rest of the afternoon while I grade essays.

When Penny returns on Wednesday for our second appointment, there is more of the same battle to get my mother to perform any of the basal routines requiring leg stretches. When Penny asks my mother to get out of bed so they can try deep-knee bends, it takes a concerted effort with carefully choreographed moves for my mother first to roll onto her side then lift her caboose in the air while her knees are tucked beneath her; then she puts her left leg out first, since it is less troubled than her right, and once she can feel the floor with her foot, she knows it is safe to move her right leg to the carpet.

All of these multistep motions are performed with excruciating time lapses. But she wants to be careful, and this is how she normally gets in and out of bed, so I can't complain. What I am enjoying is the look on the therapist's face. Somebody else can actually see why it is so painstaking for me to get her ready and out the door for any kind of an appointment.

While my mother is draped over her mattress with her feet flat on the floor, Penny asks how low she can bend her stiff right leg, then her good left leg. All the while my mother clutches the bedspread in her fists as if it is her security blanket. She says it's so she won't fall backward. I guess this makes sense. She tries to be accommodating, but she is still tired and only wants for it to be over.

Finally Penny says, "You did a good job today, Lolly," and my mother gives her that toothless grin I have grown so fond of seeing. She is proud and feels her reward should be a nap without any disruptions. I agree.

On Friday Penny returns for her third session with my mother, and this is when things begin to fall apart entirely.

"Lolly, I am here for your session. It's Penny, the therapist," she says in her sweetest voice, which sounds funny on her.

No response.

"Mom, you don't want to ignore the therapist," I say. "Remember, I told you she would be coming again this afternoon to work on getting your legs stronger." I try not to sound exasperated because we just had this conversation a half hour ago when I reminded my mother Penny was scheduled to be here shortly, and my mother assured me she would be ready if she could just be allowed to sleep until then. It is now then, and she is not getting out from under the covers.

I look at Penny apologetically because I know this has got to be frustrating for a professional who comes all the way out here to find a patient who is unwilling at least to try.

"Mom, can you please turn over on your back so Penny can stretch your legs for you?" I request.

"I want to sleep."

"Lolly, just let me see if you can bend your legs any more than you could on Monday, and then I'll let you rest." Even Penny is finding that the art of negotiating works on my mother, who folds back the covers and decides to give it a go.

Again, ever so slowly, she performs her routine of rearing her hindquarters before putting one leg, then the second, onto the floor. Throughout it her eyes are closed, and she is trying to sleep while in the collapsed position, hovering over her bed with the hope that the therapist can do the rest of the work for her.

"Lolly, can you bend your right knee for me?"
Nothing.

"Lolly, can you try bending your left knee for me?"
Nothing.

"Mom, can we try this a little more just for a few minutes? Then Penny will go home and you can rest," I try to entice her.

"I want to go back to bed." And with this she starts her climb back on top of her bed with her caboose in the air until she rolls to her side and pulls the covers up tight and begins to snore.

I look at Penny, and she looks at me, and we decide our work here is done for today. When I escort her down the hall, we stop in the living room because she wants to talk to me. She asks me all sorts of questions: How long has my mother been in this state? What signs have I seen indicating changes in her over the past year? How is her eating, and has she always been a night owl and a day sleeper?

I can tell Penny is getting to something, but I am not quite sure what it is yet.

"Your mother's resistance tells me she is not ready for more physical therapy. You need to talk to her doctor about whether she is ready for hospice care." Her voice is soothing, and her eyes are warm, but the pregnant pause is what registers concern in me.

"My mother doesn't have cancer, though, so I don't think hospice is available. What would hospice do anyway? Is it a therapy program?"

Here is where I can tell she realizes I am much younger than my age would indicate, because at her explanation I begin to cry.

"Hospice is a service for anyone nearing the end of their life and needing a team of people to help them be comfortable and comforted in their death."

I am a child at this moment. My only living parent is in the next room, and she has given the impression to this professional that her end of life is near. I do not want to think this. There is so much more I want to enjoy with my mother. She and Greg have had so much fun over dinners; I want that to continue. She wants to see her grandchildren from Brother One grow up even though they rarely come over to visit. I am a child sobbing like I did when I skinned my knee or when I burned my fingers on the hot stove for the third time, or when I broke my arm on the monkey bars. I don't want to be the grownup here. I want my mom to fix this for me too. I do not want to watch her die.

Penny can only lean in to give me a hug and pat me on the back. She has obviously seen this in patient families many times before because she knows just what to say: nothing. Sometimes this is the best thing to say. Sometimes there are no words that can bring comfort when you are at the front of something horrible.

She leaves, and I decide to call Dr. Goodcare to relay the details of the therapy appointments this week, and to express Penny's concern and her suggestion that my mother might need hospice care. Does he agree that my mother is at this point in her life? He does. Today is the last day of February. We just went to the opera one month ago, and since that time my mother has been hospitalized and gone through episodes of not recognizing anything about her life or me, then come home to sleep.

I knew this would be how her life would go. My dad got his wish to die while reeling in the big fish. My mother always wanted to die in her own home. One of these nights she will just go to sleep peacefully and not wake up. This is what I have prepared for because, of course, I am a child of my elderly parent, and a child is always a child even if she is an adult, and for my mom to sleep her way out of this life is the only possible idea I can conceive. But death is clever and comes in many different forms. I should have been more creative in my thinking.

# CHAPTER 26

# Help Is on the Way

The time has come, and I am anxious for the state writing test we have prepared for all year. It has always been the area in which my students excel. For all the many years I have worried and wrung my hands and sweated bullets, hoping that I can keep my track record pristine when the test results finally come out in August, I always write myself a little reminder not to worry half as much because each group of students does just as stellar as any group that came before. No one has let me down, and in turn I have never let down any of my administrators who have counted on me to get results for their school. The principal I had in my last district, who was a man of few words, surprised me with glowing praise in five little words that fit onto a Post-it: "Best scores we've ever had!"

So I have all the faith and confidence in the world that my students now will outshine even their personal bests when the state gives them their essay topic tomorrow. The kids always think I know in advance what they will be expected to write about, but I don't. I wait nervously like they do while I fuss with the lid secured to the box that contains the assigned prompt and the preprinted booklets with bar codes in place of their names.

I give the kids their pep talk, review the testing rules, and remind them that if they still need time to finish, an administrator will escort them to a testing room. They have done on-demand writing for me a million times throughout the year. Simulation is how I get the scores I do because the kids aren't half as nervous as they would be without it. I wish them luck, and we say good-bye, and after my meetings I go home knowing tomorrow is the big day.

Tomorrow never comes for me. It is the morning of March fourth, and when I walk in to wake my mother so I can get our morning routine started and get to school in time to pick up my box of state tests to administer, she is sitting upright on top of her quilt in a mass of warm liquid. She has just wet the bed.

"Mom, what happened?" I ask her tenderly and quietly.

And with a worried expression, she looks up into my face and says only, "I don't know." It comes out softly and with such a look of doom. We are sharing the same awful thought: this feels like it is going to turn into something much bigger than both of us want to face. She couldn't get to the bathroom because she feels her legs don't work. The toilet that is only three paces from the edge of her bed simply seemed too far to go.

"Oh Mom, it's okay. I'm going to help you. You're okay. I'm here." With this I hold her tiny hands in mine, and we look into each other's eyes. Her hands are the size of a little doll's. They are warm, and she has long fingers that are too thin to wear any of the rings that used to fit. Her dainty hands drown in my palm as I cup them gently. I never remember them being anything but strong when I was a child. She could shuck corn, milk cows, and knock my brothers' heads together if they got out of line. When did her hands become so delicate?

I try to give her an expression to reassure her that this is natural and it's no big deal to wet the bed, but I feel that something is definitely not quite right here. I just don't know what it is. I am able to get her to stand so I can walk her to the bathroom with my arm around her waist for balance. She can find her way to sit on the pot, but today she needs help wiping. I haven't done this for anyone before, not even a child, but it seems to come naturally to me. Back in her room, I yank off the bedspread. The accident did not soak through to the blankets and sheet beneath. I grab a new quilt from the plastic bags preserving the ones from the '80s that have never been used. I wash her hands and tuck her back into bed and then tell her my plan.

"Mom, I will not go to school today. I am going to stay home with you, and I will call Dr. Goodcare because he will know what to do."

She is nodding at every word, knowing I will take charge.

"But I need to go see my principal so she can get a sub for me. I will only be gone for a half hour. Will you be all right to wait?"

"Oh, Steffie, you're wonderful." She looks at me steadily and holds out her little doll hands to me. "I love you."

That is all I need to spur me on. I am going to fix this for my mom. She is going to get the care she needs. The writing test will have to be administered by someone else. My mother is falling apart.

I dash in the rain as fast as safely possible to drive, and I find my principal, Camilla, in the hallway outside her office. Thank goodness she is not already in an early morning meeting, and thank goodness no one else is around because she takes one look at me and asks if I am all right, and I burst into hysterical tears.

"My mom is not doing well." I gasp for air. "I have to go home to be with her," I say, trying to choke back the tears. "I am scared." I can't control my sobs anymore because they are flooding out of me and dripping off my nose. "I don't know what's happening to her, but I need to be with her, and I can't administer the writing test."

Camilla just hugs me tight and lets me squeak out the rest of the words, which are too inaudible for her to understand. Then she yanks me into her office, where I sit for one quiet minute with a tissue box while she tells me, "Of course you need to go home. Of course we will find someone to administer the test. You've done everything you need to do for our students. They will be fine today. Don't even think about it. Just go home and take the time you need. Whatever I can do for you, I will."

"She has tiny hands," I say, tugging tissue after tissue from the Kleenex box, "and she looks so worried. I don't know what's happening to her." I offer to do whatever else I can to get my classroom in order before a sub arrives.

Camilla insists that I just go, telling me there is absolutely nothing I need to stay there to do. "Your room looks like it's ready for Open House every day of the year. Your sub will find whatever he needs. So just go now and call me later." She hugs me again, long and sincerely, and tries to eke out a smile but I can see the tears welling up in her eyes because she has so much compassion for me. "Really, Stefania, whatever you need, just let me know what it is."

With this I dart out through the back parking lot, where it

is still too early to run into any of my fellow teachers. I don't want to have to explain the tears and the reason I am not staying on the biggest day of the year for my department.

Once I am in the car, I hit the road and don't think twice about the test that day. I have more on my plate to worry about. I call Dr. Goodcare, and he calls hospice. By eleven that morning, I have an appointment set with the nurse and the social worker, who will come out at two o'clock today to evaluate my mother. I am so surprised that they can arrange to be here so quickly, but I am quite grateful for their immediate attention.

When I meet Karen, the nurse, and Charlotte, the social worker, my spirits feel lifted for the first time today. They are lovely women with hearts of gold, and Karen's decades of working in hospice helps her to speak frankly with my mother and with me without scaring either one of us more than we already are. The assessment begins with a visit with my mother, who is in her room, still tucked in her bed, where she lives. She has wrapped herself in a cocoon of cashmere sweaters and a cap along with her two cats purring on top of her blankets. There is an assortment of decorative pillows cast about because I intended for her to have a bedroom befitting a princess, even if that princess was old enough to be the queen's mother. I move aside some of the pillows she has used to build a fortress behind her; I am still surprised that she never liked the body pillow I bought her a couple years ago that she insisted I get rid of.

Karen and Charlotte pull up chairs to sit at her bedside.

"Mom, these are nurses from the hospital to check on how you are feeling." I motion toward them. "Can you say hello?"

"Hello. You have such nice faces, both of you," she says

cheerfully. "I am going back to sleep now. Thank you for stopping by." And she snuggles back down and is nearly snoring that soon. I look to Karen, who is not satisfied yet with her exam, which has not even begun.

"Hi, Lolly. I'm a nurse, and I want to take some measurements of your bicep to see what your weight is today, is that all right?"

My mother grunts as if to say "go ahead, just don't disturb my sleep." So Karen pushes up the sleeves of her sweaters and measures her bicep. She asks to take my mother's temperature, for which my mother keeps her eyes closed and her mouth open. While her temperature runs a little low, it is better than having a fever. When Karen checks her blood pressure and heartbeat, they are both erratic and become something Karen wants to monitor more closely.

"Lolly, do you know what day it is?" she asks.

"Who cares?"

"Do you know what year it is?"

She does know the answer to this, and she knows her name and address and who I am. But when asked what time of day it is, her answer is consistent with any response she ever gave to the physical therapist: it's naptime.

"Can you move your legs for me? I understand you couldn't get up to go to the bathroom this morning. Are you in any pain?"

"No. I just want to sleep," she whispers.

"Let's just try to see what you can do with your legs, and then I'll let you get back to your nap. There is nothing worse than someone interrupting a good nap," Karen says in a loving tone that sounds playful to my mother.

"I know, and you're such a mean lady for doing it," my

mother retorts with a wide grin, opening her eyes for the single moment it takes for all of us to recognize she is joking around.

My mom has a difficult time moving her legs and keeps sleeping while Karen jostles her around and tries to get my mom to push against her hands to test her resistance. This task is a bit like asking a bear in hibernation if you can poke him with a stick for a while. While my mom does not become irritated, she is completely noncompliant.

Finally Karen and Charlotte decide their visit with my mother is over, and they tuck her in and join me at the dining room table.

"Your mother is in the last stage of her life," Karen tells me, "and we see this a lot with elderly patients who are sleeping into their next life. It would be the most peaceful death if she just didn't wake up one day. I know this is hard to hear, but you need to start preparing yourself because your mother is preparing herself."

Charlotte looks away from Karen and touches my hand as she can see my bottom lip begin to quiver. "Do you have a support system in place? Are there siblings in the area who can help?"

My lips are trembling, and as much as I fight against it, my face is collapsing downward into a frown, and I begin to weep. "My siblings have pretty much acted like I am here, so they don't need to be," I get out in one breath. "I have no friends in the area to relieve me, and my mom has outlived all of her friends with the exception of one who still sees her, but she is older too, and I found out early on that it is too much taking care of my mom and all the animals for one night."

I bury my face in my hands because I am now feeling the

overwhelming gravity of Karen's words. I am not ready to say good-bye to my mom. "How long do you think she has to live?" I ask with my eyes fixed on Charlotte, who looks at Karen, then they both turn back to look at me.

"We usually don't give out timelines because patients can bounce back. The trajectory usually looks like a stock market chart where there will be inclines and dips, but instead of moving steadily upward like on a mountain, the course is always at a lower point than where you started because this is the end of life cycle, and we are going down the hill."

Karen takes a break from speaking to let it all begin to sink in.

"This is never an easy request," Charlotte says, "but we will need the advance health-care directive, if you have one, to be hanging on the wall above her bed."

Yes, it is sinking in.

"Stefania, you are not going to be alone on this journey with your mom. We are here to help you as much as we can to make your mother feel comfortable," Charlotte continues. "You have done the hard work of taking care of your mom by yourself, and I know you have a good husband who has been able to help, from what you tell us, but you will be getting a team of five of us, and pretty soon you'll be sick of seeing our faces because we'll be giving you so much support."

Charlotte smiles brightly, like a fresh-faced girl from Iowa who could easily take the state beauty pageant if she would add some mascara and blush and soft pink lipstick to her routine. Charlotte is earthy and naturally beautiful, with flaxen hair that has likely never been artificially colored. Because of this there is a high sheen on her golden-chestnut locks. Her yoga-fit figure is lithe and petite and swathed in a long, olive green skirt and tights, and a simple, navy-blue V-neck sweater that appears tailored but probably isn't.

I ask who will be on the team, and Karen gives me all of the names and phone numbers but assures me they will be reaching out to me before I even have a chance to pick up the phone.

"Aside from me and Charlotte, who will both be sticking with you and your mom through to the end, we work very closely with Julio, the padre who will like to visit with you and your mom every other week to see if there are any spiritual needs either of you may have. Some families believe in the power of prayer, and while Julio is nondenominational, he is here to be a listener and offer you whatever help in healing either of you may need. Sometimes it can be difficult for your own clergy to visit as often as you might want, so Julio is here for you.

"You also get Annette, who is one of our grief counselors. As you move through this process, you might feel that you want to speak with her about the dying process and how to address any of the issues you feel are still left unresolved before your mother passes from this life. Annette is also available to talk with you whenever you need her—you don't have to wait until after your mom passes, but she will certainly be readily available at that time especially. Our goal is for you not to feel alone. Just as you have helped your mom not to feel alone by reminding her that you are here for her, we remind you that we are here for you too."

I cry a little harder because no one has shown such love and support to me. Aside from Greg Stacy, who loves me, what I am feeling from Karen and Charlotte is unwavering strength and unconditional support. I guess this is what some people experience within tight-knit families. I always wanted ours to be closer, but bad choices kept siblings driven apart from the family, and it is so hard to make up for lost time now that we are all strangers with foggy memories of our youth.

The fifth person on the team will be our caregiver, who will stay with my mom in the daytime so Greg and I can keep our jobs. Charlotte is quick to include that this will be a private caregiver our family will have to pay because hospice does not cover this part of the plan.

"Who am I going to get to stay with my mom? Do you like anybody you can recommend to me? This is such a big deal. I need to be able to trust this person implicitly with my mother and with all of our things in the house," I say worriedly, and Charlotte can see this gives me great anxiety.

Karen chimes in with a list of names and phone numbers of caregivers. It is the same useless list the hospital gave to me. No one there was willing to tell me who are the best ones and who to stay away from. This does me no good.

"Karen, I need to know who you know. I am not going to call through a directory of names to find some random person to invite into our home. There is no way I am comfortable with this, and there is no way I am leaving my mom in the care of a total stranger," I say emphatically.

Charlotte looks to Karen as if they should take pity on me and help me out this one time. "The problem is, Stefania," Charlotte softly explains in her nurturing voice, "we never want to be in the position of recommending a caregiver, especially since personalities can sometimes be in conflict. If it's not a good match, we don't want to feel we were responsible for steering you in the wrong direction." She looks at me with warm eyes, hoping I can understand her dilemma.

"I hear what you are saying, and I fully understand. But please, I want to know who you trust and who has been loved by their patients. I need someone warm and able to take care of my mother the way I take care of my mother. This is not just a job to me. This is my mother whom I love and adore, and I want someone who will be patient and loving too." I pause here and look into their eyes with my lashes wet and my cheeks stained with streaks of make-up. "Please, tell me who I can trust with my mother."

Charlotte can't stand my begging any more, and she looks to Karen and breathes out one word: "Elizabeth." We both wait for Karen's response.

"Elizabeth is an excellent choice," she says, "but I don't know if she's available. She's been with her family for six years now, and I don't know how her patient is doing because I am not on their service." She looks back to Charlotte. "Do you know how her patient is doing?"

Charlotte excuses herself to make a quick phone call, and Karen is left alone with me. She is less ethereal than Charlotte but funny, with a dry sense of humor that is right up my alley. She has a no-nonsense approach but is far more engaging than the physical therapist, whose style was more all-business. She tells me about her siblings, who left her in charge of her mother's care, and how resentful she felt that they just dumped the situation onto her to handle alone because they knew she would—that she could because she was a nurse after all. Still it would have been nice to get some more support.

One of her siblings offered financial support from time to time. I have heard of families having these kinds of arrangements, similar to custody agreements but with money going to the adult child who cares for the elderly parent to supplement costs. I have heard of families offering to give the caregiving sibling a night out or a weekend away, and I only wish I had this kind of relief.

# CHAPTER 27

# Looking for Support

Greg is a good one. From time to time, he will get me a night away on the ocean so I can have a spa weekend and not be needed by anyone. When I am ten minutes away from home, it takes only an hour for my homesickness to wear off, then I order room service and load up three movies for my marathon and order a sundae to splurge at midnight. It is just heaven knowing that my mom is in good hands with Greg and that he's walking and pottying and playing with Daisy, and that the cats are being petted and fed and looked for when it gets dark so that there is no fear raccoons might be eating them for their own midnight snack. Everything on Mindy Lane is taken care of when Greg Stacy is in charge, and this is the best gift to me my husband can give: the gift of time.

Speak of the devil, Greg walks in the door from work just in time to meet our hospice care providers. Charlotte and Karen are both very pleased to see him and to see us together. It is really important to their team to understand the working dynamics of the patient's family, particularly those living in the home and providing the care.

They spend a little time listening to the story of how we met. "My mom always says Greg fell from the sky through our roof. We needed to get our home-insurance policy back, and it wasn't going to happen without passing a roof inspection. Greg was the roofer referred by my brother's friend."

They are both nodding and smiling and marveling at what a story this turns out to be. I grab the small wedding album we made for my mom and happily share it with them, and they can see I am still a smitten bride.

"Greg, we know what kind of support you have been for Stefania from what she told us and how much it has meant to her especially since there are no siblings who are involved in the care, but how has all of this been for you? You kind of took on a lot with a new marriage and now Lolly not doing so well two years into your life here. How are you doing?" Charlotte asks sincerely.

Greg takes my hand and holds it tightly, and I know what he is going to say. It always breaks my heart to hear it. "I knew when I met Stefania that her priority is her mom, and I felt very much that a little girl like this would have to be a wonderful wife if she is such a loving daughter. I knew I was getting two girls in the package deal, and her mom is a lot of fun. We have had some good laughs around here, but I am no stranger to sickness.

"I don't know if Steffie told you, but I lost my wife to cancer after twenty-one years of marriage, and she was only thirty-nine. So I have had some experience in caring for someone at the end of their life because I was that guy. I was the one determining doses to give her so she would be comfortable in the end, and there were a lot of years before that when we were battling one cancer turning into another cancer. All the while I tried to raise three young boys and provide as much normalcy as I could while working too. So I know the job Steffie has been doing before I got here. And I know what she has in front of her, and I am glad she won't have to be alone when going through it."

Charlotte's eyes are glistening when she listens to Greg talk, and my tears have started dribbling down my cheeks again. Karen breaks the somber tone by saying how lucky I am to have him here with us and that he is probably a pretty lucky guy to have me as his wife too.

"Every day I feel blessed that we met. It couldn't have happened any other way. I was getting ready to leave the family business, and it was only a year later that I was out. If I hadn't met her when she needed a roof, I don't think our paths ever would have crossed, and it's funny because she went to school across from my high school, but with our years apart in age, we just never were on the same running path at the same time." He smiles at me, and I lean in to give him a peck on the cheek.

"Stefania, I have good news," Charlotte chimes in. "I made a few phone calls earlier, and while we are saddened to learn that Elizabeth's patient passed away last Thursday, it does mean she is available right now." She slides Elizabeth's number across the table to me.

"Oh, I think you will like her very much," Karen confirms. "She is in demand, and we have both worked with her for many years, so we are pretty comfortable in telling you that her patient families have adored her. The caregiver often becomes like an extended member of the family once you go through an experience like this."

I fill Greg in on our need to hire a caregiver, and we talk about what the going rates are. Charlotte explains another option—using professional agencies—and provides me two backup names in case Elizabeth needs a substitute or for some reason is not a fit with our family.

I am tremendously relieved and extremely grateful that Charlotte talked Karen into just giving me a personal referral. I could not feel better. I just want a mini-me to show up and be receptive to whatever I need and to be reliable and nice and treat my mother well. Affordability is also a priority. I have no idea how long my mother's decline will last. In birth we have nine months to prepare. In death there is no timeline.

It seems incumbent upon me in this moment, now that hospice is onboard, to update my siblings who are not regularly in contact so that my conscience is clear that I did right by them. I want to provide them with every opportunity to say their final good-byes to their mother and to hear from her how much she has loved them.

So I start with Sister Two. I get her on the phone on my first try. I succinctly tell her that our mom has been slowing down, and now hospice is involved to make sure she is well cared for and comfortable in the last stage of her life.

There is a long pause on the other end of the line. In a very weak and shaken voice, I hear her spit out the only words she can before she begins her usual silent cry, "How long do they say she has?"

"No one is making any predictions. But I know if hospice is involved, it must be pretty bad. I think all of the siblings need to be at her bedside together to say good-bye. Can you make it on Saturday?"

She follows with her usual behavior when she gets too upset to speak: a quick exit off the phone by saying she will call me back. I know she's got a tender heart, but it is buried beneath mesh and armor.

I call Brother One, who lives nearby. He is quite taken aback to know that we have gotten to this point so suddenly. He tells me I have done a good job and that, of course, he will be there with the other siblings on Saturday. He asks if Brother Two will be there, and I tell him I hope so because I don't want him to miss an opportunity to say good-bye, and Brother One hopes this will be a chance for them to heal their old wounds.

I call Brother Two, who we have not seen in a while because he usually only surfaces at holidays despite the fact that he lives in the area. He would have wished her a happy Valentine's Day if she weren't in the hospital hallucinating about dead dogs on her bed, and Mother's Day is still too far away. I gently tell him about some of the events that have led up to our mom's decline and that she never really bounced back to her old self after she left the hospital.

He wants to know when he can come see her, and I tell him Saturday is the day for all of the siblings to be at her bedside together, and he will also have time alone with her to say his good-byes. I make sure he knows there is no timeframe we have been given but that when hospice gets involved, it's serious, and they are here to help her be comfortable and peaceful in her end-of-life stage. I can tell he's upset, but he says he'll be there, and before he hangs up I tell him that Brother One is looking forward to making amends with him.

It's the most I can do, but there is one more sibling who still needs to be called. Sister Three is the one who has wanted nothing to do with my mother or really any of us, which has only brought me peace. But she needs to be told, and I gather my courage since I haven't spoken to her in many years.

When she picks up the phone, I tell her what I have told all of the other siblings. But her response is different. It is a quick cut like a sushi knife through raw tuna. "Well, Stef, thanks for calling. If there's anything I can do, let me know, but I don't think I can be of much help from two hours away." With this she proceeds to hang up without saying any of the polite, caring comments that even the greatest of enemies might offer. No condolences, no "let me know how she progresses," no regrets, no inquiries. Just a parting compliment: "Well, I'm glad you're there because I would have put her in a home." Perhaps it is only a half compliment.

The gathering of siblings at the foot of my mother's bed a few days later goes about as well as I hoped. We are a collection of strangers who grope for memories that might bond us and give us the strength we need to support one another. It is a forgery we carve at the dining room table after everyone has had their individual time to sit with my mother, who seems to be aware of our presence but not actively engaged.

The brothers had their own alone times and tentatively agree to put their history behind them and start an awkward friendship. This will make my mother so happy. Sister Two begins to cry as soon as she sees the document that spells out my mother's end-of-life wishes, which hangs above her bed, and thinks it is rather gauche to flaunt it for everyone to see. But this is exactly the point of why it is in that spot, I try to explain gently.

After a short afternoon, the brothers leave, but Sister Two sits for a few hours longer to hold my mother's hand. It is peaceful but hard to watch from the doorway as this sister of mine, who steels herself against the world, is dabbing at her eyes, willing her emotions to stop getting the better of her—a nearly impossible feat.

Karen and Charlotte get things done. Right away there are boxes arriving from delivery companies full of medical supplies and diapers and catheters in the event we should need to go this route if my mother ends up becoming bedridden, which is not likely the case today, in my perception. Besides, my mother loves her bed. She reminds me of the four little old grandparents from *Willy Wonka & the Chocolate Factory* who all share one bed and sleep and eat and live in it. This is why she has so many pillows and blankets and cats: so she can nest in her own body warmth. When she is in the midst of her sleep, it is nearly indistinguishable to tell who is actually doing all of the purring.

While supplies are coming in, I clear some drawer space in her bureau to store the tubes of lotions and ointments and jellies, and the wipes, and the gloves and grooming kits, and the medicines for pain, and the dry shampoos, and the tucks that look like what I potty-trained Daisy on when she was a puppy confined to the kitchen. I arrange them all, by size and color—my standard way of organizing anything.

Interviews for the caregiving position have been set for today, tomorrow, and Friday. I too am wasting no time. In my preliminary talks with agencies, I discover that there is no guarantee I will have the same caretaker each day because they rotate their employees, which worries me. I want my mom to have familiarity in her routine, not revolving faces of people she might not recognize. So I opt for the private route—the one we will pay for ourselves.

Elizabeth is not available to see me until Thursday, so today I am meeting with two other ladies separately. One— Beatrice—I found through church, and while speaking with her on the phone, I ask if she smokes. Her reply is more indignant than it probably needs to be. It plants a seed in the back of my brain that stays with me until it grows bigger, rooting itself in a full-blown lie, but I am getting ahead of myself.

The next lady, Hana, comes ten minutes early with her

husband, who waits in their van while she interviews with me for half an hour. I ask if her husband is taking her to lunch after the interview. She tells me she doesn't drive, doesn't have a license, and relies on him for transportation to her jobs. And if he's working, then someone else in her extended family will drive her.

This strikes me as unusual because I am accustomed to families having at least one car for each person in the household. Not that I grew up this way, but it is a lot more commonplace than having only one car to share between relatives. I worry that my mom won't be able to get to the hospital if the caregiver can't drive. So I thank Hana for coming, and while she is very sweet and willing to take whatever I am willing to pay if she can earn at least twelve dollars an hour, I am having more misgivings about her docile demeanor and feel I need someone who is more able to take charge.

Thursday comes, and Elizabeth arrives right on time at eight o'clock in the morning. I am so anxious to meet her after hearing such good things about her. I am hoping with all my heart that she will be the one. So far, every time I have told the story of my mother and me during the interview process, I could not hold back my tears. The prospective candidates hugged me, hoping their measures of sympathy would get them the job. Mostly they were sincere, and I appreciated them so much.

It is no different when Elizabeth steps into our living room. The room that was once so wretched, with piles of defecation and furniture zigzagging haphazardly, is now homey and inviting. Slipcovers have been neatly tucked into corners so all the furniture appears freshly upholstered in muted shades of linen and taupe. It's another designer trick when you need to pull off an elegant look with zero budget.

"Hello, Stefania. I'm Elizabeth." A good impression already, followed by a firm handshake. I can tell she has been practicing how to pronounce my name since most people say it incorrectly. Clearly Charlotte has rehearsed it with her because Elizabeth says the middle syllable with a flat A as in apple, just the way my parents pronounce it. Anyone who knows me well always gets this right.

"Hello, Elizabeth. Please come in."

We sit very near to one another and facing each other as if we are sisters who wish to share secrets quickly before anyone will come in to spoil our fun. Immediately I get a really good vibe from Elizabeth. She is poised and speaks lovingly of the patients and families she has cared for the past eighteen years. She came into caregiving after experiencing her father's decline and, as one of the last children in the family still on the island in the South Pacific where she grew up, she looked after him. She moved to the States, and had been married for twelve years and had a young son when her husband died of a sudden heart attack. She has been alone since then, and her faith is very important to her; the members of her church are very much like her family.

I listen and take it all in. Then it is my turn, and I talk about the story of my mom and me, the lack of support from my siblings, and Greg and my mom—how she adores him so much she doesn't call him her "son-in-law" but rather her "son-in-love." It's not a name I have ever heard her call other men who married into this family then divorced their way out. I watch Elizabeth as she listens. She can feel the love we have in this home. I can feel the compassion in her heart when I begin to cry and she also has a tear dripping out of her eye. I feel she is the real deal. So I say all the hard things that we need to get straight upfront.

"Elizabeth, I don't want to lose my mom. I have been here for four years so far, and I have enjoyed her so much. I need to know that someone will care for her the way I care for her so I can continue to stay in the classroom."

She nods knowingly and tells me that this is why she is here—because Charlotte told her there is a nice family with two nice ladies who need her help.

"I have a dog who is like my daughter. Are you afraid of dogs?"

Elizabeth assures me she has had dogs her whole life, and they ran around on the island so everyone took care of everyone else's dogs like they were their own.

"I need to know that if there is something wrong with my mom, you can drive her to the hospital, and I need to know I can count on you to be reliable because I can't be late for school ever. My job doesn't work that way. I have kids counting on me." I look at her to make sure she knows how serious I am, and she looks at me as if to convey that she is a professional.

"Stefania, I don't drive, but I have very reliable transportation. I have references for you, and I have been with three families for the past eighteen years. When one patient dies, the family calls me when they have another relative who is dying because they know how I am with my families and that I love their parent as much as they do. I have also seen families who don't all get along, and I know you are my boss, so you can count on me to be the help that you need." She smiles as if to say she is adamant that she is going to convince me I don't have to be fearful.

I was not expecting to consider anyone who did not drive, but even Greg pointed out to me last night that if there is an emergency, an ambulance will be called, so who needs a car anyway? Maybe I can be flexible on this point.

"Okay," I say. "I have one last thing to ask you. What will you be doing when my mom is sleeping? Is there a chance you can help with some things around the house?"

"Absolutely. I usually pick days of the week to do the laundry, and I like to vacuum at the end of every day so the house looks tidied before you get home from work. Usually I will read my book or watch television on low."

I interrupt here. "Well, the only dilemma is the television is in the family room, and if my mom is sleeping, I sort of want you in her room to watch her. Since hospice doesn't know how long we have, I would feel horrible if something happened and you weren't there when she opened her eyes for the last time. My greatest fear is that it won't be me she sees for the last time. My goal is to be with her right up until the end, but I have to go to school, and I need to know I can count on you in the daytime to be right there with her." I say urgently.

"It's okay, Stefania, I will be with your mom. You can go to school and not worry. I will be right there with her, and I will sit by her bed and just read my book all day. It's not a problem." She sounds sincere.

We talk about her rate—twenty dollars an hour—and I am choking since the highest anyone else came in at was eighteen. Certainly I could have hired the quiet lady for twelve dollars an hour, but I just didn't feel like she was a fit. Elizabeth ends our conversation with a hopeful demeanor and says to me that whatever decision I make for my mother will be the right one. She hopes it will be she who can come to help me, but she will trust that I am making the best choice for my family. I appreciate that.

I meet Hattie on Friday morning and can tell right away that I do not want her to provide my mother's care because her face is unsettling. She has over-plucked her eyebrows into magnificent arches that make her look angry all the time. It is a very dramatic look seen in movies from decades ago starring villainesses like Joan Crawford or Marlene Dietrich. I do not wish for my mother to be scared every time her caregiver walks into the room.

When I tell Hattie, who also happens to be a church member with a good reputation for caregiving, that I still have more interviews to conduct and that I will be calling her before the weekend is over, she leaves me with the fervent thought that she has already prayed on it and knows she will be coming to work here on Monday. I applaud that moxie. I say bravo to someone with such confidence. It just doesn't happen to be the truth, and nowhere inside me do I have the heart to tell her to fix her brows.

I tell Greg that my thoughts keep bringing me back to Elizabeth even though there are things I do and do not like about each of the other candidates. I feel like I have a good pool to consider, especially if I am not going to let the not driving thing bother me. He's right: the caregiver would first call an ambulance, then call hospice. She wouldn't be driving my mother to the hospital.

Greg asks me what it is I really want for my mother's care. In this instant I know the single most important criteria to me.

"In the end, if I can't be the one there holding my mother's hand, then I want the face my mother looks into to be the face of an angel, and that is Elizabeth."

My decision is made. I feel warmed by it, and Greg supports me in it. I invite Elizabeth back on Sunday to meet him and my mother before starting to work with us the next morning. I am a bit worried that my mother will not take to having a stranger in her house, so I arrange to have a substitute for my students for a few more days just so we can all get accustomed to the new routine and so my mother feels safe in her home. It turns out to be one of the best decisions I ever make.

# CHAPTER 28

# My Mother, My Child

On day one I can tell that my hovering around Elizabeth is going to be unnecessary and unappreciated. She reminds me that she is an experienced professional with a rhythm of doing things and explains how the day will roll. Between changing my mother's bedding, giving her a bed bath, and making some creative meals for her including pureed potato soup, which sounds pretty good to my mother, Elizabeth is holding her own and showing that she is capable of taking charge. I can be bossy. But I also trust someone who is equally confident in her own position, and I will relent when I see that everything is being attended to as it should be.

My mom is conversational, and she and Elizabeth are having an easy time of getting to know one another. I remind my mom that I am in the house but that Elizabeth is going to be her steady companion when I am at school, and in a way my mom is thrilled to have a combination of a nanny and a handmaiden to take care of her every need. What my mom wants more than anything is not to be alone. So this delights her to no end.

And as a sidenote to that nagging little feeling I had while interviewing Beatrice, months from now, when I use her as a substitute for Elizabeth one weekend, I get confirmation that my initial instincts were right after all. When Greg does a full sweep of the house and the property before I say good-bye and pay Beatrice for her stay, he finds the Coke can she is hastily scurrying to retrieve from the backyard where she forgot it. Unfortunately Greg already discovered her cigarette butt smashed into the bottom of the remaining soda. If you think a caregiver is lying to you, there is probably a good reason you are suspicious. Trust your gut.

At this point my mom is able to use the potty on her own, with the help of someone to walk her to the bathroom. I have bought another body pillow that we use to prop her up when it comes time for her to eat in bed, and I found one of those sturdy breakfast trays that have legs to straddle her lap stored in a cupboard in the house. What I am most intrigued by is the copious note taking that Elizabeth does to record events for my mother on an hourly basis, and sometimes in increments of fifteen minutes depending on what happens.

Upon reviewing today's synopsis, I can easily see the date and day of the week listed at the top of the page in the spiral notebook I provided for Elizabeth, along with the times listed down the left margin for events recorded. For instance, at 7:30 a.m. Elizabeth arrived and found Lolly still sleeping. At 10:35 a.m., Elizabeth escorted Lolly to the bathroom—the urine color was light and cloudy. Lolly took some more water. At 11:05 a.m., Lolly wanted to have some breakfast, so Elizabeth made one scrambled egg, half a slice of toast, and half a cup of coffee, and took eight sips of water.

All day long the register reads like a diary entry detailing the mundane movements of someone who likes to sleep, eat a very little bit, and then try to go to the bathroom. Blood pressure, pulse, and heart rate are also recorded whenever the nurse comes, and here on the first day, impressively, is Karen. Hospice has lived up to the expectations they laid out in my first meeting with her and Charlotte six days ago. Julio, the padre, has also called this morning to introduce himself and set a time for us to meet before the end of the week.

At 5:00 p.m. Elizabeth leaves while Karen is still checking my mother, and I know it will be up to me for the rest of the night. Thankfully Greg is up at oh-dark-thirty and checks on my mom to make sure she is breathing and comfortably resting. She usually hears him and asks if he will escort her to the bathroom, where he will wait patiently while she does her business, and sometimes he has to help her wipe her back side. There is no modesty when one's sole priority is to maintain proper kidney and bowel functions. To have some release is heaven, and it just doesn't matter that someone has to help you with tidying yourself afterward. My mom knows Greg did this for his wife for years before she passed away. She coos at him, "You're my son-in-love" while he freshens her up and tucks her back into bed.

Day one is a success. Days two and three and four are equally comfortable. By now Elizabeth knows where the vacuum is stored and is learning the nuances of where I keep things in the kitchen cupboards and drawers when she empties the dishwasher. This week there seems to be some jelly-like mucus that is coming out when my mom coughs, and her urine remains cloudy. A nurse's aide, Lulu, comes twice a week to help with a bed bath, and Elizabeth is right there alongside her to make sure my mom knows that she is not surrounded by strangers. I watch both times to see the consistency of how the bath is given, and how they warm up the water, and how they prevent the bed from getting sopping wet, and how they might jostle my mother around during the process.

Fortunately I am comforted to see that there is no jostling, but I am concerned about the pain my mother experiences when she is asked to bend her knee so they can wash her caboose. When she says, "Owwwch!" I know it's worse than that because my mother never complains about being in pain. She has never had a headache in her entire life, and to see her wincing when people are pushing against her knee is more than I can stand, so I stop Lulu abruptly.

"She's in pain, can't you see?" I scold, a bit harsher than I intend. "Is there a way we can avoid moving her legs if they give her trouble?"

I am sure the entire hospice team has seen overanxious children caretaking their elderly parents. But I am so grateful for their help, I don't want to overstep my bounds and make them so frustrated with me that they want to leave my mother. Nothing close to this ever happens, though. I really come to love Karen and Charlotte, who are so gentle with my mom and so congenial with me.

At this point the focus is on getting my mom to eat while monitoring the germs that seem to be producing the kind of phlegm in her throat that she is not strong enough to cough up. It just gurgles in her trachea as she breathes. Her urine is a very dark yellow and cloudy, and walking her to the bathroom is becoming cumbersome because her legs are getting weaker.

Last night Greg got up at three-thirty to check on her and help her to the bathroom as usual. Before she even got to the sink outside of the door to her toilet, she slipped from his arms and collapsed to the floor. I could hear his grunting through the baby monitor we installed in her room, and then the words that made me leap from my bed, jumping over Daisy, who was at my feet.

"Lolly, come on, can you wake up? Can you hear me? I'm trying to get you up here so you can go to the bathroom." Greg is almost in a panic.

I rush in to where my mother is lying on the floor while he is crouched over her, trying to brace her to stand with both of his hands tucked under her armpits, but she is like a wet noodle, and he can't get any leverage.

"Steffie, don't come in here. I don't want you to see her like this." I can hear his voice getting high and excited while we both look over her. Her eyes are shut but fluttering; she is completely unresponsive and motionless on her adjoining closet floor in a heap.

"I am not leaving her side. She is my mother, and I am staying with her." I am choking back tears and frightened that she is having a stroke, and it is happening so very quickly, with only a few seconds having passed. "Mom, Mom, can you hear me?" I grab her hand and hold it close to my cheek while I stroke her hair. "Mom, we want to get you up, can you hear me?" The tears are flowing, but I am not hysterical. I am thoughtful in this moment and so grateful that I can be here with her so that if she does open her eyes, she will know she is not alone.

"I think I must have fainted," she says, coming to. "Let's try it again."

I am so thankful that Greg is here in this moment to help me because there is no way I could manage getting her up from being splat on the floor by myself. She is still heavier than I am, and with Greg's tremendous upper-body strength he has more success maneuvering her, so long as she is not going limp and lifeless.

Hearing the news of this, Karen thinks it is time to move my mom into her own hospital bed, the kind that can be easily elevated and lowered. This will make using the toilet much more convenient because she also decides we are ready for a commode at my mother's bedside. Karen makes a call to the supplier, and they come out the same day while Elizabeth and I flip my mom's room so her queen-size bed can be tucked into the opposite corner where I, or Elizabeth in the event she ever spends the night, can look directly at my mom perched upright in her twin-size hospital bed complete with electric buttons to control if she wants to be adjusted downward for napping or upright for eating.

The commode experience is mine alone when my mother tries it out for the first time that evening. Karen's instructions to me were to put a layer of tucks beneath the commode so in case there is any drippage it won't go directly onto the carpeting. I use two of the thinly layered diaper panels just to be on the extra safe side and find that getting my mom up from the bed is as easy as Karen said it would be. Now all my mom has to do is stand on her feet, take one step toward the commode, turn around, then sit on it to go pee-pee. Everything about executing this is a disaster.

My mom is wobbly on her two feet, and getting her to feel confident enough to take one step toward the commode requires me to yell urgently for Greg, who is in the next room watching TV but on standby if I need him. He quickly comes in to help keep my mom propped upright until she sits on this pot, which meets her at hip height. My mom has to urinate so badly that in the sheer moment it takes for me to assure her the commode is safely within a couple inches beneath her bottom and she can sit directly on it if she drops down just a bit, her body is listening instead to its own urging. With legs still positioned stiffly in front of her, she proceeds to spray urine everywhere other than the commode, having only caught the open pot with her tailbone instead of her full bottom.

All I can do is watch while she enjoys the relief that comes from the sweet release of liquid that was building for hours after she was plied with Ensure, broth, juice, water, and coffee. Even if she is only taking six or seven sips of everything she is offered, her body functioning is not quite to full capacity. The only reaction I have is to quickly move my feet out of the way.

After she is finally done, my bare feet are the only things that are still dry. The entire floor is seeping with urine. The two tucks cloths I used for double the protection somehow got caught in her feet while she was moving into position. Their thin, plastic linings bunched up and twisted around the legs of the commode, sparing nothing. Even the bedspread in front of her is wet; so are the bed rails and the carpet. It is quite a scene, but she is comfortable now.

I have Greg hold her in place so I can do a quick change of her bedding before I sponge her down, put some new Depends on her, and change her clothes. She is now ready for sleep once again. While I mop up the wet carpet with towels to soak up the residue of all that should have gone into the bowl, she says to me, "Oh, Steffie, you work so hard."

"I am here to help you, Mom. Whatever you need, I am here for you. Don't even worry about this. It's easy enough to take care of. The important thing is that you are comfortable and safe," I say, meaning it because the great problem with that commode is her stiff-legged approach to using it. I don't know that her knees will ever again bend enough to allow her to use it in the way it is intended.

When Karen, Elizabeth, and I talk about this the next morning, Karen decides a catheter is going to be the easiest route at this point and orders extra-large diapers as well. I don't get it.

"Why do we need the diapers if she has a catheter?" I ask innocently.

"That's to catch the poop." Karen smiles at me. "You probably haven't changed diapers in a long time."

Oh my. It never occurred to me that I would be changing my mom's diapers. I haven't done this since I babysat for neighbor kids when I was in middle school a long time ago.

"This is going to be difficult for you because your mom is a heavy lady, and you are smaller, and the bed only elevates so much, so you might not be able to get the right angle to roll her the way you should in order to avoid throwing out your back. Let me show you the proper steps so you don't hurt yourself," Karen says seriously.

It is a lesson I will practice over and over again as I tug and pull and struggle to roll my mom sideways so I can slide a diaper off her with one hand, taking care to not mess the sheets, and quickly put a new one in its place. She does her level best to extend her little hands to meet the cold, metal bar and grasp it, doing her part to help me keep her upright, but her upper-body strength is quickly dwindling, and it takes a lot of concentration for her to hold on for ten seconds.

The more we do this, the more I get a rhythm down, and despite the sweat that builds quickly at my hairline, I manage to do a pretty good job, if I do say so myself. At least the diaper is on, and the tape seems to be affixed in the correct places, and for the time or two when I can't quite get it fastened before her strength gives out and she rolls over on my hands, I am soothed to know that she made it almost through the last stage, and even an imperfectly positioned diaper should be good enough.

But here's the universal lesson in diapering that most young parents figure out early on the job: Without a diaper securely intact, you run the risk of finding excrement coming out of the leg holes, pushed naturally to the front onto the tummy and smeared onto the blankets. There is no way of knowing in advance how much of a load there may be at any given time, and I am reminded of this in episodes that are repeated with great frequency.

There are some nights and weekends that, as soon as I get her all cleaned up and in fresh diapers, another BM decides to come out. In such moments I rush to the bureau drawers to reach for new supplies, hoping I am faster than her bowels. We are happy her body is still doing its job to keep her colon cleansed on the minimal water she has been taking.

"Keep pushing, Mom," I say in my most encouraging voice. "Your body is working hard." And I hold her on her side so it is easier for her to move her stool. When it finally does come, we are both excited, and I congratulate her for a job well done. "You did it. You did a nice big one!"

"Oh, Steffie, do you know how perfect you are?"

"I am not perfect. I'm just pretty darn good," I say with a big grin on my face, hardly affected by the smell I have become accustomed to on my shift. I always joke with Elizabeth that I hope my mom has her big one on her shift so it gets out of the way before I take over night nurse duties. I always know the weekends will be full of changing diapers and hosing off bed sheets from time to time. But I am so happy that my mom's body is still cooperating. Without her kidneys or colon functioning, she will cease to exist.

Hospice is quite pleasantly surprised that my mom is still doing all right, all things considered. She is losing weight but not rapidly. Karen can tell by the incremental measurements of her bicep that even though she is dropping by only centimeters, her arms are getting smaller, and her face is getting drawn. Her appetite has been reduced to baby food or puree soups that Elizabeth knows how to make just right. Mostly my mom just wants to sleep. There is an incessant gurgling that becomes so pronounced one night I have to call the number I've been given for the hospice nurse advice line to explain what I am hearing. My mom has not awakened for three days. She has not eaten, and she does not stir for the bath nurse or for Karen or Charlotte, who come to check on her twice a week.

This is the closest I have seen my mom to being completely gone, and when the nurse comes on the line all I can say is, "My mom is gurgling, and she won't wake up," and the sobbing begins again.

"Oh honey, I know it's hard to watch." She has the sweet voice of a mature woman with a slight accent that is nearly undetectable until I ask where she is located. "I'm in Austin. I've been a nurse for twenty-five years. Can I ask you a couple of questions?" I hear the compassion in her voice as she walks me through this slowly so I have a chance to calm myself down.

She tells me the medicine Dr. Goodcare prescribed will help to clear the congestion in my mom's lungs. My only problem is she won't wake up to eat or drink anything, so it is nearly impossible to think of getting her to swallow a horse pill. But the nurse has another suggestion: crush the pill with a serving spoon, then mix the fine granules into applesauce, which we have, and my mom should be able to get that down in a couple little bites. I put the nurse on hold and do as she says, and after shaking my mom a bit to open her eyes, she is willing to swallow the applesauce from the baby spoon we use to feed her now, and finally takes several sips of water to wash it down.

My mom continues to sleep away the month of April. Every day I come home from school, rush to her door, and peek at Elizabeth, who says, "Yeah, she's still sleeping, but she's very peaceful and her breathing sounds good," for which I am very thankful. I ask Elizabeth if she knows what it sounds like before a person dies, and she says she can usually tell and assures me that when she feels the time is here, she will let me know.

People keep telling me that pneumonia is an old person's best friend, but I just don't want to say good-bye to my mom yet. She tells me all the time, "Steffie, what would I do without you?" and I am so genuinely happy that she never has to find out. I am lucky that she expresses her love and her gratitude to me daily, multiple times. Karen tells me horror stories of patients who throw things at their children or don't even know their children, or rant and rage all day without making any sense. She tells me it's really nice that my mom and I have such a loving bond and that it will be such a happy, peaceful death— a good way for my mom to leave this world, as painful as it will be for me to be without her.

And so I wait. Every day I go to school, leaving my home thinking this could be the last time I see my mom. I am anxious every time my cell phone rings in class, and while the kids think it's a double standard that I get to have my phone out and they don't, I explain to them that sometimes there are phone calls from nurses and doctors who are caring for my very sick mother. They understand in this moment, but then they forget a few days later because when you are twelve, you are the sun that everyone else orbits around.

Their forgetting almost makes it easier on me. I find answering questions from colleagues about the condition of my mother, or the age of my mother, or what my mother is dying from either puts me near a state of tears or fills me with a fury that makes me want to scream at them for being more nosy than compassionate. It also completely derails my focus at school when I need to stay in the present moment for my kids and compartmentalize what's going on at home until I can get there after school.

## CHAPTER 29

# My Misery Compounded

During the last weekend before income taxes are due, I am consumed by the same feeling every other American who waits until the last minute is having: heavy anxiety. Fortunately my paperwork is all collected in one tax file I have kept for the year. Unfortunately I have more legwork to do: crunching my numbers prior to entering the data requested into my tax software program.

It takes me the better part of Saturday to get myself situated, and while Greg is in charge of my mom to make sure she is still breathing or to let me know whether or not I need to change her, I attend to my business. I can hear him playing with Daisy as they gallop around the front of the house, chasing each other in and out of the doors and around the pool area. There is nothing Daisy likes more than to play, especially every single time I sit down to grade papers—or work on taxes.

This weekend is no different. Even though Greg has distracted her while I am getting my work done, it really is her momma she wants. So I go and gallop with her too, and chase her with the only toy she ever likes to play with: an oversize red ant that stretches the length of my entire leg, ankle to waist. She loves to wrestle with that thing and take the challenge that today she might be successful in finally ripping its head off. I have had to sew its neck together more than a few times, reinforcing it with the same red yarn I have kept since the '90s, intending to finish the scarf I have been knitting since then. I know how to start, I just don't know how to tie off, so I keep buying skeins, and I now have a scarf that is so long and wide it could wave from a pole like a flag.

The next day is Sunday, ending my week of spring break. It was truly wonderful having Elizabeth here to take care of my mom so I could have time to manage the things in my own life that have been pushed to the back burner. It felt good to go out for a long walk on the lake. It felt good to join a gym. It felt good to go out to a movie with Greg. It felt good to have support.

Our routine starts out just like yesterday's did. After another morning of heavy play with Daisy running wildly throughout the house, charging in and out of several doors, she hightails it out the back gate where the yard, still enclosed, is safe for her to gallivant. She finally comes inside to sloppily lap at her water and gobble up her food before it's naptime next to Lolly.

While my idea of dotting my I's and crossing my T's should take me only an hour or two before I am free for the day to watch some football with Greg, I realize my time management is off because my taxes need one more triple check. Once the afternoon becomes dusk, and once I have missed dinner in favor of just finishing the last couple of questions, my methodical pace has now kept me in my dad's old den until bedtime. After I am finally sure I am squared away with my taxes, I begin filing away all of my receipts and paper-clipping my checks to my returns. That's when I hear a thud followed by some heavy panting.

My first guess is that Daisy has jumped off our bed and is about to start heaving up some form of grass or food since she loves to take swipes at the cats' food dish every time she's in the kitchen now that Nuisance, the great intimidator, is gone. But the uneven breathing I hear from outside the den door is telling me to go check. Heading toward our bedroom, I find Daisy lying on the floor with her jaws open, panting in a way she never has, not even after running on the beach.

Her eyes are following my every move and seemingly trying to convey a message to me that I am not yet picking up. I am wondering if she landed a little too hard when she hit the floor and got the wind knocked out of her, but this doesn't seem logical considering how much she has made bed jumping a way of life. I look to our bed to see if she has taken any contraband from the kitchen, and instead of the foil wrappers I half expect to find, I see a mound of steaming poo-poo.

"Greeeeg! Greeeeg! Something is wrong with Daisy!" I call as loudly as I can down the hall, hoping he is in the house and hoping to not wake my mother.

She is my first dog, so I don't know all the signs of an animal in distress, but I can tell in the thirty seconds since I have found her and found her clues that the message she is sending me is coming in loud and clear: all is not well with my daughter, my dog.

Greg bends down to look at her, and he instantly says we need to get to the emergency vet right away because her gums are discolored and turning white, and her eyes don't look right. The extra blanket I have in the first-aid box in the kids' bathroom that I originally kept to be used as a stretcher for my mom in the event we ever needed to cart her to the car is now used for Daisy for the same purpose. We put her in Greg's Suburban, and I sit with her in the back, stroking her fur and crying and telling her she is going to be all right.

"You're Momma's precious girl. You'll be okay. Can you hear me, girl? Stay with me. You're going to be all right. We're going to get you some help so you'll feel better." I am trying not to drip tears all over her face, but I am scared. I have never seen her look like this before. Anytime my dad took care of our sick cats, he took them to the vet by himself. Usually he took them out of the house before we even woke up, so I have not made this trip before.

While Greg whips around Mindy Lane, getting us to the emergency vet hospital where he has been so many times before with his own dogs since he was the dad who had to make that trip alone, I have already arranged for Brother One to shoot up to our house. I tell him just to wait there with our mom for Elizabeth, who is already on her way and expected to arrive in ten minutes. He was in the middle of getting his kids put to bed, but his wife is home, so he is able to get to our house instantly.

When we get to the hospital, the attendants are waiting with a gurney to haul Daisy inside so the vet can look at her right away. There are other families waiting in the lobby and no more seats left in the house. I don't have time to sit anyway because the nurse needs the information filled out on the chart now and assures me the doctor is already in the emergency room with Daisy. I am beginning to feel engulfed in a slow whimper that is building in my throat. It's the same kind of cry you hear from children as they begin to realize they are lost, separated from their families. The fear inside me is growing louder, and a flood of tears begins to rush out of me.

Greg says we should go sit in the car for the time it is going to take the doctor to figure out what is happening. After the nurse promises me they won't forget about me in the car, that they will come get me in that Suburban I point to, parked right there, once they have any news, Greg walks me out.

"Babe," he says once we're in the car, "these are good doctors. I've been here before, and it's always hard. But I think you need to prepare yourself because Daisy doesn't look good."

This is all I can hear before I begin wailing.

"Wh-what are you saying?" I can barely get the words out as I begin gulping for air. "Do you think she's going to die?" I can barely express this inconceivable thought because Daisy was just playing with me this morning. How could a dog with that much energy and appetite be dying a few hours later? It doesn't make any sense to me, and because I know I am being logical, I decide that I don't need to worry about Daisy dying because this is probably something doctors see all the time, and they are going to fix her right up. I refuse to think about anything else. Why be dramatic?

Just then an attendant in scrubs knocks gently on the door and says the doctor is ready to see us. I ask this guy what he knows, and he tells me he was only sent to find me. Do I believe him? If I could see his expression, I might know better, but it is after nine o'clock at night, and the parking lot is pretty blackened despite the one halogen light giving off a minimal ambient glow.

He escorts us to the door separating the lobby from the other families who are waiting for news about their own animals. We meet the doctor, who seems so familiar to me but only because his long, wavy, brown hair and dark, European features are similar to Mark Ruffalo's, who plays opposite one of my favorite actresses, Jennifer Garner, in one of my favorite movies, *13 Going on 30*, which I just rented. His demeanor, though, reminds me more of Al Pacino because he is so serious. As is his sworn duty, he advocates for animals, so he tells me everything I need to know within two minutes because time is of the essence.

"Daisy is suffering from a tumor that has erupted inside her stomach. This is common for labs her age." He can see I am not handling this news well and starts to speak a little faster so I can take it all in. "She is dying, and you have a decision to make right now. You can either prolong her life for another six months with surgery that costs several thousand dollars, and I will scrub in and do this tonight, and we run the risk of her being too weak to come out of surgery, or we euthanize her right now with an injection to put her out of her misery."

He isn't able to get through the entire speech as he had hoped before my shoulders start shaking and uncontrollable tears come from my eyes. I am doubled over with sobs that don't fully come out. It's as if someone has knocked the wind out of me; it's hard to breathe. All Greg can do is hold me tight while I squeak and snort and try to suck in my grief instead of letting it all out. I know the people in the lobby can hear me because the walls are not soundproof, and probably they were just where I am right now.

"Can I see her? Where is Daisy?" I ask urgently. Maybe it's not as bad as he is saying. Maybe he just wants to make some money from a desperate patient. Maybe I should get a second opinion.

He walks us back to the pre-op room where Daisy is hooked up to an IV and barely able to move, but she weakly lifts her head to greet me as I approach. I stroke her fur gently and lean down to let my tears spill all over her and tell her how much I love her and that Momma is going to take care of her.

"Doctor, I don't want to lose my dog. My mom is dying at home, and we just started hospice. I can't say good-bye to my dog too. I can't handle all of this. It's just too much." I am unable to contain my grief. The doctor moves us back into our little patient room where I can try to collect myself out of Daisy's view.

"I am so sorry," he says. "This is one of the toughest decisions you are going to make. I will tell you, I went through this last year with my own lab, who was also eleven and had the same stomach tumor. I operated, and I got another great six months out of her, and I am grateful I did, but there is never going to be a miracle cure, and you are going to have to say good-bye to her again in six months. There is also a very real risk that she might not make it through the surgery tonight. With your mom sick right now, imagine what the next few months are going to bring you. You don't have any more time to think about a decision because Daisy is suffering right now."

I feel like someone keeps stabbing at my heart. I want to be put out of my own misery.

"I can't make this decision so fast," I tell him. "I can't just say good-bye to my dog. She has gotten me through so much in my life, I don't want to lose her tonight." I have nothing left of my Kleenex except for the blob it has become in my fist, twisted and shredded, leaving particles of smeared little black balls stuck to my wet cheek.

"I am leaving you here for a few minutes only, and when I come back, I need to know if I am scrubbing in or if you will be saying good-bye. I am so sorry you have to be faced with this." Solemnly the doctor leaves and closes the door behind him.

Greg has sage words for me, but ultimately the decision is mine. I know she is hurting. I have never seen her in this condition. It's not fair to hit someone with a surprise like this, especially when my mother is practically unconscious at home and waiting to die. I consider what it will be like to have Daisy spared tonight and then wait for the next time, when I will have to say good-bye again. What if I am at school when another tumor erupts? What if Greg and I are both at work and unable to rush her to the vet? What if she is dying at the same moment my mom is dying? How could I handle both, and how would I be able to be at the side of whoever's suffering is the greatest? It is too much for me to predict the future. I go with what I know today. My little dog is suffering, and I need to say good-bye. Greg and I are both here tonight, together with her, and we agree that it is the most humane decision we can make.

The doctor brings in Daisy, and Greg makes sure to position her head so she is facing me instead of him. Even though he has become the one who now gets up to take her for her walk in the dark of morning, she is still my little girl, and any parent with a sixth grader who is faced with the impending loss of their eleven-year-old child knows the kind of pain that is hollowing out my soul. I pet her and hug her and thank her for being my entire life's joy and happiness. The doctor says the shot will take effect immediately when I am ready, and finally I tell him to go ahead.

For the longest time, I think Daisy is saying one long good-bye to me because she keeps staring at me lovingly with her brown eyes, which remind me of a doe's the way they slant up. I ask the doctor when the effect will kick in, and he answers that it already did a few minutes ago. My Daisy is gone. Greg and I make the somber drive home alone with only the blanket that cradled her in the car. When we walk through the front door that we walked out of two hours ago, I am greeted by

Elizabeth, who gives me a warm bear hug in the living room and weeps with me over the loss of Daisy, an animal who saw herself only as a human little girl.

Elizabeth tells me my mom has slept the whole time and that Brother One left as soon as she arrived. Greg and I make plans to call in sick tomorrow and do something to commemorate Daisy. I leave Camilla a message on her voicemail that sounds more like garbled pain in high-pitched syllables that she will likely not understand. I thought I collected myself well enough before I dialed, but how can I say the words "my dog has died" without pieces of me breaking apart?

In the days after my return to school, the students do everything they can think of to cheer me up. On the fifth day of my wearing all black, one student finally has enough heart to ask me when I will begin to feel better and says that he misses my colorful clothes. Even though I am soon back to my old wardrobe, the loss of Daisy feels like something I will never get over.

A few weeks later, as we enter May, my mom is finally awake for Mother's Day, and Greg and I want it to be special. She is getting more oriented, and the spring sun is shining. Greg brings home her favorite flowers, and I make a splashy showcase of gifts in oversized, colorful bags with loads of colorful tissue brimming from the top and helium balloons, which is really a grandiose purchase since our family never invests in things that aren't made to last. But I wanted this Mother's Day to be spectacular.

Now that she is out of her deep sleep, we are seeking out clever ways to entertain her in her room while she is bound to her bed. My mother is losing strength in her arms now too, so spoon-feeding is required. I bought a little, pink television set with a combination VCR/DVD to watch any kind of video entertainment we can find. The DVD player also allows us to play CDs, which is nice for the times when my mom wants to be lulled by the sounds of music she requests to hear, such as Spanish-style guitar.

Since she and I used to love to watch *Mary Tyler Moore* together as our nightly ritual to avoid the scandalous realization that with a hundred channels there is still nothing to watch, I buy her more collections of decades-past favorites such as *I Love Lucy* and *The Golden Girls*. I buy her new night-gowns in flannel that look exactly like what you would expect the big, bad wolf to be wearing when he poses as Grandma-ma because these sets come complete with matching flannel bonnets. It is hard to imagine that someone would need flannel in the spring, but they make a killing selling these year round at the Vermont Country Store online, and my mom is often cold.

I also buy her a beautiful, velvet-fleece throw that feels like shearling fabric because its underside is so soft. I can't decide between the celery green and the sable brown, so I buy both to trade off every week. I buy new soft sheets in a beautiful sage and another set in sable so everything is "matchy-matchy," as Elizabeth teases me. Even the flannel gowns my mother wears coordinate nicely with the sets of bedding—all by design.

Brother One comes with his preschool daughter, whom my mother planned to see grow up to become a fifth grader, and they stay for a short visit, which makes my mom's Mother's Day. There is no mail from Sisters Two or Three, and even Brother Two forgets to call. Maybe the effort that would be required to see me in the process is worth ignoring his own mother today. Since the last time he visited—in March, when I invited all the siblings to come at once so they could say good-bye—Brother Two has begun taking all of his hostility at the prospect of losing his mother out on me. He has left me harassing messages, screaming at me long enough for the recorder to run out of room then calling back to pick up where he left off. He would seethe at me because he could not get through his head why I was scheduling my mother's visits like she was in a hospital. With the new hospice team who were in and out of our house every day for check-ups or baths, some days two or three people were coming and going depending on what the needs were. These were not times for hanging out because there was so much activity going into caring for my mom.

He thinks I am being controlling. Yes, he's right. Someone has to be in control of managing my mother's health, and I am that person. He makes things so complicated. I only asked that he come in the afternoons when she is usually more apt to be awake, fed, and bathed, and Elizabeth will still be there in case I need her help. But Brother Two's volatile nature and screaming at me on the phone, so much so that I have to use Greg as a buffer, leaves the indelible impression that his emotions are running too high, and I don't want him to start a screaming match in our home when my mother is requiring peace and rest.

This is the priority that hospice establishes. They are completely supportive of my arranging the visiting hours and tell me that this kind of behavior from siblings who are feeling latent guilt for not being able to participate in the process usually manifests itself onto the caregiver. I do not want any more stress brought down on me, and I feel Brother Two is being utterly selfish in figuring it is okay to take his unfiltered anger out on me.

This is how he justifies his behavior—that he is too upset about mom and it is okay to throw his hostility my way. This is his idea of an apology when he comes back for another visit. I tell him it is never okay to take anger out on the caregiver. The caregiver needs caring for too. He doesn't get it, so I stop direct communication with him, and when I needed to inform him of a development, it is Brother One or Greg who will call. I also send e-mails so I know nothing I am communicating can be misinterpreted, and I read them all carefully for tone before I send them.

My mom sleeps for the rest of May with only the sound of that gurgling in her throat still not cleared. Every morning I change her urine bag and record in the notebook that it is cloudy and a dark-orange color with floating particles and a very sharp odor. The visits from Karen are becoming more frequent—nearly daily—and when I ask her if she thinks my mom is getting closer to the end, she tells me what hospice has thought all along.

"When we met you in early March, we honestly didn't think your mom was going to make it through the week." She pushes her glasses down an inch and looks at me over the bridge of her nose, smiling widely. "But she is our reminder of why we don't want to make any predictions because she seems to be defying the odds."

I let out a big breath feeling as though this is tremendous relief.

I tell Elizabeth about this conversation with Karen and ask her what she thinks, and she says she can tell when a person is about to go, and my mom is not ready yet. Again I breathe another big sigh of relief. The school year's end is near. I just want my mom to hold out until the summer, when I can be with her every day and not have the pressure of students to deal with at the same time.

My mom asks Elizabeth where Daisy is, and, under strict instructions from me, Elizabeth only replies that Daisy is asleep in the other room. My mom knows something isn't right about Daisy's absence even in her half-conscious state for the past several weeks. Finally she says to Elizabeth one day, "I think Daisy is not here with us anymore" and then closes her eyes to sleep some more. This is in late May.

By early June my mother is awake for my birthday. She knows it is because Greg tells her, and so does Elizabeth. She is awake while they sing to me and I blow out the candles on my cupcakes. It is bittersweet because while it is a gift in itself to have my mother awake today, I know this will likely be the last birthday she will be here to celebrate with me.

I get through the close of another school year, and my mom is still with us, so I entertain her with stories of the kids, and she reminds me how she always used to tease her classes when it came time for vacation. Some child would say, "I can't wait for summer to come," and my mom would chime in next with, "you know who else is pretty excited for summer vacation? Me." The youngster would look at her wide-eyed as if it had never even occurred to him that teachers might like the idea of playing too.

Within days of my wrapping up my school year, my mom is more awake and telling stories, and her appetite is improving. She tells anyone from church who comes to visit that we are keeping her trapped in her bed, and they look at me to see if such a thing could possibly be true. One day I decide to flap the covers back and say to my mom that if she can get out of bed, I will wheel her around the house in her chair. She can't do it. Her legs have atrophied so much that she cannot move them by herself. She wants them to work so badly, I can see her practically willing them to stir, but they just lay there still.

"Cover me back up. I can't get out of bed yet," she says, and I hear the defeat in her voice.

"Mom, if we do some exercises, there is a good chance your legs will get a bit stronger, and you can see the house again. Things look pretty good out there, just like you remember." I try to sound cheerful.

Elizabeth and my mom have become fast friends, and my mom has a whole new audience to share her life stories with. So whenever I come home from running errands, Elizabeth will ask me if I ever heard the story about such and such, to which I usually reply, "Only about twenty times." I used to ask my mom why she kept repeating her stories and if I should be worried about her forgetfulness.

Her only response was a logical one: "Why do you think I keep telling you these stories so often? It's so you never forget them and you can hear my voice telling them to you long after I am gone." And all of a sudden, this makes all the sense in the world.

# PART 7

# GOING HOME

REALITY 7
*The Critical Role Bowel Movements
and Bedsores Will Play in the End*

# CHAPTER 30

# Safe on Mindy Lane

By mid-June hospice is feeling quite encouraged by my mother's progress into the living, and they are using this month to evaluate the need for their further presence. Remember, while hospice is not only for the cancer-stricken, they still do require that criteria be met showing your end of life is near in order for them to remain on your case. I do not want to lose the support we have had in place for three months. I can afford to keep Elizabeth, who is familiar with how to order all of the medical supplies we need, but the costs for all of these medical supplies will now start coming out of our own pocket if hospice leaves.

Greg and I look at this upswing in my mother's health as an opportunity to retreat to the woods for a couple of days. We know a lovely cottage that provides daily breakfast and peace away from everything else. My mom is doing great, and Elizabeth will spend the night attending to her around-the-clock needs. Everyone agrees this is a good time to go.

While I am giddily packing and reviewing with Elizabeth the list of how to close down the house at night and how to take care of the two animals we still have left, I hear some muffled grunting coming from my mom's room. I figure she is having another bowel movement, which I will leave for Elizabeth to clean.

When I hear the faint murmuring of words that sound like "I did it, I did it," I am curious enough to go and see what she has been busy doing.

I walk into my mother's room to find her left hand bloodied. I can tell by the mischievous grin on her face that something is terribly wrong, but I can't find the source of the trouble. There are no cuts on her arm. Her mouth looks fine. She just continues to tell me that she did it. I follow her body contour beneath the covers to the smears of red painted on her gown around her lower midsection. I discover that her little right hand is also wet with red liquid, and her fingers are coiled around her catheter tube.

I follow the line to where it is supposed to be connected to my mother's urethra, inserted medically up through her lady parts. It is lying across her thighs, wet and sticky, while she is bleeding into her diaper. She has yanked that catheter completely out, which is no easy feat considering the precision threading it took to get it in there so urinating through a tube could be possible.

I call for Elizabeth, who calls Karen, who tells us she is already in the neighborhood and will be here to reinsert within the hour. This is not a sight for the faint of heart. It is scary to see, especially for me because I render any sight of blood as an emergency. But Karen says that some of the more persistent patients are able to withstand the pain when they take to yanking at their catheter lines. I ask Karen if my mom knows what she is doing and if she is being harmful to herself or if she has no idea, thinking only of her catheter line as a toy. Karen's answer is, "Probably a combination of both."

After Karen arrives and takes care of the catheter, and my mom is safe again with Elizabeth, I say good-bye, telling my mom we will be back in just two days and that we will not be far from home, and we leave feeling like this is the break we have both been needing. Greg and I breathe in the pine-scented air and rent bicycles to ride through the forest and into town for ice cream. Going out to dinner has been a rarity in the past few months since I want to be with my mom as much as possible, plus there is the added expense of having Elizabeth stay late, so this first night out we royally indulge in overeating with dish after dish.

We enjoy ourselves so much, swept away in such a vacation euphoria, that I am completely taken off guard when my cell phone rings at eight o'clock the next morning with Elizabeth's number popping up on my screen. I panic because I know this is bad news. "Elizabeth, is it my mom? Is she okay?"

"It's not your mom. She's sleeping, and we had a good night last night." She pauses there to let me relax but only for a moment. "It's your mom's cat, Friend. I went to look for him and found him sleeping in Daisy's old spot in the guest room, but he's not breathing, and his eyes are still open. There is liquid all over the bed, so I am sorry to say this to you Stefania." I know what's coming next because we live in the house of death. "But Friend has died."

For some reason the news of Friend's death hits me less hard than when Nuisance died in October and Daisy died in April. It is now June, and I have to surrender to the idea that the decks are being cleared for a reason. Every living thing in our house is slipping away. It makes me anxious because I cannot foresee the reason for all of our pets to be going in succession while my mom is dying too. There must be a plan.

I give Elizabeth instructions about which neighbor I trust

to help her handle the remains, which need to be taken to our vet's office nearby. Elizabeth carefully wraps Friend in the fresh blanket I tell her to use then packs him in a pillowcase and ties a plastic garbage bag around him like he's a present. With the death of Friend, the most loving of cats, and Nuisance, the fat cat whose belly would sashay across the rug while he meandered through the family room, we are left with their scrawny sister cat, Sissy. She mostly stays outdoors all day then sleeps under beds in the hollows of dark, unused rooms. She careens around corners so quickly we catch only glimpses of her shadow as it fades in a wisp. She runs from human interaction, but she will sleep on top of my mom at night. This is when I see her, and from time to time she will let me pet her, putting her skittishness to rest.

When Greg and I return home, my mom is still in good spirits. I break the news to her about Friend, and she takes it in stride as any animal person who grew up on a dairy farm would. She has seen her share of animals come and go. "Friend was a friend to all," she eulogized. And that was that.

Now that the end of June is nearing, hospice is about to create a new plan for my mom that eliminates their involvement. They can hardly believe how well she is doing, and Karen and Charlotte tell me over and over again how they thought this would be a short-lived case because they did not expect my mom to make it beyond a week or two when they first came to me in early March. I fret a bit over what it will cost to keep her in medical supplies and all the diapers and tucks, and what it will be like if my mom pulls out her catheter again because I won't be able to call the hospice nurses to assist me.

It will mean returning to regular doctor visits, and I don't see how this will be possible when my mom still can't get out of her bed. But I know Karen and Charlotte have seen patients through all stages of the dying process, and they remind me often that they are not gone permanently because as soon as it is evident that my mom needs hospice again, they will be back.

While my mom has resumed her old cheerful nature and is eating again, my worries over what kind of future care she might need and for how long are beginning to weigh heavily on my mind. She could stay this buoyant, yet bound to her bed, for many years to come since longevity runs in her family. We are running out of money. With only three trees left in our bank account, I call our family accountant for options. Since qualifying for any government assistance will mean having to spend down all of her resources first, forcing her into an assisted living facility, he thinks a reverse mortgage is the most likely scenario for her situation. However, others in the family are not so sure.

I do not doubt any advice I get from our trusted CPA, but I also feel compelled to buy every book pertaining to senior finances written by well-known financial advisers so I can educate myself even more. I am nervous because I don't want to make the wrong decision, and there are mishaps that can occur if she outlives her money source. This is what is keeping me up at night. This and the constant company my mother would like me to keep with her at two in the morning since she is bored in her bed.

It is nothing shy of a miracle that when I continue digging through the last tower of boxes in the garage that I have been poring through for four summers already I come to the eighty-fifth and final box with a discovery that makes me gasp out loud. There are stock certificates I have never seen. They are typed onto paper I do not recognize for company holdings I am unaware of. But since I have become overzealous in scrutinizing anything I cannot explain, I gather them together inside a manila envelope and make an appointment to see an agent at Charles Schwab.

While I am unwilling to relinquish these certificates until I have catalogued each of their reference numbers in the agent's presence, she recognizes the serial codes on the first batch of papers I have held together with a half-inch clip. She wants to be sure, so after placing a couple of calls to verify, she gives me the sad news.

"These certificates are held in Canada for a company that is no longer in existence. They aren't even worth the paper they're printed on. Sorry."

So am I. She returns the worthless pile to me.

The next stack I hand over is equally thick. I sit silently watching. With each stroke on her computer keyboard, her incredulous expression begins to warm. She tells me I have luck on my side today. The stocks I have unearthed that have been tucked out of sight for the better part of fifty years equal at least a hundred trees, providing enough cushion that I won't have to pursue a reverse mortgage after all.

I feel much more comfortable knowing my mom can stay in her house longer, and my fears for her long-term care are alleviated by the contents of this one box. Let this story be the only reminder you need to avoid throwing out papers haphazardly until you know exactly what they are. While it will take weeks to convert the certificates to cash, I relax without saying a word to anyone until it is a done deal and the money is safely in the bank.

Karen and Charlotte have begun the official paperwork to release my mother from their care since she has been improving slightly every week. However, the signatures required from hospice managers who are on vacation means Karen is getting stymied by a paperwork jam. Greg and I are dreaming of a long Hawaiian vacation that we have been saving for. School is out. Elizabeth is here. Daisy is gone. I am tired. So Karen and Charlotte recommend that Greg and I take this vacation now, and the final exit paperwork can be signed off when we return. Karen reminds me that hospice will reenter when my mother's condition worsens and that this is typical for a lot of patients. This will be our final hurrah before I come back to a summer of no more support from the hospice team that has been filtering in and out of my house like worker bees for nearly four months.

With Elizabeth in charge, I know everything will be taken care of. She knows who is on the visitors list, and she knows the personalities of the siblings and is not afraid of turning Brother Two away if he is hostile at the door. When Greg's son takes us to the airport, my eyes begin to leak while I am sitting in the backseat of the car, and I cannot control the gushing of my silent tears. I want to go on a vacation, but I don't want to leave my mom. I didn't have the heart to tell her we would be across the ocean because that sounds like we are too far away, so I only told her we will be back in just a few short days even though we will be gone for one whole glorious week.

My mom told us to enjoy ourselves and to take good care— her parting words for the times any of us ever leave the house, whether it was going on a date in high school or driving two states away for college, or whether we were just going to the beach for the afternoon. Her last words are always resounding in our ears with her enthusiasm for life and her love for us.

Hawaii is exactly what I need. The weather is eighty-two

degrees and breezy enough to keep cool while basking in the sun all day. Our hotel has cabanas on the sand in front of the ocean, and when we put up our orange flag, a waiter will appear within minutes to take our order, returning with trays so we can eat beachside without any worries about getting sand in our food. With another raise of the flag, the waiter takes it all away, allowing us to get back to our leisurely reading and relaxing.

Once Greg figures out this system, he reserves the same cabana for the rest of the week so we won't have to worry about them all being taken by others before we get downstairs. It goes like this for the first two days. Pure heaven. And then I get the phone call from home. It is Elizabeth sounding quite worried on the other end of the line.

"Stefania, it's your mom. She's not doing very well," she says as I plug my other ear with my finger to drown out the pounding surf. "She's not making any sense. She has been hallucinating all night and hasn't slept." Now I really hear the doom in her voice. The only kind of hallucinating I saw with my mom was when she was in the hospital and seeing dead dogs at the foot of her bed and hundreds of cats outside her window.

Elizabeth continues to tell me that Karen has already been to visit a few times, and the doctor prescribed medicine that Karen has given my mom to help calm her hallucinations. But my mom is still calling for me and misses me very much.

"I want to talk to her," I say. "Can you hold the phone up to her ear?"

Elizabeth agrees to try, but my mom is quite agitated, and I can hear her calling my name in the background before Elizabeth tells her I am on the phone.

"Hi Mom, it's Steffie. How are you?"

"I don't know where you are. I'm all alone."

I can hear the rasp in her voice after having stayed awake all night.

"Mom, I am with Greg, and I will be home very soon. Elizabeth is with you just until I get back. You're safe at home on Mindy Lane."

She interrupts me with her tears, telling me she is trying to make a pail lunch for Brother Two.

"I can't get the lid to stay closed. I am trying to fix his lunch, but the pail keeps spilling over. I don't know how to do it." She is nearly beside herself as she speaks about a pail lunch that doesn't exist as if it is the most important thing on earth.

"It's okay Mom. He will be happy to eat whatever you put in the pail," I say to try to soothe her, but she continues to fret.

"I can't get his pail together. Where are you, Steffie? I am all alone. I need your help."

And this is more than I can bear because she sounds so completely desperate and abandoned. I would no sooner leave a toddler to play in the curbside of a busy street than I would leave my mother, who feels equally lost, and I ask Elizabeth if she thinks I should come home and if she thinks my mother is going to die.

The answer is obvious. Even if Elizabeth does tell me no, which she does but only to buy enough time to see if my mother will calm herself and get to sleep once Karen returns with more meds, it doesn't matter. I want to be with my mother. I wait the whole day to see if there is any improvement since California is three hours ahead of Hawaii, and by nightfall back home my mother is still hallucinating and still desperately calling for me.

She has not slept in two days and is completely hoarse, having worn herself out. Nothing she says is making any sense to Elizabeth, and none of the anti-hallucinogenic drugs are having an impact. At this news I book the next flight out, which won't leave until tomorrow as there is only one flight out per day from this island.

When I do make it home on what would have been the third day of our vacation, I rush to my mother to assure her I am here. I comfort her and stay by her side for the rest of the morning. After staying awake for forty-eight hours, shouting all the while to Elizabeth that she was falling, reaching skyward for things, and talking about wanting to go home, she has finally relaxed into a deep sleep knowing that I am with her and she is safe on Mindy Lane.

## CHAPTER 31

# Witness to Her Life

I am worried sick about my mother. I do not want to leave the house because I have a feeling of horrible fear that if I turn my back, she will be gone and I will not be at her side when she goes. After all this time caring for her, I do not want her to feel alone in her last minutes. Thank goodness Greg is willing to run all of my errands. We stay home for every meal, and while we miss going out to dinner, I am simply too afraid to leave the house.

Hospice has provided one more support person on my mother's team to relieve me for four hours a week. Grace is my lovely volunteer who offers to stay the entire four hours with my mother if I want to see a movie with my husband and grab a bite, or I can break it into increments of two visits for two hours each if I want to go to church or get my nails done. It is a wonderful offer. But it takes me many weeks before I feel like taking Grace up on the invitation to leave the house and do something for me.

With Fourth of July behind us and my mom's hallucinations subsiding for days at a time, I am trying to gauge if there is a pattern. As soon as Greg and I returned from Hawaii, the hallucinations stopped immediately. My mom slept for a couple of days, and then when Elizabeth came to greet her one morning, my mom said there were ants all over Elizabeth's face. It took a few minutes for her to convince my mom that no, there were not ants all over her face, to which my mom just looked at her quietly, studying her face. But before that day was over, the hallucinations began again with talk about death and dying and heaven, and ramblings about a range of topics that were completely disconnected.

I called Brother One, who came to visit that evening. He didn't quite know how to handle all of her rapid chatter, which wandered aimlessly. It is very disorienting to watch someone as their mind charts a course over choppy waters, drowning in their thoughts that slosh over the sides of their once sturdy boat, now capsizing from all the holes that have torn it apart.

By bedtime I have been instructed to give my mom medicine to help alleviate the hallucinations and allow her to sleep. This small dosage does not soothe her at all; in fact she becomes panicked. She begins seeing snakes, acting out in fear, and feeling as if she is falling again. She will not close her eyes because she keeps insisting she is meeting "the man" for her "nine o'clock appointment." This makes me nervous because I am sure it is some code for her maker who is coming to get her and that she is about to leave this earth.

I cannot take my eyes off of her. I do not want her to be alone. I hold her hand until she pulls away to busily pick at imaginary fruit from imaginary trees off imaginary branches high above her head. She peels them, sucking their imaginary juices, while I sit in the chair next to her bed, watching her directly. When I get cold, I move to her big bed that we placed in the corner, and I cuddle up with the blankets that used to be hers. I squish myself into all of her pillows with the smell of her still among them, and I watch over her through the night.

I sleep here for the rest of the week. Some nights she is very quiet with her very active hands still picking at the fruit and pretending to eat their lush centers after peeling their outsides, or still struggling to get to branches that are out of reach above her. Other times she is very talkative and quite intent on not missing the train. The more she speaks of appointments with "the man" and the bus she cannot ride and pleads with someone I cannot see to please let her go home, the more I know I have to prepare myself for the death that is certainly coming.

I cannot do it though. I am willing it to not happen. It is my fervent prayer that I not lose my mother yet. I am not ready to say good-bye. I call Sister Two about all the hallucinations, and she comes to visit that Saturday. Even though we are not the close sisters my mom intended for us to be, I take some comfort in knowing she is, for once, willing to drop everything and get in the car to come sit with her mother.

In fact she sits all day for several hours. When it comes time to change my mother's diaper that has filled with another overreaching bowel movement, Sister Two willingly helps me to clean her. I realize my mother is her mother too. I only wish these siblings of mine could be the kind of people who pull together with me to do more of the heavy lifting.

Just before Sister Two arrived, Charlotte the social worker had come to check on my mother, visiting for an hour. She tried to set my mind at ease about what the hallucinations mean to the patient and said that it is very typical for a person facing death to become so busy with visions when they are straddling two different worlds. Whatever religious beliefs one has, it is very hard to deny the gravitational pull I see luring my mother away from this world. By nightfall, Sister Two is on her way out, with a two-hour drive ahead taking her back home. At the door she greets Elizabeth, who I've made arrangements with to stay the night so I can get some sleep.

By Monday morning my mom is back to normal, feeling jovial. The irregular pattern of hallucinations means that hospice is not going anywhere, and I am eternally grateful for this news. A couple days later, my mom tells Greg that she is covered in ants all over her face and blankets. Later that day she is adamant that I have taken away her peach pie before she finished. What I was feeding her in actuality was a hard-boiled egg, and when I tell her this she calls me a liar. It is another reminder that the hallucinations act with a mind of their own.

Karen makes her rounds before the day is over, and my mom confides in her then that she doesn't expect to be here when Karen comes back the next day because she will be exiting. Hearing my mother talk so assuredly about her time-frame for dying is speeding up my anxiety. I call Sister Two and Brothers One and Two to tell them if they have anything left to say now is the time even though I cannot know if my mother will be lucid when they choose to visit. The pattern goes on like this for weeks and weeks. Nevertheless, the brothers do not come again.

Every few days my mom sinks into her hallucinations and then comes out for a couple of days of good banter and clear conversations. She even talks to me about her episode in the spring "when I was dying," which leads me to think she is more aware of what is going on with her body than I have realized.

"Mom, why did you think you were dying in the spring?"

"I just could feel it, and I knew it, but it wasn't my time to go yet. I didn't want to leave you."

This puts a big lump in my throat. She smiles at me and grabs for my hand. I hold back the tears as hard as I can and tell her, "I am so glad you held on for a little while longer. I love having you around, and I am going to miss you so much if you are not here." This is the most I can get out because I don't want to cry now. I don't want to scare her and make her feel horrible that I won't be able to cope in her absence. I want her to be able to do what she needs to do to move forward into her new life. I just can't tell her as much yet.

On a random day in July, my mom tells Karen that we won't be doing this for much longer. Karen asks her why, and my mom tells her it is because she only has somewhere between one and twenty days left to live. When Karen shares this with me as a way to prepare me before my mom just blurts out this information in my presence, I begin making sure that I have thought of everything.

The gift ideas I have for Christmas I buy now. The warm and cozy flannel nightgowns for the winter are ordered today and enjoyed by my mom for the next three weeks. I call the clergyman to alert him to the fact that these are my mother's last days and he should come to visit, which he does. I call my mother's best friend Constance, who also comes.

I call my mom's oldest friend in the Midwest, but I can only speak with her daughter because this elderly friend, named Eunice, died back in January. It is a solemn conversation we have because she knows what I am going through, having been there herself. I cannot bring myself to share this news with my mom because she and Eunice were like the sisters they never had. They were close for eighty years, having known each other since grammar school.

In August another death comes, this one completely unexpected. When Constance calls me one evening, I can tell her voice is shaken. Her husband died suddenly the day before while at home. He just came back from his morning jog and was tying his shoes for church when he suffered a massive heart attack. She wants me to know because she will not be able to visit my mom for a while. Another death I cannot share, and I keep silent about the fact that Reed too is gone.

I do everything for Constance that I think my mom would have done herself. I bake macaroni and cheese from scratch thinking that this might be the best time for comfort food and make enough to feed twenty out-of-towners. I help with arrangements of where to hotel some of her extended family. I drop off a tray of lox and bagels for the morning after so Constance doesn't have to think about what to feed a houseful of guests, and then I leave her in peace until she is ready to come up for air. My mother loves Constance so much, and Constance has been the one visitor to appear at my mother's bedside several times this year. I will always be grateful that my mother has known a friend until her very end.

For the rest of the month, the routine is more of the same. We keep my mom clean and bathed every other day when the bath nurse comes, feed her when she is awake and hungry, diaper her when her bowels are fully functioning even though her mind and body are not, and all the while monitor her bouts of hallucinations that run for days at a time. One night she is so loud and active I am impelled to sleep in her room because there is so much she is excitedly watching. Of course I can't see any of what she is seeing, but I become a witness to her life as she moves fluidly from one decade to the next, talking with people who knew her intimately in every stage of her life.

The first person I come to know is her babysitter Anna. My mom's conversations are so fascinating, but she moves at a rapid-fire pace, and I can hardly think to leave to find a pen and notebook so I can record all that is unfolding for fear of missing a decade or two. So I stay. She is calling out to friends she knew when she and my father were a young married couple in Fresno. Just as she is sharing her joy at reuniting with them, another friend from a different direction pulls her attention away, and she calls after them by name, names I don't know from her history. Excitedly she continues to wave and to stare at the ceiling until she is eagerly pulled toward a different direction of the roof where there are other friends who have already passed on calling for her now.

What is clear to me is that she is surrounded by throngs of people she recognizes and that they are anxiously waiting for her. This is something I could easily have presumed her to be making up if it weren't for some hard evidence that stops me in my tracks. She begins to call out for people I know who have very unusual names. Through the crowds, toward the back, she will wave and shout, hoping they can spot her. She does not stop until she makes eye contact, and I know I am a witness to something more than just her life.

"Eunice, Eunice, I am here!" She waves excitedly to her beloved friend who is like her sister, whom she does not know has died. If you are reading this thinking Eunice is a common enough name that this could be a coincidence, let me remind you that all of the names in this book have been changed, and the real name behind Eunice is so unique that when my mom shouts it across the room in the middle of the night, I know she has actually seen her dearest friend in person. Eunice responds to my mother, and I can only tell from a one-sided conversation that they are eager to embrace one another.

"Reed, Reed, what are you doing here?"

Death is comforting to me in this moment because I now have a sense that my mother, who has not been told of these passings, is actually meeting the dear ones who have left this earth and are part of the committee sent to greet her. I do not have another logical explanation for what I see unfolding in front of me. I know that the loneliness my mother has experienced on this earth over the last seventeen years without my father will be made up for in spades with the throngs of people who are waiting for her now. My heart fills with happiness that she is so beloved and that she is not forgotten after all.

Then she calls for the name that hits me the hardest. As she reaches upward with both of her arms fully extended, expending as much effort as she can manage, she calls like a toddler from the crib, "Mama, Mama," and smiles tearfully that her mother has found her through this crowd. In this sweet moment, she is not alone anymore because she has her mother with her. It's the moment I find bittersweet because as much as she wants to be held by her mother, I want her to be here to hold me. I begin to sob into the blanket, which covers my face as she cries and cries for her mother.

I get a sense that there is tremendous movement on the other side of what she is chasing. People are going, trains are coming, buses are loading, and my mother wants to get on. She begins to beg and plead, "Please take me—I want to go home," but there is some problem because her next response is, "How am I supposed to get on the bus when you see I can't walk?"

Her conundrums are not yet solved. There are many conversations in her hallucinations this month about "the man" who is coming for her nine o'clock appointment. She is pleading for the people in charge to let her go home. Sometimes I sit next to her little hospital bed, patting her hand softly while she looks to me and says she wants to go home. I can see the desperation in her eyes and hear the strain in her voice. I can only take this to mean she is preparing herself to die.

I say only what I can offer in this moment: "You are safe. I am here. You are home on Mindy Lane."

This becomes my mantra to soothe her daily worries. Much of the time it seems to work. Even a couple of times I have been able to bring her out of her hallucination and she will say to me, "Oh, Steffie, do you know how wonderful you are? I love you so much," and I echo all of the same sentiments back to her and lean over to cradle her head close to my heart. Tears drip silently down my cheeks because I do not want to get in the way of the preparations she is making, but I do not want to let her go.

Before August ends, on a sunny day late one morning, I hear my sleeping mother cackling heartily. I peek inside her door to see her tossing her head back and forth and making giddy protestations—"No, Daisy, I don't want my face washed"—while her head darts to the left, quickly to the right, and then back again to the left as if she is watching a tennis match.

We all know, Elizabeth and Greg and I, that my mom has finally met Daisy again. Three months after her passing, Daisy is still jumping on her and wildly licking her face as she always tried to do in life. My mother's giggles and chortling are the most heartwarming sounds to hear, and again death reminds me that I do not have to be afraid because my precious dog Daisy is also waiting for my mother to join her. Still, even this does not ready me to say goodbye.

# CHAPTER 32

# High Alert

School has resumed, and I am agonizing over being back with the children, in the routine that I love, because I thought for sure summer would allow me time to grieve privately, away from students and the workload so I could collect myself and be steady for the beginning of the year. But my mom is still here, and I am ever so grateful. I just want to be at home with her where I can watch her instead of teaching.

Elizabeth and I have worked out a system that if she cannot reach me by cell phone, she is to call the front office secretary. I have put through a protocol plan to everyone who might come in contact with Elizabeth about how to proceed. I basically crafted a military drill in case of an emergency for both of my colleagues on either side of my classroom who would know what to do with my students in the event I needed to abandon my class to race home.

My principal, Camilla, knows I am operating on high alert and any day could be the day. I create emergency lesson plans for a substitute that can be can be carried out for a ten-day stretch. Each morning I leave for school praying that my mom will still be there when I get home. All I want is to be there with her at the end so she won't feel alone.

My mom is becoming more intent on preparedness in her hallucinations. One night before bed, she insists that she wants to go back to Fresno, where she was secure and where she had friends. She will not let it go no matter how I try to assuage her and reassure her that she is safe, I am here, she is home on Mindy Lane.

"No, I want you to get my suitcase. I want to go back to Fresno," she says. That was where she lived with my father when they were a young married couple in their thirties. The only thing I can do is oblige, and this will be no different from the other hallucinations I participate in. Sometimes I will pick up an imaginary key that she says she dropped. I will even remove one from my key ring to use as a believable prop, after which she will insist I still didn't pick up the right one. I will pull down fake fruit from fake trees lodged up in the beams of the ceiling just so she feels validated. Elizabeth goes along with her charades in the daytime when I am at work. I always read her notes at the end of the day about the furniture that was up in the ceiling that my mother insisted Elizabeth move. After she cleared the beams of the one hanging flower pot we had, my mother was still not satisfied, so Elizabeth would climb imaginary ladders to pull down imaginary chairs until finally my mother told her she got them all.

With suitcase in hand, I lay it on the big bed and ask my mother what we should pack.

"Well, I want my cosmetics and my lingeries," she says, and this gets the biggest hoot for weeks to come when I tell this story over and over because she pronounces *lingerie* as if it is plural, by adding the same hard S that ends in cosmetics.

One time I hear my mom wrestling with Sissy the over-grown kitten, the last remaining of our pets. She no longer sleeps under beds; she is stuck to my mom like Velcro on top of her belly. I hear the cat making faint meowing sounds, and she doesn't seem happy. There is something in that meow that strikes me as odd, and when my teacher's ears hear something out of the ordinary, I bound to where I need to be. Thank goodness I get there as fast as I do because my mom, in her state of hallucination, has Sissy in a chokehold, trying to strangle her while the poor cat is wriggling the best she can to get free.

I immediately unwrap my mother's fingers from Sissy's neck, which she was twisting, and tell her we need to be gentle with Sissy. My mom only says, "She can't come where I'm going, and I don't have anyone to take care of her."

"Mom, I promise you I will take care of Sissy. I will love her like you do, and Greg and I will feed her and make sure she is not alone. I know you love that little kitten and wouldn't want to hurt her. I will take care of her for you if you have to leave." And she relaxes a little.

For a few weeks in September, my mom is lucid once again and excited to hear about my tales of school. She wants to know about all of the new students I have in this year's crop of seventh graders, and I tell her they are wonderful children except for a handful who might be rotten to the core. They are used to getting their way, and the reports I have heard from other teachers are just as bad, so I try harder to be friendlier, more authoritative, more creative, more sympathetic, and more rewarding of good behavior in others, hoping this will set an example—and yet I am counting the days until these few will be gone, and sadly I have ten months to wait.

During these weeks of clarity, there are many nights when

I am awakened with a start at two or three in the morning by my mother's screams as she calls for me at the top of her lungs: "Steffie! Steffie!" I throw back the covers, scaring Greg halfway out of his sleep, and sprint down the hall with a frantic expectation that she has somehow fallen from her bed even though it has rails around it to prevent it or that she has yanked out her catheter again, or that she is bloodied by something else, or that she is having night terrors again.

Instead I am greeted by her sweet smile, incongruent with her bellowing of a few minutes ago. "Whatchya doin'?"

"Well, Mom, I was sleeping. What are you doing awake?

"I was lonesome for your company. How are you?"

And this is how most of my nights go when she is not in a hallucination phase. It is very hard to tear myself away from her, but after about twenty minutes I need to beg off so I can get the rest I need to teach my classes in the morning.

I have no choice but to respect my mom's predictions because maybe she does actually know something the rest of us are only guessing at, but her timeline until death has not been met according to her crystal ball. Nor were the predictions hospice made after I begged them to tell me what they thought about how much time was left. Nobody can believe my mom is still hanging on.

She eats when she is awake and not hallucinating, which makes her eating schedule erratic. We make sure to keep her hydrated, giving her sips of water even if she is hallucinating. When liquids become too hard to swallow, we moisten her mouth with damp sponges. Greg and I have a routine for this through the night. I have learned that during the times when she is straddling two worlds, I should leave her alone. Once I mistakenly interrupted to see if she wanted a meal, to which she tersely replied, "Can't you see I'm busy here?" So I figure this business about planning for death is serious. There seems to be a lot that needs to be done before one is fully prepared to go.

Karen and Charlotte are checking my mom's vitals and mental state one afternoon when I get home from school, when very suddenly my mother bursts out with how much she misses my father and then begins wailing like a baby who has just been pinched by an old-fashioned diaper pin. It lasts for only about two minutes, stopping as abruptly as it came on.

I have never seen her cry before, so I am not quite sure what just happened, but it makes me cry too because I still miss my father very much and have convinced myself that when we cry, it's because the person we miss is looking down upon us in the same instance. At least this is what I tell myself so I can self-soothe.

Before September ends we celebrate her ninetieth birthday, for which she is clear and present. Greg and I do more helium balloons and big bouquets of flowers—much to her distaste because she tells us it looks like a funeral parlor in here. This time, for her video-viewing pleasure, I have found train travel tapes that can take her through Canada or the Rocky Mountains or the East Coast.

She has always loved to travel and has probably seen many of these places firsthand. I figure it will comfort her and connect her with some of her fondest memories. I also get her more of the Spanish acoustic guitar music she wants to lull herself to sleep. I never knew her to love this music before this year, but it is important to her because she is setting her stage now.

None of her other children sends a card or calls. I don't

know why, but I know she is aware of the silence of the phone. I try to make up excuses that Brother One will be by soon after work, or that Sister Two plans to visit on the weekend, but I know she must be wondering where her other children are. Greg thinks I shouldn't have to make excuses for grown adults who have better things to do than visit their mother, but I can't let her live with that truth; it's too hurtful, and it's too painful for me to watch.

Finally Brother One decides to visit, and he picks the wrong day because my mother is not lucid. I call him every day that she is coherent and tell him now is a good time to swing by, but he doesn't come. When he sees her in this agitated state—working her hands as if she is knitting, picking at blankets, throwing off quilts, and reaching for things in the sky we cannot see—he tries helplessly to carry on a conversation with her, but she is too busy to participate.

After he meanders down the hall to what used to be his bedroom, I silently creep behind him, and when I can hear no more of his rustling, I peek my head around the corner of the doorway just like we used to do when we were kids and we would spy on each other. I find him down on one knee with his head buried in his hands, which are clasped together in a silent prayer.

It is gut-wrenching to see him this way. I know he is hurting even though he has left me here alone to suffer through this with just my husband. I move in to comfort him, which I should not have done, because it just makes him cry harder, and as he chokes back his tears, he makes a play to leave, telling me he just needs to be alone.

When I catch him at the front door, I sincerely offer my gratitude that he has come to visit. "She loves you very much.

She talks about you all the time, and she loves your daughters too." This just makes it harder on him—I can tell.

"It's just too much to see her like this. I remember her on trips we used to take, and I never thought she would end up like this. I just don't know that I can come back," he says while heaving sobs he is trying to collect before he gets into his car. I can't stop here because he needs to know one more thing.

"As hard as it is on you," I say with the softest, most compassionate voice I can manage, "how hard do you think it is for her to wonder where all of her children are when she is alone?"

"Stef, I just can't do it. I can't see her this way."

And so I gently let him go. I understand. I get it now. Maybe it's not that he didn't want to help me; it's that he just does not have the capacity to deal with losing her. They have always had a tight bond, and I believe she helped to pull him out of a dark hole at one point in his life that he couldn't climb out of by himself. I close the door behind him, and I cry for the way this is impacting all of us.

# CHAPTER 33

# Talking to the Man

October comes, and my mother is excited for Halloween and especially to see my brother's daughters in their costumes. I hope he actually brings them around this time instead of reneging on us like last year. We have the whole month ahead of us. I hope my mother can hold out. Her pattern of being lucid for a few days and hallucinating for a few more has us all baffled. I keep wondering if there is a connection between this and the days when she is constipated, causing such discomfort she cannot sleep, thereby beginning her stage of hallucinations again.

I create a bowel movement chart to track the size and frequency of her body functions, and now we are all looking at it for a possible explanation. Karen has always said how critical it is that elderly people be able to function with their bowels. Becoming blocked is extremely uncomfortable and can become life-threatening, so whenever this happens for more than two days we give my mother a suppository. Only once have I had to administer this by myself on a weekend, and it is nerve-wracking because if you do not get the proper placement, you will not get the result you need.

On her good days, my mom still asks for her favorite mocha from Starbucks; however, I have taken to draining it of its regular flavor because sweet things are highly unappealing to her now with the change in her taste buds. After the recipe is altered to mimic her custom flavor with a lot less syrup, her drinks now taste more like a soft version of hot chocolate.

I soon discover, though, that this presents a different problem for her colon because her body can't absorb even this modification. After a few of the same reactions, I know that within twenty minutes of her finishing a mocha, I will be cleaning explosive bowel movements that will shoot down her legs and up her belly. I hate to tell her "no" because I feel like I am depriving her of the one last pleasure she looks forward to, but it wreaks havoc on her system.

There are times when, as soon as I get her all cleaned up and am just about to put on a fresh diaper, another movement is gushing out urgently. I will have to twist myself around quickly to grab a tuck with one hand while holding her in a good position with my other hand to allow free flow, hoping for the least amount of damage to the fresh sheets I just put on.

I have learned a lot about catching a rhythm when it comes to diapering a grown woman. I have a little wooden chair next to the bed that serves as a holding station for all the supplies I need. My goal is to diaper her quickly before her strength gives out and she loses hold of the rail she has grabbed on to while helping to keep herself propped up. On this little wooden chair, I hang a plastic, handled grocery sack for quick disposal of the dirty diapers and tucks. On the seat of the chair, I have all the products I need lined up in the order of when I need them.

Two oversized tucks are layered to create a large sheet beneath her. The wipes are opened, and I have already yanked at least half a dozen from the dispenser so I won't need to wrestle with them swinging from the plastic container and wait impatiently for them finally to pull apart. The ointments I use to prevent diaper rash and bedsores are also at the ready and have been lifesavers in closing up skin tears that can become hazardous to my mother's health if neglected.

I have become very adept at changing sheets while she is still in the bed. I learned early on from Elizabeth and Karen how to roll my mother gently from side to side as I fold up dirty linens beneath her in exchange for fresh ones, moving her deftly while I finish the second half of the bed. I have this routine down to less than ten minutes. I have learned how important it is to change the top blankets frequently because the weight against her toes can not only atrophy her feet; it can actually produce so much rubbing that the skin begins to come off, taking nails with it. This is why we now cover my mother only to her ankles and use a much lighter crocheted blanket for her feet.

Two more things take me by surprise this month. First, on a bad day when I come home from school, my mom is hallucinating again, only this time she doesn't know me at all. She does know Greg, though, and she has determined that he is her husband. She is holding on to his hand while he is standing over her, facing me as I walk into greet everybody. Elizabeth is sitting there watching with a wry grin, waiting to see how this is going to unfold.

I can tell something is going on because my poor husband looks like he has been caught in a net, a "fish on" unable to swim his way out of this one.

"Hi, Mom," I say cheerfully, still standing in the doorway.

She turns to my husband with her hand elevated from her bed, clasping his hand tightly within her grip, and says to him directly, "What are we going to do about her?" She tosses her head in my direction to make sure he knows I am the one she means.

"Well, what should we do about her? She is your lovely daughter," he says with a warm smile, leading her into the same dialogue they already had before I arrived home.

"Tell her we're married now," my mother says to Greg intently. "Tell her you're my husband."

He looks at me partly like he hates to break her heart, and partly like he does not want to deny that he is already married, to me.

"Well, your lovely daughter is who I am already married to," he says, and he kisses her hand. "Remember when Steffie and I got married?"

"You mean you and I are married. Tell her." She does not want to let go of Greg, his hand, or his image of him as her husband.

"Mom, you were married to Dad for a long, long time," I say, approaching her bedside, taking her other hand in mine. "And I am sure he misses you very much, the way you miss him." I try to hold back the tears, but my eyes are misting up. "And Greg is married to me, but he is your son-in-love, and he loves you very much too." I am hoping this will all sink in.

Elizabeth just smiles broadly because it really is hilarious that my mom is trying to think of ways to off me so she can steal my husband. She has always loved him though. I remember the first time I invited Greg to have dinner with us. I cooked tilapia, which isn't complicated, but I never made it before, and

I don't know what possessed me to experiment with something new when I was trying to impress a man.

Fortunately the entire dinner looked spectacular and tasted as delicious as I had hoped. I baked my famous brownies for dessert, the kind that have little marshmallows and heavy walnuts and chocolate chips. My mother would blare loudly from the couch when I put them in the oven, "My daughter can bake the best brownies!" as she eagerly anticipated their arrival on her plate.

Since this first dinner was going so well, she decided to put Greg to the test and said to me, "Let's see if he has our sense of humor."

I thought it was much too soon to find out because if he didn't laugh in all the right spots, he would never be able to fit in. But my mother proceeded to plop herself on the couch while I put in the video of Ellen DeGeneres doing her recent stand-up comedy routine called *Here and Now*. It is a retrospective look at how our world has become so dysfunctional because everybody is so much busier now, and news information comes blaring at all of our senses at once, and she longs for the simpler times when we had phone cords that would take a good half hour to unwind while you stood there and waited. It is hysterical.

The best part is toward the end, the place where my mom can recite the routine by heart, which she did for Greg. Ellen was speaking about how embarrassed we get when we accidentally trip and we think everybody is staring at us when they're probably not. Her point was made when she illustrated how even pain will take a backseat to embarrassment. For instance, she imitates a person who walks right into a plateglass window, and while everyone laughs uproariously, she just holds her hand over her eye, laughing along, agreeing with how funny it must have been to see her walk into that window. She continues to earn the audience's howls by stretching it out so that now she is bleeding, and isn't that just hilarious.

Finally, when she has the audience roaring in the aisles, she removes her hand and says, "Can someone help me find my eye? I seem to have lost my eye." The audience is in stitches. It's her mannerisms and her Ellen expressions that draw this scene out for a healthy amount of time until you are unable to breathe because you are laughing so hard.

My mom chimes in just at the right moment with her little hand covering her face: "Have you seen my eye? I just can't seem to find my eye," and she pretends to look all over the floor for it. We thank our lucky stars that Greg is howling along with us for all of the funniest parts, and he passes my mother's test with flying colors. I can tell he means it because he practically has tears coming out of his eyes too.

There will be so many times in the future when we will watch this video together, all three of us, that Greg decides to go to a gag store and buy some plastic eyeballs. When we get to the part where my mom starts saying Ellen's line—"Have you seen my eye?"—he rolls one of the plastic eyeballs across the floor. My mother hoots and hollers at this because she loves that his humor can keep up with hers. I always used to think I was the funniest person in the room, but being around these two has made me feel rather dull.

For the rest of October the night hallucinations are grabbing such a tight hold of my mother that she is bound and determined to get out of her bed so she won't miss her bus to go home. I still have the baby monitor in her room so I can tell when she is being restless. Tonight is bad, and she is conversing with somebody who seems to be in charge, begging him to let her go home.

"I can do better. I will try harder. Please let me go home." It is all she keeps repeating hour after hour, into the dawn. When I peek in on her, I can barely stand to watch. She has her little face pressed up against the bars of the side rails on her bed. She is actually trying to wriggle her head through them, and if she were any smaller she might actually fit, but her forehead thwarts her efforts. Her hands grip the rails tightly, with white knuckles, clinging to them as if she is locked behind a tiny jail window. In the morning there will be imprints from the metal rods fixed along her cheeks and above her brows, reminding me of her will to go home.

"Please, I want to get on the bus too. Let me go home." She is desperate to be where everyone else has already found a seat. "Isn't there room enough for me?" Her voice is becoming hoarse. "Please, can't you see I haven't got the strength to walk?" Her helpless cries are met by blockade after blockade. She is apparently not getting on this bus tonight according to the person in charge, much to her terrible disappointment.

I feel such a sense of urgency. Time is of the essence. I never know when I turn to go down the hall for a minute to use the bathroom if she will be here when I get back. So I have taken to using her bathroom a lot, where I can sit on the toilet while I watch her. I am so nervous to let her out of my sight. I do not know how long I have to continue this deathwatch.

By the end of October, Brother One has met his obligation to bring his little preschool-age daughters to see their grandmother dressed in their costumes. They are more interested in looking for Daisy than they are in showing off their outfits to a very old woman who is stuck in a bed that is guarded by rails.

We usually—if my mother is lucid and there is no chance of her falling out—pull the rails down on one side when visitors are here, but she is getting weaker, and it's not a good idea for the kids to climb up to her.

I have discovered that my mother's gradual weight loss has suddenly left her skeletal over night. I changed her diapers the other day with my usual routine of rolling her away from me by yanking quickly on the tuck beneath her so she can have some momentum to grab onto the rail in front of her as she faces away from me. As I pull her tuck this time, I nearly flip her off the bed because she has become so emaciated.

I don't know when this happened, and I stare at her backside for a long, quiet moment. I can see the knobs of her vertebrae poking through the skin. I tell her she can let go of the bars now and rest because I can easily support her full weight with just one hand while I maneuver my free hand beneath her to change her in one fell swoop.

I gently cradle her toward me and fold her diapers neatly around her hipbones, which are protruding just the way I have seen in videos of concentration camps. I am flabbergasted. My mother is shrinking away. When I think of it, it has been months that her hallucinations have detracted her from wanting to eat, and in between when she is catching up on the sleep she missed during those active days, she is not interested in food. She gave up needing insulin months ago, before Greg and I went to Hawaii, which was one more reason why it was easier for us to get away in early July, but the reality that my mother is wasting away before my very eyes is just now resonating with me. We move from ordering diapers in large to diapers in small, and soon we will look for child-sized diapers.

Just a few days after Halloween, something very strange occurs that reminds me how completely vulnerable my mother is to potential danger. At five in the morning, someone is ringing our doorbell. I can't imagine who would be playing a prank on us at this hour, and while Greg has already left for work, I still have some time in bed before my alarm goes off. Maybe I only thought I heard a bell. Then it rings again, just once. If it were Brother One, he would ring multiple times; in fact he would just call first, or he would come to my window. There is no way this is him. I call Greg on his cell phone, and he tells me to go see who's there, but not to hang up with him.

In my most gruff voice, I call through the front door, "Who is it?"

"It's the police. Open up!"

"Greg, it's the police," I whisper into the phone, and my heart begins beating hard because I didn't call the police.

They begin pounding on the door. "Ma'am, open the door now. We need to come inside."

My underarms begin to perspire, and I tell Greg the police are banging on the door and wanting to come in.

I get a dining room chair to stand on so I can look through the glass at the top of our door to see if it really is the police, and I see two officers, both in full uniform with their hat brims pulled down over their eyebrows. I am scared to death because Halloween was just three days ago, and all I can suspect is that a couple of guys know I am here alone with my elderly, invalid mother, and they are impersonating officers with uniforms they got at a costume store.

"How do I know you are real policemen? I didn't call you," I say, trying to sound strong and smart.

"Ma'am, open this door now. We got an emergency call from inside your house, which requires a mandatory search. Open your door." They are not fooling around.

"Greg, they won't go away. They say they got a call from

inside the house," which is reminding me of every scary baby-sitter movie I ever saw as a teen, when the bad guy was already upstairs in the attic, prank calling the sitter. Greg tells me to get their badge numbers and confirm with dispatch that they were actually sent.

The officers won't relent. "Ma'am, who are you talking to? We are coming in."

"I am talking to my husband because I didn't call you, and he wants me to get your badge numbers first."

After they ask me if my husband is inside, which I really don't want to answer because if they are imposters it makes me look so much more vulnerable, they become suspicious of me and what I must be hiding since I won't let them in. I finally get their badge numbers and do confirm that they were officially sent here to investigate an emergency call.

When I let them inside with great trepidation, and they ask if there is anyone else in the house, I explain to them that my elderly, bedbound mother is in her room. I checked on her before letting them in so she won't be worried, but it feels very ominous while they are flashing their lights under her bed, behind her doors, checking the backs of draperies, and looking inside closets for culprits. I still half expect one of them to turn to me and say what a fool I am after all for letting them in.

The officers do a thorough room-to-room check, insisting that the call came from inside this house. When they get to my den, which I keep locked because I don't necessarily want Brother One poking around my things when I am not home, a habit I learned long ago when we were kids, the officers insist I open it. I try to convince them that no one has been in there all night.

They ask me if my mother could have placed the call. My

mother is in a lucid state, but she is terribly weak. Her arms have atrophied, and she can't lift her hands even to feed herself when she will take applesauce or broth. By looking at her, they agree it seems unlikely. I ask them how they know the call came from this house. Maybe it was a wrong number from another house. They read me the telephone number, and my heart stops for a moment. It's not our main house number.

"Officer, that's the private line to my den." I look at them, and they look at each other with hands on their gun holsters because they are expecting to find someone on the other side of the door to my den. I get the key for them to unlock it and stand back in my bedroom.

Once they are in, the whole house is very still. There is not a person whose heartbeat can't be heard at this moment. They ask me if there is a window inside, and I tell them the four-by-four skylight opens with a crank handle, and they suspect this is how someone could gain access. But then, I have to wonder, why would a criminal hide inside my den and call the police? It doesn't make sense, but I still hang back until they check inside the closets and behind the overstuffed chair. Once they are satisfied that everything is fine, they leave.

It takes hours for my jittery nerves to calm down. Greg has a hundred questions I cannot answer. All I knew was that the officers were growing more anxious every minute I refused to open the front door because when they heard me talking to Greg on the phone, they believed we were together plotting a stand off and stalling for time. I can see they have a legitimate point. But, the question remains, how did that emergency call get placed from my den? We never find out. Considering the alternatives, I push the curiosity out of my mind because I feel so lucky that we didn't end up with real criminals in our home.

Before Thanksgiving, Sister Two has made it back for another all-day visit. I think maybe we can become close again. Maybe I can trust her. Maybe I don't need to understand everything about her life that is foreign to me, and maybe I can ignore all the covert things I do know about. Maybe. Today she is a good daughter, holding my mother's hand while tears stream silently down her face. Today my mom is sleeping and doesn't even know she's here.

Sister Two has missed out on so many opportunities to see my mother when she was healthier, but I am not going to bring this up. She is in pain, I can see, and it will be hers to live with. I am just so disappointed that she never lived up to her potential in life. She could have been something great.

Greg is trying to keep our family traditions alive while everything around me is dying. This year we order Thanksgiving dinner from a restaurant, and he puts it together in the kitchen so I can sit with my mom in her room until Greg's sons show up and we can sit down for my third year of sharing a holiday feast with my new family. Greg wants the boys to visit with my mother and pay their respects if she is awake, which she is, particularly if she is lucid, which she is not quite.

When the middle of these three brothers, who are young men in their mid-twenties, walks in to greet her first, she takes him for a longshoreman. I can see how she would get this impression because he is dressed accordingly for the weather with his short navy peacoat and dark knit cap.

"Did you just come in from sea? Did you catch anything good out there?" she happily asks.

"No, I wasn't fishing today."

But this doesn't stop her. "How was the sea today? I bet it's rocky out there. You have to stay bundled up."

He smiles at his brothers and looks to my mother again with a bright little chuckle.

"I don't really know," he says because he is not really sure how he should respond.

"What did you catch out there today?" my mom still wants to know.

"A lot of fish. It was a good day today," he finally chimes in, and then the younger brother keeps the yarn going with tales of fishing disasters that make the middle brother laugh.

My mom is so intrigued. "Are you going back out, or are you on leave?"

"I'm heading out again. That's why I came to visit you before I leave." He feels so pleased with his contribution.

And my mother says what she would normally say to any one of us leaving the house: "I love you. Take good care of yourself."

He tosses back to her the only natural response: "I love you too," complete with a Dentyne smile. All three boys meander out of her room while I sit there to collect myself for a moment longer because I am so appreciative of his tender exchange with my mother, a woman he barely knows.

It is the beginning of December now, and there are only three weeks to go before winter break. I feel if I can make it to Christmas, I will at least have two weeks to sit by my mom's bedside, making sure I am with her so she doesn't feel alone if indeed her time is coming. When I arrive home from school one day, I find my mother agitated and hallucinating again with Elizabeth, who tells me my mother has been worried all day about me and talking to "the man" about her plan.

"Hi Mom, I'm home from school," I say gleefully as I stride toward her with my hands outstretched, having just cleaned them in the kitchen after freeing myself from my workbag that I dumped on the dining room table just like every other day.

"Oh, Steffie." She reaches out for me and takes my hands in hers through the little metal bars of her bed's railing. "I want to take her with me," she says, looking up to someone who is not there.

"No," she says more firmly. "I want to take her with me." She grabs my hands a little tighter, clasping both of hers around mine. "I can't leave her. Don't you see? I want to take her with me."

The lump in my throat begins to push through to my eyes, and the tears begin to stream again. I can tell what she wants. She is desperate to leave this world, and she is equally desperate not to leave me. It is a conundrum for her, and I do not wish to be the one thing that keeps her from reuniting with my father and all of her loved ones who have shown themselves to her and are anxiously waiting.

"Mom, who are you talking to?" I ask because sometimes I wonder if my dad is there giving her instructions.

"I am talking to the man," she breaks from her conversation to inform me. Then she says again with tremendous strength and urgency in her voice, "No, I want to keep her with me."

All of a sudden I feel like the child who has been ripped from Meryl Streep in *Sophie's Choice* as my mother pulls my hands as far as she can through the railing, trying to make them fit so I can be on her side of the bed. She is wrapping herself around me up to her elbows, and she does not want to let go.

Elizabeth is crying in the other room because it is so difficult to watch. I keep getting advice from a friend who says I need to set my mom free, that it will happen as soon as I give her permission to leave, and that maybe I am being selfish by keeping her here to suffer. Those are sobering words to hear, yet I ponder them carefully before discarding both them and the friend.

I am not selfish for wanting to keep my mother here with me. I am heartbroken by the prospect of losing her. I am suffering every day that I am in the classroom, keeping my emotions compartmentalized so I can have success with these students of mine the same way I have with every other group I've taught, and then coming home to cry as soon as school is out.

I don't know what to do. I ask Elizabeth if she thinks my mother's time is here yet. And she thinks it is hard to know for certain. She tells me that when she feels she knows, she will share it with me. Karen has been reposted at the hospital— a promotion for her, but I feel saddened that she won't be finishing this journey with me. I do not love the new nurse Darlene but mostly because she is just not Karen. Darlene does not share my humor. Darlene was not here from the beginning. Darlene does not know how funny my mother is, and Darlene makes me feel like this is her job, not her family.

I ask Darlene if she feels like the time is getting close for my mother, and she tells me it is always hard to predict these things and my mother is obviously preparing herself. I beg her to tell me when she thinks the time is near because I want to be at home with my mother. I tell her I have emergency substitute plans in place and that my colleagues and administrators know I am on high alert, so I can leave my students if I am needed at home. But I am hoping my mom can make it to the last day of school.

Every night that my mom is awake, I read to her from the

book of poems she wrote in a college course she took with my father during his retirement years. She was dissatisfied with the A+ the professor gave her because she thought her writing worthy of an A++. I always thought she was biased because any time I heard her speak publicly, I thought her work required editing. I could not imagine that her poems would be as good as she said they were until I started reading them aloud to her. They struck me, especially a few, in the way that art does when it hypnotizes the patron who is immersed in what it says and how it speaks.

My favorite is the one about two willow trees that she created to symbolize the dreams she and her young farmer boyfriend imagined for themselves. They sat in their respective trees before their dreams became two very different paths in life, with her willow tree leading to my father and away from the life of a farmer's wife. I love it so much I never tire of reading it to her. Every night she is lulled by the rhythm of her words, the memories of her past, the lifetime she lived, and the future she holds in her hallucinations.

# CHAPTER 34

# My Privilege

By the end of the first week of December, my mom tells me she doesn't think she has much longer to live. I try to take this in stride, but it is hard not to take someone seriously when they are this close to the other side, even if her previous predictions in the summer rang false. So I renew my school plans with the front-office secretaries, Camilla, and my colleagues next door. I send my emergency substitute plans by e-mail to all five of these point people, and I leave a folder with a copy inside my top desk drawer and remind my best pal where to find it in the event that she needs it.

I just want my mom to make it to winter vacation. This is all I pray for. I can handle whatever I need to over break and steady myself so I can return to work after the holidays if she does indeed pass away after Christmas. I do not want her to go. I do not wish it so. I want to keep her here with me. Yes, I want to be selfish. And then, a week later, with one week to go before we are out of school, I see something I have only heard of but could not ever imagine.

While I am diapering my mother, I gently roll her onto her

side to find a gaping hole in her back where her flesh has come off the bone. Had the little bedsore become all this in just a few days? My first reaction is to feel the way soldiers must during war when their mates are sick with diseases that waste them away, or when they are shot and part of their flesh comes off with the wound. I could lay my palm over her back and it still would not cover the area that has fallen away. I realize here and now that my mother must be suffering more than I can know, and I will not be the reason to keep her here on this earth if she is indeed ready to leave.

So I pull up a chair after I finish freshening her and giving her water to sip. I put down the rail and hold her hands and look into her sweet little face while she casts her blue eyes up to mine.

"Mom," I start with a quiver, but I do not want her to know how much this pains me to say, so I speak slowly, controlling my breath so I can get my words out evenly. "I know how much you love me. I know it, I know it." A smile forms on my face as a tear trickles down from one eye.

I continue, "I know how much you miss Dad, and I am sure he is watching over you and waiting for you to join him." I breathe so I can get through the rest of this. "I love you so very, very much, and I am so grateful I got to come home and spend these last years with you." There are trickles of more tears I am hoping to hide from her with my long hair stuck to my wet cheek.

"I know there are old friends waiting to reunite with you, and your mother is waiting for you too, so if you need to go, I want you to know I will be safe here with Greg." I have to close my eyes for a minute to blink away the tears that are blurring my vision, and I finish, "But if you can stay, then I am looking forward to enjoying all the time in the world that I am allowed to have with you. It's whatever you need, Mom, whatever you need to do. I know you will be watching over me, and I won't feel alone knowing that you will be with Dad so that the two of you can watch over me together."

It's all I can say. It is the permission I have been told that those facing death sometimes need so they can feel un-entwined from this world. I don't know how much of my words my mother hears or understands because she is so very quiet. But I got it out. I also promise to take care of Sissy, to love her and to make sure she feels safe and that nothing ever happens to her.

After this my mom sleeps for a really long time. I count the days until four have passed, and then she awakens.

I am there when she opens her eyes on the Saturday six days before school will be out for winter vacation. Greg has bought a little fake Christmas tree to put in her room and strung it with lights, and we made sure the gifts we expected to give her were already opened weeks and weeks ago. Her room is beautiful and festive but not commercialized with holiday flair. It is soothing, and from time to time the strings of her Spanish guitar music play in the background.

Last month *Mary Tyler Moore* episodes were showing; a time or two we put in Ellen's familiar act, but mostly now my mother wants things to be still. She is very quiet, and hospice tells me this is typical when one is getting ready to pass over. The last sense to leave the body is hearing, so while my mother is sleeping peacefully, Greg and I are sure to tell her lovingly how much we adore her and how grateful we are for the time we have had together.

On this particular Saturday, when my mother awakens with a start from her sleep, she tells me in an urgent way of something she needs me to know. "Oh, Steffie," she says, a long, pregnant pause stuck in between her thoughts as she struggles with her contemplation. "There is so much I want to tell you about what I've seen." She looks worried, as if she has said too much already. "But I promised I wouldn't." She reaches for my hands and shakes them as vigorously as she can. "You've just got to find out for yourself."

I can tell she is debating about whether she should just spit it all out or honor this promise. The suspense is killing me as I see her mulling it over, her tongue circling her lips as if she is just on the verge of saying what she wants to say. But she doesn't. She leaves me there with only the foggiest idea of what she is talking about.

But I never forget the urgency in her voice, as if she wanted to share with me the secret we have all been searching for in this life, as if she truly learned what is waiting on the other side. As much as I want to know, I do not want her to break her promise. There have been many times when I have caught her hallucinating and she said aloud that she could do better, that she will try harder, in the midst of being left off the bus again. So I don't want to be the reason why she misses the next bus because she broke a promise.

I settle for my wild imagination of what must be waiting for her in the sky, what all of those imaginary fruits that she seems to salivate over and pretend to eat must taste like, what the throngs of her old, dead friends must look like, what it will be like to play with Daisy again, what it will be like for her to see my father again.

I have just this week to get through before school is over until January. The weather is cold, and I am wearing my gray wool grandpa sweater that I got to match the one my mother bought a couple of years ago when she and I went on a little spree to spruce up her wardrobe. When I walk into her room to kiss her good-bye, she opens her eyes with such amazement.

"Where did you get that sweater?" she is almost frantic at the sight of it.

"Mom, we bought this one for me the same time we bought yours. Remember, we have matching sweaters?" I stroke her arm and hold her hand.

With the mightiest of wills that I answer this next question correctly, she takes a deep breath and asks in a hushed voice, "Do you know where my sweater is?"

"Of course, it's right here. I keep it in this drawer with your sweatpants." I go to retrieve it from her twelve-drawer dresser that she has had since the '60s and drape it over her front.

She wraps her little arms into it and hugs it tight to her chest, and says to me with huge sighs of relief, "Oh, Steffie, I am so relieved. I thought I had lost it and I couldn't find it anywhere." She is at once swimming in it and hugging it and tightly squeezing it. "You have no idea how important this is to me." She looks at me lovingly and tells me again that I am wonderful and that she loves me before she ends with, "Thank you."

I am lucky. My mother does not let a moment pass that she doesn't say something complimentary to me or to Greg, or to anyone who comes to visit. Her demeanor has always been to embrace people, and her reasoning has been "because it's pretty hard to dislike someone who likes you so much," so she cheers others on and finds the good in all people. I admire this quality in her and try to practice it, but it's not always as easy as she makes it look.

The week is coming to a close, and early gifts are beginning to topple over on my teacher's desk. On Friday morning, I feel a huge sense of relief that my mother has made it to Christmas vacation, and I will be able to be with her now for two whole weeks. My first class of the day is enjoying a movie, a rare treat, and I have even let a few of them sit together on the floor, so these kids are particularly good-natured right now. The front office is calling me for what I imagine will be the first of many kids getting checked out early so their family can make haste to the snow four hours away.

But I am wrong. It is the principal's secretary alerting me that Elizabeth is on the line. *Oh God, I know what this means, please let my mother still be alive when I get home* is all I can think as I wait for Elizabeth to speak.

"Stefania, your mom's breathing is not right. You need to come home. I think this is the time now."

I ask no questions. In the blink of an eye, I have asked all the kids to return to their seats to finish the movie, and I have signaled to my colleague next door with my coat in hand and my purse on my shoulder. When she comes out of her classroom to meet me in the hall, she knows right away what it means.

"Oh, Stefania, I'm so sorry." She doesn't know how exactly to comfort me, and she is trying to hold back her tears because she can see I am about to lose it. "What do you need right now? Is there anything I can do?"

My first words to her are intended to be soft and urgent, but a gust of air bursts from my lungs with the pain of a dagger in my heart as I tearfully choke out, "I left my keys on my desk and I can't go back in there." I am heaving sobs now, aware that their echoes are traveling down the cement hallway, amplifying to be much louder than what is actually coming out of me.

My dear friend finds my keys, and, as she hugs me good-bye, I see Camilla dashing up the hallway from the opposite end to see if I need anything before I go.

"I am so sorry. Don't worry about school today. Just go home. Everything will be taken care of here. You've prepared us well," she says, and she tries to give me a little smile, and I cry harder while she hugs me tight.

Within three minutes I have left campus and am driving home quickly in the rain, making my ten-minute trek arduous. When I pull into the driveway, I leave everything in the car and fling open the front door to run to my mother's room. She is still breathing, but it is uneven. Darlene is on her way, Elizabeth tells me.

"Hi Mom, I'm home from school." I stroke her forehead gently. "It's Christmas break, so the kids are pretty excited to be out for two weeks, and I tell them I am too, just the way you used to tell your students." I try to sound relaxed because I know she is in a peaceful state, and she can still hear everything I say.

I called Greg on my drive home, and he is on his way. I look at my mother, with her gaunt cheeks and the bones around her neck and shoulders pronounced. The flannel nightgown I bought her months ago just hangs on her frame as if she is a little paper doll. Darlene arrives and checks her vitals. She thinks the time has come, and we are within days of a final exit.

I am not satisfied with this answer because I want a more precise time. I am a planner, and I want to know to the minute when this will be occurring. But Darlene will not be more specific, and I somehow feel that she is keeping something from me. When she leaves, I ask Elizabeth what she thinks.

"Her time is very close now. I don't know how many days, but she is close, Stefania."

At this I cry because all of the false alarms that have rocked me for months and months are now seeming to ring true. I am faced with the very real prospect that in a matter of unspecified days, I will lose my mother.

I call Sisters Two and Three and Brothers One and Two to tell them all what I have uttered many times during this year: "Mom is not doing well. Hospice thinks her time is near, but I will keep you posted."

It's almost like the little boy who cried wolf. This family has become so conditioned to expect the worst-possible news every time I call that it is hard to believe that one of these days it will actually happen. I sit vigil at my mother's side all weekend. I figure a few days could actually turn into a good long week, or maybe even two weeks, so I'd better get a good book to read while I am holding her hand for the unforeseeable future.

I decide to delve into another presidential biography, and this one is going to be about George Bush—the son. I want to know about all of the haunting decisions that are part of his legacy. My plan is to invent creative avoidance. I figure nothing will happen to my mother during the time it will take me to read through this three-inch book. And when it's finished, it will be time to come up with a new plan to create some more avoidance.

I make it through an inch of this book on Saturday, holding my mother's hand the whole day, staying in her room at night, watching her continue to sleep. I make it through another inch of this book on Sunday and am so happy to be in the chair right beside her bed when her eyes open and she looks directly at me as she mouths the words, "Thank you, you're wonderful" and falls back to sleep.

Very early Monday morning, I am awakened by the sound of the phone ringing incessantly. I let the first call go to voicemail, not knowing who would be calling at six a.m. on my first day of Christmas vacation. The second attempt I pick up, thinking it might be Greg in an accident on his way to work. It is our brokerage firm confirming that the sale I initiated last week will be placed today for the trading rate I specified. The East Coast doesn't care that we are three hours behind them when they are calling about stocks that need to be sold. Now that I am up, and since Elizabeth won't be here for another couple of hours, I decide it is the perfect time to be alone with my mother and enjoy some peace and quiet together.

Clad in my flannel pajamas and my fuzzy robe and slippers, I amble down the hallway to sit on the little chair at my mother's bedside. I find her hand, which is cool to the touch. It has been left out of the blankets all night again, so I tuck it inside and pull the covers up to her shoulders. She is sleeping peacefully; I can tell because I have learned to watch her breath and wait for it as it falls.

I sit and relax in the sound of silence, with the darkness outside and the rain coming down. Sissy has found her spot on my mother's tummy as usual, and I watch her rise up as my mom breathes in and fall downward on the exhale. The breaths aren't very deep, so the kitten has no worries about falling off my mother's belly. I watch my mother, who looks so cute in her matching flannel nightgown and granny cap. I speak to her softly because I believe she can still hear me.

"I love you, Mom. You are safe, I am here, you are home on Mindy Lane." I sit with her for a half hour, just holding the hand I untucked from where I placed it a few moments ago. "I am so grateful I got to be here with you these past years." There is a catch in my throat. "You are precious to me, and I love you so very much." I wipe the tear that is dripping off my nose. "Thank you for everything you have done for me in this life. I know I will never be alone with you watching over me."

And then it comes. Her last breath. It is a big exhale of wind. There is nothing more dramatic about it than that. She is very rigid, and her face is feeling cool. There is no soul left in her, for when she lies this still now, she seems different. The possibilities of her living through another day are gone. My mother has left me.

I gush tears of sorrow, but I have not one single regret. In this moment I am comforted to know that in every thought I had of what I could do to make her time on earth more enjoyable or more comfortable I did not delay. I acted on her behalf with the purest intentions, and I maintained ties with siblings so they could be informed of their mother's progress. That was the hardest part of this job.

My mother told me in our early days together that it would be my privilege to care for her, and yes, it became my privilege indeed. I got to be a witness to her life. I got to enjoy another five years with her, and she got to meet my darling husband. My greatest reward is being here in this moment, alone with my mother, just the two of us in peace. This is the gift my mother has left me. I will be forever grateful that my wish was granted.

Once I have had enough time to pray with gratitude for my experience here with my mother, I call Greg, who will turn around to come home and should be here in an hour, and Elizabeth, who insists on coming to me even though I told her I want to be alone. Before they both arrive, I have the presence of mind to write each of them a letter of gratitude for the support they have been to me through this long year.

The sentiments flow easily because I love them both. They

became the family I did not have to comfort me in my most difficult days, when my heart was hurting the most. I expressed to both of them how much my mother adored them and what they meant to her, and then I sealed their letters and handed them out when they arrived with bear hugs for me.

I first call Sister Two, who is at her office. Upon hearing the news she finds that words won't come out of her mouth. I know she is crying on the other end of the silent phone, then she finally spits out the phrase I've heard from her my whole life: "I'll call you back." Most of the time she doesn't. I call Brother One and Brother Two, who both are equally short on the phone because they need time to process. Each of them thanks me for what I did for Mom—a gesture, maybe, the first sign of peace. I call Sister Three and get an answering machine, which is no place to leave a message.

Once the calls are made, I sit with Greg while the business of the day unfolds. The coroner sends a wagon to pick up the body, and Greg shields me from viewing my mother being wheeled down the hallway of our house to the vehicle waiting outside. I am glad the last image I have of her is our quiet time together. This is what brings me peace. Knowing that she got her wish to die in her home also brings me peace.

I go to sleep in my room, the room where I was a little girl, the room I now share with my husband, and I try to dream. I try to dream of the place where my parents are together, happy at last and watching over me. I know after I awake there will be funeral arrangements to be made and more death business to handle. But for now I sleep.

# PART 8

# ESTATE MANAGEMENT

---

## REALITY **8**
### *A Preplanned Funeral Is a Gift to Your Family; Binders, and Lots of Them, Are an Executor Trustee's Gift*

---

# CHAPTER 35

# The Funeral Playbook

Death has come, and you think this means your work is done; sadly for you it has just begun. These should be lyrics from a song because it will become a familiar tune in the coming days, months, possibly years you have ahead. The first task is to make funeral arrangements, which can be just as involved as planning a wedding only short on time and sad as hell. Assuming you are the executor trustee, the second task is the massive job of sorting out the estate.

Fortunately I had the benefit of a great example of how to prepare for this day because my dad had a playbook for his funeral. It was entitled "If I Should Die Before I Wake," and it included several typed pages of instructions laid out step by step. When he first showed it to me, I was twenty-seven years old and quite taken aback when he began talking to me about his mortality. I had seen my father cry only twice before, both times when I was a teen and he had been relegated to taking our cats to the pound on two different occasions after they had both coincidentally been run over by cars.

He wanted me to know in advance what to do so it would be less of a shock for me when the time did come. But to see him before me trying to explain his plan for his death was no less shocking for me hearing it for the first time that day. As his eyes began to water and he ran the handkerchief he always kept in his back pocket beneath his eyeglasses, quickly swiping his face in one swoop, I was nearly devastated. My first reaction was to wonder if his heart condition had worsened, if the doctors had told him something new. My next reaction was to cry.

It was a difficult conversation to get through, but I am so glad my father took the time to speak to me directly about the wishes he had and the plan he had put in place so we wouldn't have to fret in the midst of our grieving—if we were doing the right thing. It was a sobering moment. Ten months later, one month after my twenty-eighth birthday and three weeks after I had sat in the pew with him for his last Father's Day, my father passed away on a fishing boat. It hit me like a ton of bricks, and while I was hanging on to him alone in the hospital room where he was cold and lifeless, with my face buried in his chest, heaving the tears of a grief-stricken child, there were others who were already assembling and putting his plan into action.

These others were his pallbearers—his closest friends from church and associates from the company where he had worked for twenty-seven years before he had retired. They were men he had regularly gathered with on the sea where it seemed they truly worshipped, or over miso soup at his favorite restaurant. The first caller to reach us when my mother and I returned home from the hospital was Gil, a company man. He extended his condolences to me and then told me not to worry about the arrangements because he and the others were handling the details that my dad had laid out, and then he spoke to my mother for quite a while.

This is how it went. I did not need to be involved in any decision making because my mother was just nearly seventy-three and capable of handling anything that required her attention. But, as I recall, the only thing she really needed to do was write a check to the funeral parlor covering the expense of the casket and the transportation to the military gravesite two hours away, where my father's remains would be buried in a field of long wheat grass that blows gently in the welcome breeze of the hot valley. My father had prearranged with the funeral director, who was another personal friend, all of the details including the selection of his casket, so there were no questions to bother my mother with.

His friends all had a copy of "If I Should Die Before I Wake," the document my father carved out at the typewriter in his den with hours upon hours of time to plan. His thoughtful preparation saved us from having to make tedious decisions that would take us away from the only thing we really had any energy for: answering the telephone to receive calls from well wishers who had just gotten the news.

The phone tree was working. Each of the pallbearers had a list of numbers for those they were responsible to notify as soon as the first person received my mother's call. Gil was one of my father's best friends and a fellow retiree from the company where they had forged a bond that lasted well over forty years. Gil made sure to contact the rest of the retirement crew, some of whom I hadn't seen since I was a little girl when they would visit our house, but I knew their names and the fun-loving stories attached to them.

If Gil was the quarterback, Charlie was the receiver. Equally important, Charlie took care of corralling all of my father's contacts at church and in the neighborhood where we all lived. Charlie also knew the funeral director, and it made it much easier on everyone to have a master diagram of the plays laid out on paper so everyone was on the same page.

The playbook read like a top-ten list enumerating the steps to take in the event of my father's death. Each succeeding page was dedicated to a particular topic like burial details or estate management with a new list of bullet points that needed to be followed. It was very well executed because it was easy to follow. So I borrowed from this version to create my mother's playbook and, later on, my own.

This playbook is designed for the surviving spouse. It is simple and straightforward, and you don't need a financial expert's best-selling book to understand it. For a basic overview of the first eight calls we needed to make, this came in handy. At the end of this chapter, you will find the more detailed version of my own playbook.

Here starts the list of steps from my father's playbook. Additionally he remembered to include the names and phone numbers for all contacts within each step. It saved immeasurable time because we didn't have to scour through phone books or address books to find what we needed right away.

*Step One: Notify my primary care physician. If time of death is after hours, call the coroner.*

*Step Two: Notify my cardiologist.*

There should be contact information here for any specialist who treated the deceased.

*Step Three: Notify my clergyman.*

*Step Four: Notify the funeral home.*

There are further instructions here on where to locate the folder labeled "Funeral Arrangements" in a filing cabinet in the den, in which safe-deposit box to find the military discharge papers the funeral home will need to forward to the cemetery, and a reminder, in case my mother had forgotten, that my father had reserved the plot space for her as well.

*Step Five: Notify the cotrustee who is next in line of succession on the trust.*

Hopefully a trust has already been set up. When the trustor, the person who initiates putting his property into a trust, dies or becomes physically or mentally unable to manage their own affairs properly, then a trusted trustee and his or her backups will manage the estate accordingly. Know who your trusted friends are; you will need to count on them in this case. Do not make this decision lightly. When you name someone to assume the fiduciary responsibility of managing your affairs according to your wishes, remember this role is a serious time commitment for that person. You can always reevaluate your estate plans in a year or two, and you should.

*Step Six: Contact our family accountant about the next steps that need to be taken with regard to your change in taxes, looking ahead to the next tax returns.*

*Step Seven: Notify the people listed in the "Funeral Arrangements" folder who agreed to be my pallbearers and inform them of funeral services and burial arrangements at the cemetery.* If, like my father, you have prearranged for this, then have the names and phone numbers of the pallbearers listed here.

*Step Eight: Notify Social Security about my demise.*

Here my father listed his Social Security number along with the phone number for Social Security. He also provided the contact information for the company where he retired from so my mother could ask for survivor's benefits, which would have a bearing on her own Social Security and retirement benefits.

He signed it, "With love and thanks to all." Fitting.

Beyond covering his funeral arrangements, including the preselection of hymns he wanted sung, on the next page my father went on to provide a new set of instructions on how to manage the estate. He laid it all out, giving clarity to the importance of notifying the estate attorney who set up the original will and trust and getting in touch with managers of pension plans and institutions where investments are held.

Plus he typed up useful guidelines on how to draw down assets and wrote out a list of standing bills for my mother to pay rain or shine. He also provided a list of contents in filing drawers containing financial papers that would need to be accessible. There were more lists of contents in safe-deposit boxes as well as types of checking and savings accounts, highlighting the fees charged at each institution. I was exhausted reading it all.

Probably sweetest among these lists was my father's parting checklist to my mother for how to maintain a car to last longer and cost-cutting measures to take, including the sage advice to watch the filling station attendant when he pumps your gas or, better yet, fill the tank herself. This was something my mother learned how to do in her seventies. This list is good enough but, as you can see, largely outdated for the twenty-first century.

In planning my mother's funeral, I know it will be completely different from my father's. He was a man who was beloved at age seventy-five, who still had many, many active friends who kept in regular contact with him. My mother has lived long enough to outlive most of her friends and relatives, which leaves only a handful from church, many of whom do not drive anymore, and a few immediate family members, many of whom do not visit. My worst fear is planning a service wherein loving speeches about a mother who was dearly adored are given to largely empty pews. This would not do my mother's life justice, and because I protected her from her greatest fear of being alone, I do not want her service to feel just that: lonely.

So, I start with the funeral parlor that handled my father's arrangements seventeen years earlier. This is my first mistake. I fall into the trap of sentiment, ignoring the inner voice telling me each time I meet with my "host" that these people are disorganized, that this place has not been kept up. The word *shabby* not only comes to mind when describing its appearance; it also fits what I think of their customer service.

The first director I met was a nice enough man in his middle-aged years, but he was very distracted, seemingly too busy helping someone other than me. The problem was I did not see anybody else around. I was the only person inside this old and tattered building despite its charming curb appeal, which was still intact. So, he passed me to Martha, the director he introduced as the one who would be consoling me through my time of need.

Martha wore nurse's shoes in black along with the requisite black polyester pants. Her long-sleeved burgundy top made of some acetate fabric hung loosely with a ribbon tied tightly at the base of her neckline. It appeared she hadn't combed her hair maybe for days, but it didn't much matter. I imagined she hoped the ponytail dragging down to her waist would disguise this. There was no makeup on her face, only large, drooping brown eyes and leathery olive skin that would have benefitted from more sunscreen.

Martha's hands were warm when she greeted me, but her smile was not. I immediately got the impression that either she had done this too many times to still be compassionate or she had not yet done this enough and had no sense of the pain I was experiencing. She invited me to sit in an office that didn't feel like it belonged to her because she didn't know where any of the forms she needed were kept.

She pulled at drawers one after another, frustrated that she was not having any luck. Finally, after finding what she needed behind a desk in another office, she asked what she could do for me. I explained to her that our family had a very positive experience when my father's death was handled here, and this was why I was coming back. She popped out of her chair to retrieve my father's file from the archives, which meant leaving me to sit by myself for several minutes until she could find the manila file buried in a storage room in the basement.

While she was gone, the phone never rang. No one came through the front doors. No one left. I felt like no one else was in the building except for Martha and me, and since she was out of view, my solitude in the funeral parlor was eerie. When Martha did rejoin me, she dusted off my father's file and let me take a look. The rates back then were modest and completely affordable by today's standards.

Unfortunately the price of funerals had gone up with inflation, which I could understand, but with the price-gouging of weddings, funeral parlors apparently decided somewhere along the way that they too should be charging a lot more since people had no other option in death. Weddings and funerals are solid businesses to be in: you will always have customers regardless of the economy. Seventeen years after paying for our last family funeral, the rates had now tripled.

I signed the paperwork only after I inspected the costs of travel for the mortician to go to the gravesite two hours away, and picked out a casket in beautiful steel with a velvet lining at a surprisingly attractive price. This concluded my first experience with Martha. I met with her early on before Thanksgiving because I did not want to be caught unprepared when my mother's time did come. Prearranging details was a reoccurring thought that nagged me in my sleep, constantly telling me that I should be getting things in order. I had no idea that my mother's life would be ending in the four short weeks we had left before Christmas.

My second visit with Martha happens the day after my mother's passing. I return to firm up all of the details, write the check, and find out how many easels will be available for me to create a grand photo-gallery display of my mother's life. But Martha can't find the original contract we signed, so she has to fill out a new one. This time the price is different because she has checked off boxes for higher-end features I never wanted in the first place.

It is a good thing that in the midst of my grieving, I still have my wits about me because Martha is overcharging me by fifteen hundred dollars. I pull from my clutches the folder I have been carting around for a month, clearly labeled "Funeral," and show Martha the previously agreed-to price. While she tries to hem and haw a bit more, haggling over why the increase is needed for the driver's time to go such a great distance with the procession, I point out to her that this was settled in our initial visit, and I am only paying what I originally agreed to in the contract that was signed by both of us.

This exchange leaves a bitter taste in my mouth. But it gets better. Actually, I should say, it gets worse. The viewing room

I initially wanted has leaks dripping from the ceiling due to recent heavy rains. The dilapidated walls, which are badly in need of fresh paint, look yellowed, and the plaster of Paris appears to be sliding. When she tells me that the other room can be made available—for an additional charge since it can accommodate triple the amount of guests than the smaller room I have reserved—I decide to keep our room as planned. It is already larger than we need, big enough to hold a chapel meeting. A smaller, more crowded room is the look I am hoping to achieve.

I have determined that we will be doing an open-casket viewing only, followed by a private burial ceremony for family at the gravesite. My mother passed away a few days before Christmas; the fact that there were only thirteen mourners in attendance a week later is easily explained by the holidays that have taken everyone out of town. The dearest friends who come are the few we have seen in our home on my mother's infrequent good days. Constance brings her grown daughters, childhood playmates I remember vividly and fondly. The neighbors across the street come to pay their respects too.

The elderly couple from church hobble in with their canes. Both are in failing health and nearly my mother's age; they slowly teeter together up to the casket to say their final good-byes. The rhythm of their syncopated canes on the downbeat of each footstep lulls me with the familiarity of a sound I have grown accustomed to hearing for years. As they near the front pew and head toward my mother, it is at the same moment they both trip over the loops in the throw rug that has been laid beneath my mother's casket station, toppling them to the ground, one onto the other.

I am petrified that they may have each broken a hip, or

that perhaps he has done the falling first because of a heart attack he is having. Thankfully Greg rushes to them immediately while I run to find the mortician, whose extra pair of hands we need. As we check for broken bones, we gently begin to untangle the couple from one another. At Mr.'s insistence, we help his wife up first and seat her in a pew where she can catch her breath. It could have been so much worse. I should have known about the loops in the rug given all the trouble my mother had catching her lazy toe, which landed her in the emergency room.

I excitedly say to the director that we need to remove the carpet, but he hesitates, and now I can see why. Beneath the throw rug is a carpet stained by water damage probably from the leaky roof. There is no hiding it, so we rearrange the flowers to mask the markings on the burgundy carpet, sliding my mother's casket forward a bit to hover over the stains. It looks better this way anyhow; she didn't need to be set so far back in an empty chapel. This feels more intimate, more welcoming.

# CHAPTER 36

# Photo Gallery

I relied on my dear husband for the advance work I needed done to prepare for my mother's funeral. I put Greg on the task of enlarging a poem I had written for one Mother's Day while I was in college. I had written it the morning of the holiday with some last-minute inspiration, and when I read it over the phone it was very hard to get through without tears. When I returned home to care for my mother in the last years of her life, this poem was the first thing to greet me in her bathroom. Sitting on the sill of her sink, with the ink in the frame faded from basking in the brightness of the skylight above, my words for the mother I adored were still there.

She had saved this poem for all those decades, and I read it to her on every Mother's Day we had together. It is called "Blessed Mother," and its universal message is one that you and your mother could probably connect to on some level. In it I share the sentimental reasons why I felt blessed to have been raised by her.

I sent Greg to the office supply store with a typed version

for enlarging, using letters big enough to be read from a distance by the failing eyes of the seniors who would be visiting.

Next to this poem, on the other four easels, are poster boards all measuring twenty-four by thirty-six inches. The first one of these is for a photo gallery I configured to reflect my mother's stretch of time. I combed through old, tattered albums to find photos I could get scanned and reprinted to be equal sized photographs, four by six in size for uniformity and ease of placement on the board. I arranged them in chronological order beginning with her toddlerhood, wherein she was dressed in a turn-of-the-century, long, flowing white gown as she stood on a box next to a wooden child's chair. A black and white photo, it looks like it was staged in an old-time picture booth at an amusement park.

This board feels complete as I was able to fit at least thirty photos for a very nice pictorial synopsis of her ninety years on earth. This is another reason why we who do not like to have our photos taken should go to greater lengths to make sure there are some pictures of us for every decade of our lives: we change more than the mirror lets on. My mom never could reconcile that the thirty-five-year-old gal staring into the mirror was the reflection of an eighty-five-year-old looking back. In her mind she never aged.

The second photo-gallery board is dedicated to the love story of my parents. It includes early pictures from when my mother and my father met as teenagers. The most fun ones are the prewar photos my mom would send to my father in the South Pacific with pinup likenesses of herself in a full coverage, one-piece bathing suit paired with a short coat thrown over her shoulder. The review of her married life alone with my father segues to the third board, which completes our family with a gallery of images of each of us kids as we entered the picture. I made sure to punctuate what she meant to us by finding a single moment in which each one of us kids was photographed separately with our mother on some memorable occasion.

This was a lovely idea; however, there were no photos of Sister Two with my mother beyond her babyhood. I scoured drawers and albums and begged my sister to look through her own memories, but nothing ever surfaced. So, the only solo moment my mother has with Sister Two is when she was a tiny girl looking ever so joyful in my mother's arms. This is another reminder why it is crucial to have copies of all family members in photos together, and individually with parents, throughout one's lifespan.

The final foam poster board sits on the fifth easel with a duplicate version of what I intended to be my mother's funeral notice until I was rudely awakened by the rates for each line the newspaper charges for obituaries. I decide instead to make the newspaper version the size of a tweet with the fact that my mom did not die alone and listing where services would be held along with the requisite date of birth, date of death, and residence.

For the extended version of the news of her passing, I thought long and hard about how to capsulate a modest life lived in a grand amount of time—over the course of ninety years. This was a lot of living to cover even on a large poster board. It seemed logical to dedicate each paragraph to a different part of her life, giving a sense of the woman she became and all that she held dear.

The first paragraph shares the intimate details of her death and how she spent her last years surrounded by love in her home. The second paragraph provides a sense of how and where she was raised and the thirst she had for learning through college and into her professional years as a teacher. The third paragraph is reserved for how she met my father and their path to raising a family in the postwar decades. The fourth paragraph speaks of her passion for traveling, noting a trip to Jerusalem that was particularly dear to her.

The fifth paragraph is dedicated to the memories those who called her their friend will always recount when they think of my mother. The sixth paragraph thanks those who cared for her, and the seventh and final paragraph recalls the platitudes that were her way of sticking important lessons in our heads. "We were put on this earth to learn" was heard weekly when we were teenagers.

Between the poster boards that tell the story of my mother's life, the spray of lilies on the casket, and the deliveries that arrive from family and well wishers who cannot be in attendance, it is a less dramatic send-off than what I had steeled myself for. The one piece that makes it easier to stay all day in anticipation of visitors I might need to greet is that I cannot keep myself from blabbering to each guest, "Please go on up to see the posters. My mother looks nothing like herself in the casket, so you'll hardly recognize her."

My husband keeps trying to get me to say anything else, but it is the only thread of robotic impulse I can get comfortable with. I worked so hard to prepare the mortician, whom I entrusted to make my mother look natural and to get her hair just right like in the picture I submitted, which I snapped a year earlier when my mom was dressed up, looking so pretty. I even supplied the ruby lip liner and the matching lipstick so they could be applied meticulously. Her smile was her most notable feature, bringing a jubilant glow to her face.

I made an emphatic point about how her bangs should

hang forward. Instead her hair is parted on the side and swept back behind both ears with some sort of grease to hold it in place, making her look more like Victor from *Victor/Victoria*. I keep tugging at her bangs, trying to weed them out of the man's hairdo, which was utterly wrong for my mother. I don't know who is responsible for this, but in a way it makes it easier to stand around tending to business because the person resting in peace looks so unfamiliar to me. Perhaps I should thank the person who was in charge of makeup this day.

Afterward, it would be one more reminder of things that did not go according to what I had planned. All of these missed details led me to think I could do it so much better if I were a funeral director. In fact, I got so carried away with the idea that I think seriously over the course of one full day about switching my career.

If I were in charge of a funeral home, the first thing grieving families would find would be some compassion from someone who extends the same kind of warmth that veterinarians do when their client loses a family pet. I would reduce the prices of caskets so people aren't made to feel guilty if they choose a more modestly priced coffin instead of one made of bronze. The depth of love should not be measured by how deep one's pockets are.

I would have an inviting place for a family to sit instead of in front of a messy office desk where they are made to feel as if they are unexpected and perhaps even unwelcomed because the staff is busy attending to some other distraction. The files of the last customers would already be put away, and the files of the current customers would be filed accurately, not lost when the time comes that they need to be retrieved.

I would shower my newly bereaved family with a meal service that included my macaroni and cheese with homemade croutons along with my famous coffee cake, dropped off at their home within the first twenty-four hours of signing their contract and again within twenty four hours of their service, both with notes attached that read, "We hope this gesture will bring some small comfort to you when your hearts are so heavy."

I resent the fact that funeral parlors are in the business of making money, forgetting that someone beloved has been lost. Why do payments need to be made in full within twenty-four hours of the service? Maybe the logic is to get all the grief and pain over at once instead of dragging the memory out with every monthly installment check that needs to be written.

If I were a funeral director, I would make sure to upgrade the look of my parlor so it feels inviting, creating a feeling of respect for the deceased so families could know that their loved ones passed through a really nice place on their way out of this world. For goodness's sake, I would at least make sure my roof didn't leak and that my walls and carpets weren't ruined.

I would also make sure there was chocolate on hand next to the Kleenex box. I would be sure to have pretty soaps in the ladies' room and good lighting around the mirrors. I would make sure there was a lounge in the ladies room for sitting as long as you like, in private, to cry your eyes out before returning to the rest of your guests. I would be sure the hand towels were soft enough to wipe your tears without tearing that delicate skin beneath your eyes.

Furthermore I would be sure to send a thank-you note for choosing us as your primary mortuary along with a comforting reminder that the file from today's proceedings was safely tucked away in the archives drawer, where it could easily be accessed in the future. I would also include at this time a one-page synopsis of what was ordered, who your personal escort through the process was, and a comment card for any feedback and ideas we might incorporate into our future services. This is how I would run my funeral parlor.

While the viewing continues, following the elderly couple who took a tumble and, shaken, went on their way home again, Greg Stacy and I wait for who might show up next. It isn't until well after lunch that Sister Three arrives, announcing herself at the door in a boisterous fashion, unsettling the peace and quiet we had settled into for most of the morning.

My adult nephews from Sister Two are already here keeping us company in silence, tucked slightly out of Sister Three's view. She finally turns around from the sign-in book to greet me with her fake smile and her fake hug. I am lassoed by her robustness, which pulls me in to her plume of heavy perfume that reeks like something made popular in the '80s, a thick combination of cinnamon and bark, and as I am caught in her swirl she presumes to give me advice.

"Sister dear, I am hear to tell you, don't sell the house. It's a down market. You should just live in it," she says, setting her wild blue eyes on me as if she hardly recognizes me. After all, it has been two decades since her eyes were last cast upon me.

I tell her that the plan is indeed to sell the house within the year since it will take some time to prepare it, and that my goal is not to live in it indefinitely since it is the major asset and I am sure the siblings will want their portions. I also find a way to finally muster up the courage to retaliate for all the years of condescension she has tried to rain down on me by lobbing one parting remark: "*Sister*. You're throwing that term around loosely, don't you think?"

To which she can only reply, "Well, *acquaintance* is perhaps better," and out of my peripheral vision I can see my two nephews bracing themselves for a cat fight, pleased that at least I am willing to make a stand on behalf of their mother, Sister Two. Even though she may not be anything like me, and we may not ever be close, she is more of a sister to me than Sister Three ever tried to be.

By evening, Sister Two has trickled in within the last hour of the time we have scheduled. At least she has made it. We all know what it is like to wait for this sister. She has spent a lifetime being late for everything, including both weddings—hers and mine.

Brothers One and Two slipped in earlier and left after a while. I still have no idea why Brother Two's wife was crying so dramatically. They saw my mom only a handful of times over the entire five years I have been back. Neither Greg nor I has forgotten Brother Two's episode of screaming at me in March, so I keep a polite distance, hoping we can all just get through the day by faking whatever we have to in order to keep the peace.

My dad would be so disappointed to know the family has turned out so differently from what he and my mother had hoped. I think he would be ashamed that my siblings could not extend themselves more to help their mother. I think he would be sick to know that we all get equal shares of the estate he left behind according to how he and my mother set up the trust. At least I am sickened to know this is the case. So be it.

With today's viewing concluded and the drama contained, the next day will be spent at the gravesite two hours away, for family only. Sister Three doesn't come. She makes up some excuse at the last minute about having a conflict with her husband's uncle, who is coincidentally being buried the same day, which is where she will be instead. I think in the hierarchy the unwritten law states one's own mother will always trump the uncle of a husband.

Our clergyman has been out of town for the holiday week and returned very late last night. He, of course, will be happy to make the two-hour trek to the cemetery early this morning to deliver a few words of prayer, said his wife in her phone message to me a week ago. I was not sure I wanted to put him out. It felt like such an imposition to ask someone to travel so far after having just driven five hours the night before, but he insisted, and I relented.

Now I am glad I did, because I can't imagine how the service would have gone if he had not been present to conduct it, giving my mother the proper spiritual send-off befitting a woman who was faithful her entire life. I don't know how I even considered for a moment that it would be too much trouble to ask him to participate in this important service.

Once the family all has a chance to say whatever few words they can manage to get out of their hearts, it is done. The luncheon I host at a nearby restaurant gives those who are on speaking terms a chance to collude at the opposite end of the table from where I sit with my nephews and Greg. The brothers have been trying to forge a bond, and it looks less awkward today than I imagined it might be. I see the proverbial water rushing under the bridge. Maybe they can heal after today.

# CHAPTER 37

# Communications Binder

The reason, I think, these services went so smoothly is the advance work I did within the first twenty-four hours of our mother's passing. After speaking to each sibling, I took time to carefully carve out a road map so they and I were all on the same page. It included the plans for the services that I sent in an e-mail to the safest point person I could rely on for distributing the information: my adult nephew. His instructions were first to forward this e-mail to each of the family members I had listed on his mother's side then to connect personally with them as a follow-up. He did not let me down.

This e-mail was organized into three main topics. The first was the obituary, with the dates of when the local newspaper would be carrying it, how long it would be made available online for free, and a directive to pick up enough copies of said newspaper to distribute to family members as keepsakes.

The second topic provided details for the viewing with the where and when, and with phone number of the mortuary listed. I explained that this viewing would take the place of a formal funeral service and that friends and family were invited to come and pay their last respects and were free to sit as long as they like in the pews to offer silent prayers. I provided directions and made sure they knew flowers could be sent directly to the funeral home.

I reminded them that there would be no specific time the family needed to arrive, but the funeral doors would be closing at seven o'clock that evening. I made sure they knew that Greg and I would be there all day and, while no reception would be following, I did invite everyone in the family to join us for the lunch I would be hosting at the restaurant near the burial site the next day.

The third and final topic was entitled "The Burial". It held details of many questions I anticipated. Along with date, time, and location, I provided insight into the rules of a military burial. This very brief ceremony would be closed-casket and held in a small chapel, not at the gravesite because of the military restrictions that would have to be enforced while the plot was open.

There would be no admittance to see my father's grave, where my mother was to be lowered into the ground to join him, until after 4:00 p.m., when the burial had already taken place. I went on to note that the headstone would be revised to add a line of my mother's information beneath my father's line; in the month it would take to prepare this, a temporary marker holds its place.

This e-mail was simple and clearly delineated, and it alleviated a lot of headaches from people asking for clarification because I already anticipated their questions. There was nothing left to be asked. The plans were set, the invitations were made, and the family got together peacefully for a lunch honoring my parents in a way that would have made them pleased.

Once we leave the restaurant and the business of burying our mother is behind me, the rest of the plan needs to be put into place. I will not return when school resumes after winter break. I have arranged for my favorite substitute to stay for the month of January so I can catch my breath and gird myself for what is ahead as trustee. But, rather than lick my wounds and sleep away the heaviness that makes me feel like I am wading through quicksand, I instead become inundated with the phone calls and paperwork that propels me into estate management.

The first piece of business as the trustee is to start your own binder system to stay organized. Keep all of your loose paperwork easily retrievable in a moment's notice, filed away behind tab dividers with categories that make sense. The impression you want to establish with those you come into contact with is that you are prepared. You want your paperwork to be easily retrievable when making those time-consuming phone calls to people who are difficult to reach because they might be in different time zones.

My binder system will be an essential part of maintaining my sanity. There are three that I will refer to religiously while I carry out my duties as trustee. The first is binder one, labeled "Communications." Here I keep a running log of my communications with the principal players with whom I will be in regular contact. The best way to keep track of conversations is to start a new sheet for each professional or company you will be speaking with often. For instance, on a single sheet of paper I write the name of my accountant in the top right corner along with his phone number, e-mail, and address. Every conversation I have with this person begins with the date and time listed on my first line, followed by notes on what we speak about. Ideally your concise note-taking will allow you the room for two columns to the right: one for your to-do's, the other for their to-do's to help you keep track of next steps.

The people I need to communicate with on a regular basis are divided into tabs inside binder one. I have three categories: accountant, attorney, and siblings. There will be other binders used for people holding our assets, but this is covered later on in the chapter. Behind each corresponding tab, I file copies of correspondence I mail out, including e-mails and their replies, and keep documentation of phone conversations as the first page I see when I flip to that section.

Filing papers in reverse chronological order with the most-recent activity on top and being sure every piece of paper is three-hole punched will make your future business seamless. Avoid the habit of stuffing loose documents into side pouches because the first time you drop your binder—and you will—anything not on the rings will go spilling across your hardwood floors. A two-inch binder will see you through the duration of managing your estate for the next three years or so.

Lest you think I am overzealous in my organization, here is the most relevant scenario I can provide as to why keeping track of conversations can become so critical for you. Every professional I meet prepares me for, as they say, the inevitable worst that comes out in family members whenever money is involved. They tell me fights can ensue over who gets what, and the long-held resentments of imagined or not-so-imagined favoritism begin to bubble up to the surface.

While our family has had a trust in place for decades, I am reminded that this does not cover the property inside the house. For years my mother was openly vocal about her wishes as to which kid would be inheriting which china pattern and who would get her prized blue vase. Whether we are interested in it or not, it will become ours to unload if we so desired. So I expect my next e-mail to my siblings, about tagging and retrieving the personal property in the house, to go off without a hitch. However, this e-mail will cause a stir before the chapter ends and makes me glad I started keeping track of conversations I had with individual siblings early in my process.

My message outlines the four phases we will be moving through over the course of this first year. Phase one is for tying up loose ends on the burial now behind us. I remind them that the new headstone will be ready by March and invite them to come by the house to visit our mother's room, which I have turned into a shrine. All the photo-gallery posters from the viewing are spread around next to tables of cards addressed to our family. I want my siblings to find comfort in knowing how beloved she was by her friends.

Phase two is for legal. I inform my siblings we will all be receiving letters from the attorney within the next month advising us of the next steps per our mom's wishes since there were many meetings held behind closed doors with my mother and her attorney that I was not privy to.

Phase three is for real estate. As I prepare to put the house on the market this year, I inform my siblings, they should plan to meet on two specified dates: they will first come to tag the items they want on March 5 then bring them home on April 2. Whatever is left unclaimed will be donated the following week. The idea of running a rummage sale for curious neighbors and passersby to snub their noses at stuff that holds no real value to them is not how I want to be tortured. To me this junk is filled with achingly personal nostalgia.

For the first tagging date in March, I give my siblings a window of time to be here and tell them lunch will be served.

For the items that are up for grabs, I do an inventory of the house room by room so we are all reminded of what is here and give everyone the chance to reflect upon which of these items holds the most significance to them.

I issue one color of sticky dots to each sibling so they can tag any possessions that are not already reserved for them on the "Items to Inherit" list, which I also attach to the e-mail I send out about the phases. I give a caveat for siblings wanting the same item to work it out peacefully. I finish this message with a chart delineating every single item that, according to our mother's wishes, we already know we are to inherit.

For the retrieval date in April, I advise my siblings to bring trucks large enough to accommodate the personal items I saved from their childhoods when I purged the house. They will take home the oversized gray crates and two bankers boxes stuffed with photos kept in Mom's closet drawers plus report cards she saved from our school years. I end with an invitation to join Greg and me for lunch on this day and a reminder to bring extra boxes to hold the hanging wall art, recipe books, or books from the library shelves in our living room that they tag in March.

Phase four will be dedicated to memorabilia. Beyond the small photo albums from our childhoods that I plan to scan and duplicate into hardbound memory books so we can each have the same set, I find some priceless treasures I just know we would all love to keep. There are legal pads of Mom's writings, much about her life, and some letters to each of us through our younger years, and there are film reels I have begun transferring to digital formats. I tell my siblings that if they can be patient, my goal is for them to have wonderful gifts of memories before Christmas.

With this one e-mail, I unearth the wrath of Sister Two. The timing is coincidentally such that we have all received copies of the official trust, and she is not at all happy that the loan extended to her against her inheritance was not forgiven as she hoped. In a livid state, she e-mails her reply to me, saying that I have had some hand in her undoing. She rationalizes that because I was there with our mom in the end, I must have changed things in the trust. Aside from the fact that I was not on the scene when her loan was initiated, legally I didn't have the power to change my mother's wishes in her last years.

She insists that our mom told her the loan would be forgiven and uses every word in the book she can think of—and she thinks of them all—to describe me. She says I have ruined her life and robbed her blind. Sadly for her, copies of her signature accepting the loan against her inheritance were also entered into the trust for all to see. The loan is not going away no matter how much wishful thinking she has done.

Does she show up on tagging day? No. Do I repeatedly call her in the days approaching to remind her? Yes. All she keeps saying is that I have ruined everything and she doesn't care about whatever stuff is left in the house; she only wants her money.

Does she come for retrieval day? No. Do I leave multiple messages reminding her and send e-mails trying to get confirmation that she will be here to get what our mom wanted her to have? Yes. Communication has shut down. She is not coming. I finally realize this after everyone else has come and gone from getting their items and lunch has already been put away. No word from her.

There is not much I can do to extend to her any more time. Plans have been made to evacuate the house to prepare it for market. Greg is looking for rentals while we are hurriedly packing. We will be out in thirty days, and the house needs to be bare.

So, I call my adult nephew who helped me communicate funeral arrangements to that side of the family. He drops everything, calls his brother, and makes plans to drive their big truck to haul away their mother's contents the next morning. They drive two hours each way to help me make sure their mother gets what is intended for her plus everything else that we can fit into that monster truck.

With ropes and pads, we stuff and ply mirror after mirror, crate after crate, box after box and add in all the fragile pieces of china we can hold in the backseat. I am so grateful they made haste in coming. I am so appreciative that I can count on them to rearrange their weekend plans to help me.

Their mother's next e-mail to me is scathing. She tells me that I managed to squeeze her out of everything. She makes up several excuses as to why she couldn't come for tagging or retrieving—all false as I know the lame truth of what kept her away—and she isn't happy with what her sons were able to cart home for her, referring to the china that has been in our family for three generations as "dishes I don't want." These are the travails of Sister Two.

Sister Three also rears her ugly little head and nearly makes mine spin. She decides not to come on the day that the other siblings will be at the house tagging and retrieving, so we set up a separate time for her to come privately to load her car. She is very pleasant when I give her a tour of the home she has not been to for at least ten years. She is surprised by how clean it is because she remembers it only from its early days of being filled with junk—the junk that has taken me five years to unload so my mother could enjoy a fresh home free of tripping hazards.

Sister Three pores through glass cabinets in the breakfront where all the china figurines and tea sets that were too good ever to bring out in my lifetime sit on shelves too high for little hands to touch. They hold special memories for her, and even though they aren't on the designated list of "Items to Inherit," she is here to take what she wants, and I am happy to give it to her. I don't want it, and Sister Two has forfeited a chance to claim anything else.

Once our nice reunion is finished, Sister Three has bundled up so much that her cargo car can't carry it all. It takes Greg and her husband two attempts at packing and repacking before the doors will all close and the trunk can be tied down.

It takes only a week for my attorney to call me with the news that Sister Three has made a claim against me.

Her version is that when she got to my mother's house, the entire place had been cleaned out—that there was nothing in fact left for her to retrieve. She wants an inventory of household items that were retrieved by other family members and a list of which items were donated. She believes that all of the household items have gone to me. I don't get it. When she was here, she seemed so sympathetic to me. She even agreed that indeed no one had helped me in the years when I cared for our mother.

From this conversation with the attorney, I decide it is best to craft a letter in my defense, explaining the history prior to the claims, and to provide copies of letters and e-mails I sent to both sisters. I want to provide assurance that I have covered my bases as diligently as my legal duty bound me to, but it takes painstaking hours to write it all out. Fortunately nothing more ever comes of these scenarios.

This is why it is so important for you to keep a communication log. It will be worth your time in the end to carve out these minutes upfront, getting details jotted down as conversations take place. You never, ever know when someone's misperception of their misfortune is going to be lobbed against you since you are the only living person to defend those last wishes.

CHAPTER 38

# Estate Assets Binder

Binder one—Communications—soon becomes filled with more of the same copious notes I have been taking with siblings. Now I am detailing what needs to get done from my phone calls with the estate attorney, the accountant, and the many financial institutions that require every single account naming me as the successor trustee to be revised accordingly before they will give me any information.

Your binder system will save you from many headaches in the role of trustee because it will allow you to be readily able to access the last conversation notes or the recent financial statement being discussed or the follow-up questions you prepared. You don't want to have to hang up when someone finally comes on the line because you need to spend more time scouring your drawers for that misplaced paper.

Plus, I find that flipping through pages in a binder is a lot easier than digging through files kept in drawers, which is quite cumbersome when you have a business call placed on hold.

Besides, when you attend meetings with your estate team

of attorneys and accountants, a binder is very portable and makes you look like you are amply prepared. This will help your credibility in the new role of someone who is shouldering the tremendous job of carrying out the wishes of the deceased.

Within a couple more weeks, I realize that one binder is not enough to store all the legal documents that I am to carry to banks and investment houses to ensure I am indeed the correct person. I have three inches of papers showing the original will for each of my parents, their trust, and the durable power of attorney plus letters from my estate attorney arming me with enough credibility to show I am the one with the legal authority to make financial decisions.

Would you believe I am still treated like a cat burglar by many bank managers? I sit for two hours in some places, even worse asked to return in a couple of days, until I can jump through several hoops of different layers of verification that finally allow them to believe the information they are parting with is safe in my hands.

Binder two—Estate Assets—is created because your system must expand with your needs. It is set up much like the Communication binder, however this one is reserved only for paperwork pertaining to the financial institutions where you are doing business. Every place must have a tab divider created for it. Again, be sure the first paper you see behind each tab is the communication log sheet for that company so you have a good record of the many, many conversations you will surely be having before this account is cashed out and closed.

Behind your communications log sheet, file any current statements you are receiving, and keep them in reverse chronological order with the most-recent dates filed on top. To make your filing even easier, be sure to alphabetize all of your tabs. Preplan how many tabs you will need, and don't forget that you may be selling your home soon, so prepare a tab in advance with the name of your street.

Also do not forget that you will need categories for the IRS and for safe-deposit boxes if your family owned any. My greatest adventure in managing my family's estate has been traipsing around to various financial institutions within two to twenty miles of our hometown on a scavenger hunt to find out what contents, if any, still remain in safe deposit boxes that haven't been active in decades. The even greater challenge comes from scouring through a house of drawers for unmarked keys to unlock these safe-deposit boxes. I have to think like Depression-era parents to find keys that are tucked tightly inside an empty Hershey's cocoa tin underneath old nightgowns in my mom's dresser. Only a few of the keys are labeled. The remaining thirty are copies of keys we had for cars we sold when I was in my teens and spares of house keys for locks that were changed eons ago. The keys with unrecognizable shapes are my best clues that these might be the ones I need to open the boxes after all.

Sadly, after all of the effort it takes to match the key to the right financial institution, whereupon I need to return for a second or third time with proper identifying paperwork that can only be satisfied with more copies my attorney needs to make of a half-inch-thick swath of legal documents, the box is empty.

My points are twofold when it comes to safe-deposit boxes. First, keep your keys to the box visible in your Estate Assets binder, which I will explain how to create before this chapter ends; second, don't have so many safe-deposit boxes just because every financial institution offers you a free one for your first year if you open a new checking account today. It will be easier on survivors if you have ten at the same institution. Even stealth spies like Jason Bourne only need one safe-deposit box to hold a slew of fake passports for changing identities on a whim and enough currency to avoid the need for a stop at the bank when slipping into international territory.

Most importantly, be sure to file in these tabbed sections copies of any correspondence you have mailed out to these financial institutions. If you do not have a personal letterhead, make one on your computer that states your name at the top with your new title of executor and trustee for the trust, naming it exactly as it is written, along with your address, phone number, and e-mail address. Underscore this information with a big, bold line to separate where you will begin the body of your letter, and you will look like you take your job seriously.

In addition to the tabs you created for your accounts, be sure to include more for your bank account and investment houses. A tip for you: create a second tab for the bank and call it "New Tax ID Account" because if both of your parents are now deceased, the Social Security number of the last surviving parent will soon be expiring, and an entirely new federal tax ID number will be issued and used in its place forever more. This will make your sorting more simplified when looking for the correct bank statements you will need to provide to attorneys and accountants in the coming years.

Considering your fiduciary role as trustee obligates you to create an accounting prior to the year's end of all expenses for the estate, you will want to be organized. Your accounting will need to list in microscopic detail every penny that was spent from the estate and every penny that was deposited into the estate—literally every penny. The more work you do upfront, the less time it will take you to account for your estate assets, which you are legally required to do for the beneficiaries and for the IRS.

Binder two—Estate Assets—will need two additional tabs before you are done planning your categories. One is called "Expense Reports," which is where I keep copies of reimbursed expenses that go to me or to Greg for anything related to the estate. When preparing a home for sale, which can be a nightmare in itself, instead of writing estate checks all over town including on your many stops at Home Depot, it makes more sense to pay as you go. Hang on to those receipts that come out of your own pocket, labeling each one with the reason for the expense, then reimburse yourself at the end of the month from the estate. If you have not accumulated a lot of expenses, you can go three months before you write that reimbursement check.

The point is, keep exceptionally detailed notes on your receipts, and do not lose any original receipts, or you will not get reimbursed. I tape my receipts onto blank paper and then number them in sequential order corresponding to a spreadsheet I use. I create columns for the date of receipt, the receipt number, the place of business, the amount, and the reason for the expense. I staple this spreadsheet as a cover for the receipts that are affixed to the multiple pages beneath and turn this in to the attorney's office so there is a copy on record and all spending is transparent.

The second required tab is kept at the front of my binder because it is that important. It is called "Accounting," and this is where the year-end accounting is filed. Once I submit my work product to the attorney, the process of triple checking my math, matching the expenses against the receipts, and categorizing each of the expenditures for legal accounting begins. When I have passed inspection, the official copy of what the attorney has reconfigured into a legal balance sheet gets filed on top of the copy I kept of my original work.

All in all my Assets binder has about fifteen tab dividers. This all fits into a two-inch binder, but I am stretched to capacity, and an upgrade of a third inch would probably be better. You will discover your needs as you go. But it will take you a fraction of the time it took me because you are benefiting from my experiences—she says hopefully.

# CHAPTER 39

# Legal Documents Binder

Binder three—Legal Docs—contains all of the original documents that need to be turned over to the estate attorney, who will keep originals and return copies to you. Do not separate pages from the documents; leave them how they are originally stapled. Do not lose sets of documents that are part of a succession either. Every change that is made to a will gets reflected in a separate document called a *codicil*, which needs to travel with its companion, the original will.

There are four essential documents you legally need to have in place in order to protect your assets and to ensure your wishes—both financial and medical—will be carried out beyond your death. The first is your will. A will decides who will receive your assets after you die. A will is important for naming guardians for your children and an executor trustee for managing your estate. A will can be used for naming your beneficiaries, who are family members, or friends, or charitable organizations that may receive either your money or your possessions.

Typically you will need to create a separate list of valuable items that are not named in your will, as property usually isn't, so that if you intend for your friend Eleanor to have your button collection there will be no dispute from anyone else. In a will you are also able to list separate bank accounts for special loved ones where you would like to set aside money that will be transferred on your death; if you were to name them as beneficiaries, you would unintentionally give them decision-making power on your behalf, thus making your surviving spouse beholden to them.

If you do not have a will, in the state of California where I live your estate will be distributed in the courts through probate, which requires a court-appointed time to prove that you are the executor. This means that all monies are tied up until a decision is made as to how assets should be distributed. This also means that someone will have to pay out of pocket for expenses the estate is incurring while awaiting a judgment.

Think about the monthly costs of running the household including a mortgage, property taxes, attorney and accountant fees, and realtor fees, and determine if this is an affordable amount for someone to pay for the several months or longer it will take the courts to decide. If the cost seems too high for the family members left behind to pool together, a trust avoids the necessity of court intervention because you avoid probate altogether since all named assets move directly to their designations upon your death.

More importantly, if you do not have a will and you are unmarried without any children, your assets will go to your parents; if they are deceased, your assets will go to your siblings. This one line is enough for me to get my own legal documents in place with both a will and a trust because if something happens to my husband and me at the same time, I do not wish for my inheritance, which is not subject to community property laws, to be redistributed to my siblings.

Keep in mind there are many ways assets can be rerouted to beneficiaries of a person who dies without a will in place. Depending on if you are married or not, have children or not, and have living relatives or not, the money will go to the next living kin, and this is why there is always some poor sap at the end of a hard-luck story who winds up getting money from a fourth cousin he never knew existed. Happy endings are not just for the movies. If you do not name your heirs in a will, the government will name them for you.

The second document you should have in place is a trust. This is different from a will in that your will is the first set of instructions for where to move your assets when you die; if you have specified that your assets should move into your living trust, then your existing will becomes known as your "pour-over will," allowing all of your assets to spill into your trust.

A trust skips the middleman, avoiding probate altogether and moving the process of distributing monies along almost immediately. The only thing that takes time in getting that first distribution check written is determining where all of the assets are actually held. If you have a trust, you will name your property in it so instead of your home being listed with just its address, like "66 Monroe Street," the revised deed will be titled with your family's name along with the date the trust was created, like "The Johnson Family Trust—January 2, 1997, 66 Monroe Street." If you have a trust, you will rename your checking and savings accounts with the "Johnson Family Trust—January 2, 1997" title so the executor can continue to write checks for bills without any interruption.

The third legal document you need is a durable power of attorney for finances. This legal form permits the person you name as executor to make decisions on your behalf when it comes to your finances. This is a formal, multipage oath that the executor assumes in good faith. I read the whole document. It scares me. There is a lot of legal responsibility for the executor, who is under a microscope and beholden to the beneficiaries, who are seeking transparency at all times with regard to the accounting. I make sure to dot my I's and cross my T's every step of the way.

I also discover very early on—luckily, saving me from making a horrible mistake later—that if you distribute all of the money from the estate at once to the beneficiaries, and the IRS performs an audit of the estate determining that you owe money to the government, it is solely the personal financial responsibility of the executor to pay this bill.

If you think you will have an easy time retrieving monies that have already been dispersed to beneficiaries, then you have nothing to worry about. In my case I have reserves on hand in the bank until four years from the time of my mother's date of death have passed, which is the duration for the statute of limitations on an audit of an estate of a deceased person.

The fourth legal document you need is a durable power of attorney for health; in California, we call it the "advance health-care directive." This document allows the specific person named to make health-care decisions for you when you can no longer make them for yourself. It should also contain your wishes concerning life-sustaining treatment, other health-care issues, organ donation, burial instructions, and your funeral. This will be quite uncomfortable to think about today when you are healthy, but it will save those you are leaving behind from immeasurable grief because they will never have to wonder what your wishes are.

When my mother passed away, I was not only managing her life but, in effect, my father's life as well because both were now deceased. I needed to obtain legal documents for each of them. A will is only for an individual, not a couple. Therefore I needed to find the original will for my father plus the original will for my mother. I also needed every single codicil that was ever created to amend those wills, and I needed to have them in chronological order.

I needed a copy of the trust and all of the changes that had been made to it over decades. These changes were listed at the top of documents named "amendments" and "restatements of the trust." These too had to be in sequential order. I had a copy of the advance health-care directive in my legal documents binder; the original was hanging on the wall above my mother's bed ever since hospice entered the picture. The durable power of attorney for finances also needed to be filed in this Legal Docs binder along with the death certificates for my father and my mother.

I found what helped me the most was to have my attorney put in order all of the amendments to the trust and codicils to the will, then I went back to the office-supply store for more tab dividers and a bigger binder. A two-inch binder was not roomy enough, so I opted for a three-inch instead. I filed all of my legal papers accordingly behind tabs placed in this order: death certificate for mother, death certificate for father, power of attorney for finances, power of attorney for health, amendments to trust, trust document, codicils to wills, will for mother, will for father. This equals nine tab dividers.

Within each of these nine sections, I used clear-plastic

sheet protectors to store the individual documents because I found early on that it was easy to get papers out of order; I had no idea what codicil went where because I am not an attorney, and it is hard to understand the language on headings sometimes. So I wrote a header in permanent marker on the top right corner of each sheet protector.

This made the process of re-sorting so much simpler, especially since I was making multiple trips to banks that asked to make copies of each of my documents. This way I knew if my sheet protector was still empty, the bank manager had not returned the original document to me because it was still on the Xerox machine. This happened once. It would not happen twice. At my insistence the representative at another investment institution allowed me to join him in the copy room so I could watch that the nearly one hundred-page document he removed from my binder was actually being returned to me in its entirety. It will save you many headaches down the road to be organized.

This entire process of managing my family's estate leaves a nagging voice in my head urging me to get my own estate planned. It will be so much work, I know, and I don't have the time to spare while I am still in school. I don't have time in the summer when I am selling the house. I don't have time in the fall when I am finishing memory books for my siblings. I put it off until I can't put it off any longer.

When I finally do follow through with my promptings two weeks before Greg and I return to Hawaii, three years after the last time we were suddenly called home, I put together a very comprehensive estate plan intended to guide my successor trustee easily in the event that Greg and I both go down with the plane. In a three-inch binder, I have twelve tab dividers with the following categories.

The first tab is titled "Instructions to Husband," wherein I have written a love letter to my sweetheart who, no doubt, will be saddened by my demise. I have remembered to capture some specific moments here from our history together that should bring a smile and give him permission to live out his days in whatever manner will bring him happiness. I also attach a seven-page letter of instruction to help him navigate his way through every area of my life that will require decision making.

Within my letter of instructions, I create subject headings with bullet-point directives for each. The first subject is "Medical Matters" with contact info for my primary physician, the location of my advance health-care directive, and additional details of the care I do and do not want. I also list my health-insurance information.

In the event my husband dies with me, there is a separate letter addressed to my successor trustee, who has already been advised of where to find the master documents.

The second subject within my instructions is "Funeral Matters," wherein I specifically spell out the plan I would like to have followed along with the location of my original will and where charitable donations should be made in lieu of flowers. I also have instructions pertaining to the video will I have created and who should be in attendance for its viewing.

The third subject is "Legal Matters," reminding Greg that all the legal docs he needs to prove he is my successor trustee are filed inside my estate binder. There are also instructions for how to proceed if I die before I have closed out my family's estate, contact information for the estate attorney, and where all of the estate files are kept.

The fourth subject is "Financial Matters." In it the contact information for my accountant is listed along with the location of the safe-deposit boxes I keep and where the keys are. I have listed my financial accounts, the institutions where they are held, and phone numbers for the bank managers I have relationships with plus my pension details.

Most importantly I have listed the location for passwords to my accounts and where to find information stored on electronic devices. I explain where pending bills are kept and where IRS returns are stored. I also make note of the TOD ("transferred on death") account I have set up for assets to be transferred to individuals named on that account. This separate savings account is designated for certain people whom I wish to receive money from my estate without naming them as beneficiaries, which would legally complicate matters for my husband.

The fifth subject is "Literary Matters," since I am a published author, including how to distribute any remaining inventory I hold and what to do with drafts of unpublished projects.

The sixth category is "Personal Matters" wherein I have listed updated contact info for beneficiaries and friends along with instructions for viewing the video I want them to see.

The seventh category is "Property Matters," which deals with real estate, jewelry, clothing, furnishings, family photo books, classroom curricula, artwork I have created, electronics I own, and my automobile. All of these areas are delineated with specific instructions as to who gets what.

The eighth and final category is called "Professional Matters," and in it I identify my place of employment and the names of my boss and my human-resources contact.

The very last page is a list of the contents in my safe-deposit boxes.

The complete twelve tabs looks like this: "Letter of Instruction to Husband"; "Letter of Instruction to Successor"; "Letter of Instruction to Wife" because my husband figures since I am already organized with a binder, he will put his letter here for me in case he goes first; "Communications with Estate Attorney"; "Communications with Accountant"; "Trust"; "Will"; "Power of Attorney—Financial"; "Power of Attorney—Health"; "Property Distributions"; "TOD Gifts," or the funds I want transferred to individuals upon my death; and finally "Safe-Deposit Boxes," where I have kept another copy of the list of contents.

I was such a nervous wreck at the prospect of traveling over the ocean because I had not put any of these instructions onto paper. It compelled me to get it done, and within the two weeks it took to accomplish I am now able to sleep peacefully again knowing that if our plane does go down, the people who need to know will be informed.

I make sure my dear friend who is my second successor trustee behind my husband receives a love letter of sorts for the kind of friend she has been to me along with a simple note that tells her where to find the seven-page list of instructions in my house and how to access my house if I never return from that vacation. Sure, it makes her laugh because she believes travel by air is the safest kind. But it brings me tremendous peace of mind to know I have all my ducks in a row.

Either I have just made you a nervous wreck too thinking about how much there is to be done, or I have brought you a tremendous sense of peace because you know that you have a pretty good guide to follow for getting it all organized within the next month. Think of it like a book report, the kind you hated doing in high school. Break it down into manageable chunks and plug away. Your family will be grateful you did. And the surest rule of karma is that when it's in place, it won't be needed.

# PART 9

# GRIEF COUNSELING

## REALITY 9
### *Do Everything You Can to Self-Soothe, but Include Grief Counseling; You Need It More Than You Think*

# CHAPTER 40

# Depression

Many people have heard of the five stages of grief—the different emotions categorizing your pain after a loss. These are not necessarily experienced in any particular order, and you may not hit all five on your path to healing. The stages are denial, anger, bargaining, depression, and acceptance. While the original study was done with terminal patients chronicling their feelings about their impending deaths, the grief stages are widely applied to many of us who have hit hard times. The loss of a job or a marriage or the death of a loved one or a pet can be a trigger for setting in place emotions you never knew you had.

I never felt denial or anger because I was so grateful that I got to be with my mother in the last years of her life. I never had time to go through the bargaining phase because so much of what was unfolding in front of me felt like crisis management. I didn't feel I had the luxury to slow down. I was busy preparing financially for a decline that could be a long one, taking years perhaps. I had no idea what to expect, and hospice gave up trying to make predictions that my mother kept outliving. I only learned what I learned from hindsight— our best teacher.

My grief jumps right into depression. I am so very depleted after my mother's death that I can hardly hold my eyes open. The smartest decision I make is to take off the month of January from school. I rely on one of my favorite subs to interpret the lesson plans I have simplified and e-mailed to him over winter break for the novel he will be teaching. I cannot return to my students. I am so weary, all I want to do is sleep, but no amount of rest I get is enough. I can sleep for eighteen hours and still feel as though a Mack truck has hit me when I awaken.

But these are my good days, when sleep numbs the pain. The other part of my sleep problem is the anxiety that keeps me awake on other nights when the enormous busy-ness of managing my mother's estate plays over and over in my mind. It is drowning out my grieving heart. I am not taking the time I need to care for me. I am not exercising. I am not eating right; I am eating wrong. Anything that tastes like comfort goes into my mouth.

I love to bake. Gooey, chocolaty desserts are my first tier of go-tos when I am sad. So I bake almost every night. Sometimes I start to cry when I simply turn on the oven. Greg asks me what is wrong, and I tell him I can still hear my mother's voice bellowing proudly, "My daughter bakes the best brownies!" It is her voice in my head silencing all other thoughts that keeps her close to me yet levels me at the same time.

This is another reason why I cannot sleep. I am down the hall, two doors away from an empty room where I have built a shrine to my mother. The lovely cards from her friends for our family are not what make me so forlorn. It is walking by the stillness of a room that once beckoned to me to come to it several times throughout the night. In those hours, when the quiet felt more ominous than comforting, my first steps toward her bed were always filled with trepidation because checking for signs of life was a job I couldn't get used to. There is no greater dread than this, which is why it would become Greg's routine before every dawn.

My only exit path to the front of the house is the hallway leading me by her room before I can turn the corner, pretending I can start another new day without her. This slow path bringing me to her door fills my eyes with visions I have seen a hundred times before. I still see my mother's face in front of me, her head tilted just enough to look through the little bars on the rail of her bed like a toddler peeking through the slats of her crib, hoping to make a connection with someone who will carry her out. It is getting to be too much for me.

I decide to call the lovely doctor who treated my mother years earlier, when one more fall landed her in the emergency clinic on a Sunday afternoon. Dr. Vita Patel is in the right profession. She made my mother feel so tenderly cared for that I know I want to have her as my own doctor because any time I ever see my physician, who was randomly assigned to me, I feel the complete opposite. I have kept Dr. Patel's card for nearly three years, and when I do finally make the call, I am completely disheartened to find that her service has been closed to new patients for more than a year now.

It figures—once I finally have the time to look after myself, it turns out I have waited too long. Looking after my mother was always my first priority; now who is going to look after me? I learned a long time ago through a successful career in sales that if you don't like the first answer you hear, find a different person to ask. When this approach ultimately leads me to Dr. Patel's voicemail, the best I can do is to leave a heartfelt message with as much detail as I can fit into sixty seconds.

Fortunately Dr. Patel calls me back within a half hour to say that any patient who values the care of a physician this much is the kind of patient she would love to have. She sets my first appointment for the same week. In her office she pulls up a stool, puts down her chart, looks squarely into my eyes, and simply asks me how I am.

I begin to cry right there. I sob and sob and tell her I want to sleep, that I could crawl beneath this portable bed and sleep undisturbed for the rest of the day. I don't remember if I have brushed my hair this morning. I am pretty sure any lip gloss I attempted to put on earlier has already smeared from the Kleenex I am rubbing against my face. I am still wearing the black cashmere turtleneck sweater my mother bought me because I can't ever seem to get warm and because it matches the black wool cape sweater that used to be hers when she was once twice my size, before she shrank to half of what I am.

I like wearing key pieces from her wardrobe because I feel her arms are wrapped around me. I stay like this for many, many weeks. Depression is my uniform. It makes it so much simpler to decide what to wear when I have only a couple of black, oversize sweaters to choose between. I didn't keep much from her closet for myself. What could fit them was given away to Sister Two and Elizabeth. There were many days and nights while waiting for her hallucinations to break when I had hours to stare into my mother's closet, calculating its contents' fate. I had a plan for how I would attack her possessions, clearing the racks as fast as I could, like ripping off a Band-Aid to avoid the sting.

Dr. Patel gently asks me about what happened, and I explain that I cared for my mother in the last five years of her life, and she just passed away a few weeks ago. There is some relief in sight now because when I tell her I am not sleeping, she says we can try prescription medication, but she will want to check in with me regularly for the next few months to see how it is working—or not working.

I really appreciate the interest she takes in me. I feel like a little orphan being taken in by a kind lady who will feed and clothe me and give me pills to help me feel better. I thought the only doctors who insisted on regular follow-up appointments when meds were issued were psychiatrists, so I am pleasantly surprised to know that this doctor insists on building a rapport with patients who seem like they are on the verge of a break-down. She has other recommendations for me including what to start eating and exercise I should begin gently incorporating into my schedule. I am really looking forward to seeing Dr. Patel again in two weeks.

I keep my appointment for the next visit, and even though I haven't made any progress on exercise or eating, I am beginning to sleep better. When she asks how I am functioning now that I have returned to school, I explain that I am the master at compartmentalizing. I get through the day pretty successfully so long as none of my colleagues tries to show me any compassion by asking how I am doing. Then, as soon as the bell rings, I want to go home so I can pet the cat and cry for the rest of the afternoon.

It becomes my way. After Greg walks through the door, usually to find me sound asleep in my skirt if I haven't managed to change into pajamas by four o'clock, he lets me rest until I am awakened by smells of the dinner he is cooking in the kitchen. Sometimes it's not until nine when I hear the rustle of him getting ready for bed that I realize I have slept away another afternoon. On the evenings when I am awake before dinner, he is happy to see that I am interested in food. He is even happier to sit with me for the little while it takes before I determine I am simply too exhausted for conversation and head back to bed again.

This is my routine. It has been four months since I lost my mother, and spring is here. The sun is shining, and I am numb. Over Easter break my eldest adult nephew calls to check on me. He is old enough to have been a good traveling companion for my mother when she had the itch to go abroad. They had a wonderful bond, and mostly she enjoyed the fact that she had a strapping, young grandson to push her around the airport in a rented wheelchair so she could get places faster and cut to the front of the lines easier.

He sounds genuinely worried that I am having a hard time with the loss of Grandma. When he hears my voice breaking beneath the false pretense I am trying to keep up for him, he says, "Aunt Fanny, it's okay. You took great care of Grandma, and she loved everything you did for her."

I cry harder. I tell him I am not really doing that well. I tell him it is hard for me because I still hear her voice calling for me in the middle of the night. "Steffie, Steffie" rings in my ears. Sometimes I wake up frantic that I need to go to her. But no one is there. I see her face in this house every time I pass her room.

Soon after this conversation, and once the siblings have come and gone from retrieving their tagged items from the house, it doesn't take long before I tell Greg I don't want to stay here any longer. My mom intended, and legally provided in her wishes, that we live in the house for a year so we can take our time to figure out our lives and determine where we want to live. Greg's adult boys are pretty comfortable living in their childhood home, so our plan has always been to avoid displacing them since it will be easier instead for us to find our own little place where the two of us can be comfortable. Once Greg knows my wishes, this man moves heaven and earth to help me turn the house upside down so we can get it prepared for sale.

# CHAPTER 41

# Distraction

In exactly thirty days, every remaining item that has not been tagged or retrieved is donated or dumped. All of our possessions get boxed. Our extra beds are given away to friends of friends until the entire house is emptied truly and finally. I could roller-skate through the halls like I did as a third grader when we first moved in if I had roller skates now and if we still had linoleum throughout the house.

In the midst of packing, Greg also looks for our new home. He does all the heavy lifting and the trekking from place to place after work so he can narrow down the best of the options out there before I need to come along. He does everything he can to spare me the hassle of driving 'round and 'round looking at places that sound great in ads but that I would never consider once I see them up close. Finally he finds the right fit, and a change of scenery does me some good. Now that we are settled, I start the next major task of hiring a realtor and preparing my childhood home for sale.

I am counting down the weeks before school ends and summer break begins. During the most anticipated school event—Open House Night in May—I will be greeting parents who have been like rocks of Gibraltar to me after the loss of my mother. One such mom, a teacher in another district, pulls me away from all of the other parents who are bustling around my classroom, eagerly escorted by their seventh graders, who are anxiously showing off their work from the year.

She holds my hand softly and, with glistening eyes, offers me the ultimate compliment with sincere words of praise from one teacher to another. "Thank you for all you have done for my daughter. You have no idea how you have helped her to grow. I know how hard the loss of your mother has been for you, but she must have been so proud of not only the daughter you were to her but the teacher you have been to these kids. You have worked hard to instill something special in them that they will not soon forget." With this she gives me a squeeze, and I begin to cry again.

I have nowhere to hide; however, I do look at my curriculum closet as a place I would like to retreat inside now. All I can do is catch the tears beneath my eyes with the back of my hand, turning away from the crowd, hoping that no one else approaches. Her comments remind me of things my mom used to say and, if it's possible, make me miss her even more.

On Mother's Day Greg and I make the drive out to the gravesite where my parents are now buried together. The headstone has been newly inscribed with both of their names, and the seedling grass has begun to fill in. I try to offer a word of prayer, but I can't because my emotions are all stuck in the back of my throat, and I am choking on all the tears pushing their way forward. Greg does it better anyway. He manages to inject thoughts filled with tenderness, gratitude, humor, and the love we have taken away from our time when the three of us were together—memories we cling to brightly.

I wonder when I will feel stronger. Weeks earlier Greg took me to lunch on a beautiful Saturday afternoon to eat at an outdoor café that is always populated even in inclement weather. Luckily we didn't have to wait for a table, and as we were making our way through the restaurant, we stopped mid-path to allow an elderly woman being carefully guided out by her middle-aged daughter, who had carefully locked elbows with her mother, grasping her free hand tightly.

"It's okay, Mom, I've got you. We have just a few more steps to the car," the daughter said in a tender voice, trying to reassure her mother that she was in good care.

I saw it. I refused to let it seep into my heart. I had had enough pain. I would not cry in public again. Greg and I sat down, the waiter brought our menus, and as soon as he turned away to get our waters, Greg could see my resolve cracking all over my face.

"Oh babe, people are going to think you're mad at me. What is it?"

"It's the la-ady, and her m-m-mommmm," I said, and the rest came out as sounds of unintelligible words that only squeaked when I tried to finish my sentence. I had to rush away from the table before the pain I thought I had buried well enough to enjoy my lunch came out in tears that gushed while I gulped for air. I darted through the back door to the patio, where I stood behind the bushes, hiding by a parked car in the back lot. I could not pull myself together. It did not matter that the cooks out back on a smoke break were watching me curiously. It was ten minutes before my grief subsided well enough for me to return to my table, but Greg dared not mention the lady again because he could see I was not on steady ground. I never was able to control when the waves of grief would come over me.

During my first summer off from school with nothing to do but care for myself, I still only want to stay home and pet the cat. It soothes me to take care of this cat, Sissy, who became attached to my mother like Velcro. In one year this middle-aged cat has lost both of her brother cats, Daisy my dog, and my mom and has been displaced from the only home she's ever known, where she could roam freely as an outdoor explorer. Now she is forced to live indoors with us in our temporary condo. I cry every day. I can't help it. I feel sorry for the cat.

I take walks around the new neighborhood and stare longingly into garage messes left unattended beneath roll-up doors that should be rolled down to hide the decades of life spilling out of stacks and piles. I remember what my mother's garage looked like, and I want to knock on this stranger's door to ask if they need my help. Maybe busying myself with another project is what I need to take my mind off my unabated despair. Greg convinces me these are not the kind of tasks I should be taking on right now, so I change my direction, walking through parks instead.

I have other urgent obligations; I feel compelled to put together memory books for my siblings from the piles of tattered photos that have come unstuck from decades of old glue that held them in the cardboard albums chronicling our youth. I do not wish to rob my siblings of their childhoods, and the only way I can see fit to preserve the memories is for each of us to have our own copy in its entirety of what was stored in the living room cupboards beneath the built-in bookshelves for forty years.

Before Greg and I moved, I packed every important memory into a couple of bankers boxes to cart with me until I had the time to sort. That time is now. I sit on the living room carpet, photos sprawled out in front of me every night while watching reruns of *Mad Men* until the wee hours of the morning. I am not sleeping unless I take one of my special pills, and right now I am feeling energized by the progress I am making on this project.

The several hundred photos I have strewn about the room are methodically staggered into categories so I can easily put them away without losing my place when I start at it again the next day. I thought it would be easier to look through photos and that it might bring back happy memories to sustain me. I was wrong. The first picture I see of my mom looking lovingly into the camera flattens me.

My heart has such heaviness. I am at a loss. I do not know how I am going to fill this emptiness. I hurt all the time. I really don't care that there is sunshine outside. I want to stay in. Baking becomes an effort. Cooking becomes an effort. Cleaning the house is an effort I make, though, because I like a straight closet and tidy drawers. So I wile away afternoons undoing compartments that were just organized when we moved in a few months earlier. I vacuum because it is the one chore that relaxes me. And then nighttime falls again, and I return to sorting family photos.

I begin my work by filling shoeboxes that will later be dedicated to separate memory-book themes. The first box is for pictures of my father alone in his childhood and through the war. The second box is for my mother's life before she met my father. There are plenty of photos of her as a child because she was a darling baby girl and the first child whose conception was not miscarried. After her parents lost three children in the womb, there was a lot of praying and hand wringing that my mother would make it to full term and come out healthy. Thankfully for all of us, she did.

The third box holds photos of my parents together through

their courtship, extending into the years when we became a family; all the photos of us together go into this box. Then I sift through more piles to create a book for each sibling's singular childhood so all of the spectacular photos showcasing just his or her images can be captured in one album.

The memory books total seven in all. I buy a brand-new Mac computer for this very purpose of creating digital photo albums presented in custom books so each of us will have a complete set for our keepsakes. This way, I figure, no one will fight over who got which photos, and I won't have to worry that they will think I claimed all the best ones for myself.

I spend all summer learning how to use my Mac. Since I was always a PC person, I am bracing myself for a total shift in mindset. I keep hearing I will be so happy with what I can do on my Mac. So I keep sorting. When I finally have my seven boxes segregated, the best advice I get is to have a professional camera store do all the scanning, and the place I find is affordable because they are running a special.

This is the smartest thing I have done because it saves me hours upon hours of trying to manage a project that is bigger than my skill set. Within just a few days, the photo store has my complete order, and I am ready for my first lesson in building a custom book. I spend multiple hours in tutorials and learn things I have always shied away from.

By fall my feverish pace at building digital albums means I will be on track for sending the gift sets to my siblings by the time their first distribution checks from the sale of the house will be ready in the coming weeks. In the meantime I have started another new school year with another group of wonderful students who are eager to soak up every bit of knowledge I put in front of them. They become my little academic sponges, and teaching them is fun. It is also exhausting. I sleep better now naturally, having weaned myself off of the pills, but I still want to rush home after school to pet the cat.

# CHAPTER 42

# Orphaned

There is a flyer that has been sitting on my desk for a couple of months now—an invitation to join a grief counseling group specifically for daughters who have lost mothers, hosted by hospice. I penciled myself in knowing I could easily cancel at the last minute. I thought maybe I should give it a shot; maybe I would feel better. But by the second visit to my mother's gravesite in time for her fall birthday, I am actually feeling like I am self-managing reasonably well. I know it will take some time to get back the bounce in my step, but I am functioning with daily responsibilities, and my regular check-ins with my primary physician have been scaled back to every few months, so I must be making progress, I tell myself.

The first of my ten Monday night sessions of grief counseling are set to begin the day after that visit to the cemetery for my mother's birthday. I did great that day. I was able to offer the prayer this time and did it without coming unhinged. I was able to reminisce with Greg in a restaurant without losing it over lunch at the table.

I intended to cancel before this first meeting because it

feels like I won't need it after all. But a long day at school has left me no time to call ahead and since I don't want to appear flaky, I go. I am feeling very upbeat, very light on the drive over. I am hoping this three-hour session will fly by, then I won't have to come back. I don't want to add one more weekly obligation to make me feel even more overextended when I already have regular meetings for committees, papers to grade, lessons to plan, and test results to analyze. Blocking out one more night of the week just takes time away from me and the cat, and me and Greg.

I arrive early, smiling and nodding at others as I walk in. I find the placard with my name on it reserving my place at the corner, and then it's the strangest thing. After moving into my spot at the long conference table set up for a dozen of us, I become engulfed in a convulsion of tears the moment my bottom hits the chair. I don't know what has happened. I was completely fine just a second ago. It's as if a string has been pulled from my base where I sit, and when it lets go I become the baby doll that cries and cries.

I am so flummoxed I cannot even look up while everyone is solemnly making introductions. The tears are flooding my eyes, streaming down my face. I am incapable of collecting myself even to say my name. I have lost control of my wavering voice. I am trying to mute my grief, embarrassed by the spectacle I have become. There is not even a thought in my head that says I should go to the ladies' room for a moment because my feet are frozen, my body paralyzed.

When the second loop around the table lands another question in my lap, something easy enough to explain like why I am here, I choke even harder. The emotions I am trying to swallow finally come out in a soft wail, which I immediately work to stifle. I am mortified by the shame I am feeling at having brought so much unwanted attention to myself, possibly derailing this meeting.

The leader, in her compassion and wisdom, keeps the ball moving. She allows me to take another polite pass and invites everyone else at the table to recognize that we all are in different stages of pain. She reminds the group that this is why we are here tonight—to discover what hurts us the most about our losses and to strategize ways we can connect to our pain so we can begin to heal.

I sit and listen while the tears slow and my breathing becomes more even, until someone else tells the story of losing their mother, and my whimpering starts all over again. It is so difficult to stay in control of my emotions when they have pushed their way out of my throat. I have so much empathy for the other women who are here. Some of them have lost their mothers only within the past few months. I am on month nine.

I sit like this for three hours. Tears are just dripping off my nose while I try not to hiccup between waves of pain that pulse through me. I am as invisible as I can make myself, but I feel that everyone must be staring. I am the lump at the table, still in her down coat, hiding beneath the brim of her newsboy cap, hoping the session will end early.

What I learn this evening is that I am not doing as great as I think. I have been compartmentalizing my grief and busying myself with enough bigger priorities so I do not have to get in touch with my feelings because I don't have time. After tonight's session, I decide I owe it to myself to take the time needed to heal my heart.

Listening to the other women speak brings two immediate thoughts to mind that stay with me: First, my problems aren't worse than anyone else's, which is humbling since going in I thought I had the heaviest burden. There is tremendous suffering in our room. I soon discover there are dysfunctional families worse than mine, and suddenly I am relieved that what I have dealt with is minimal compared to the nightmares I am hearing unfold.

Second, the story of my mother's decline is not even the worst at the table tonight. I feel grateful to share in others' burdens. Together we will spend ten weeks bonding while we move from being strangers to becoming sisters in spirit. Each time we meet, we draw on the strength of those who are managing a little better than we are this week.

Both of these eye-openers immediately take me out of myself and my woes and allow me to listen to others, to hear their hearts, and to feel compassion for them. I also make a friend, the kind you can count on for keeps. We spend hours in the dark parking lot one evening continuing the discussion of how difficult it is for the friends we have in our circles to really understand what it means to lose a parent. How it feels to care for a parent whose life is unraveling before your eyes, and what it feels like to say the lonely words "I am an orphan," cannot be known by those who have not felt this void.

*Orphan* is a word most people attribute only to children. But for us it does not matter that we are grown women or that many of us have children of our own. Being a child who has lost both parents is disorienting no matter what age we are. None of us wants to go through life with the sense that our parent who has guided us skillfully is now departed. The path is now ours alone to carve. There is no one in our corner to applaud, or to suggest we do it a different way, and while this may have driven us crazy at one point, we long for it when this presence is gone.

Some at our table do not have strong relationships with their father figures, and now that their mothers are gone, their entire lives are crumbling. This helps to put a lot of things into perspective for me. As escrow finally closes on my mother's property, I have one final opportunity to stand alone in my parents' house, the one that was my childhood home, the one wherein I had once built a shrine to a mother I still miss dearly.

On the night before the new owner takes possession of the keys, I stand in the master bedroom lit only by the sunset and pray in the place where my mother lay for several months in her little hospital bed waiting for death. I stare at blank walls that, in my mind, are still filled with framed photos beside towering shelves lined with books, amid laughter that was robust. I finally muster some strength, and I make a promise to my parents that I will live the remainder of the life I have left on this earth to its fullest capacity, in a way that will honor them for the rest of my days.

As the daughter they raised, I will live to fulfill my potential in the dreams they saw for me. I will not wallow in despair. I will take what I learned from them both and carry myself forward knowing they will be watching over me, guiding me better than if they were here beside me. I feel tremendously positive after this last encounter alone. I am able to gain closure as I shut the doors to my childhood home, turning my key in its lock for the very last time.

I never drive past the house again after this night. I never feel the need to see what the new owner has thoughtlessly done to ruin all the details I put into making our house just right. But Greg fills me in from time to time. I am satisfied with the memories I carried away from Mindy Lane and so very grateful I got to spend the last five years there with my mother.

The next week our grief counselor has a new exercise for us to try. We have been meeting for several weeks, and it is time to gauge our feelings. She has pretended to mark the wall behind us with invisible lines to measure our pain on a scale from most miserable to least miserable. Anyone who stands nearest to the window side of the wall she points to is at the lowest number, one, and experiencing pain that is still too unbearable after suffering the loss of their mother. At the opposite end of the line is the spot for tens—for those whose hearts have healed.

Once she confirms we are all clear on where the positions fall on the wall, she invites us to insert ourselves into the number line. It is so illuminating to see who stands where. The friend I have made, the one I'd like to keep, is still somewhere around a four. One other woman and I are at the eight. Most of the group hovers near the five. It is a hard thing to get over the loss of one's mother.

The leader asks what has prompted me to feel so positive now after feeling so miserable during that first meeting several weeks ago. I relay for her and the group the good-bye I said alone at the house and the promise I made to my parents. I want to live in a future that I believe will be bright. My mother's mantra was always "you never know what's waiting around the corner, and it might turn out to be something pretty good." I am feeling it.

I continue to say that I have no regrets because I followed through with every thought I ever had to make her feel more comfortable. My mother's last words to me were, "Thank you, you're wonderful." She would want me to feel full of life. In my heart I believe my parents are together watching over me, and I take comfort in this.

I capture these sentiments with enough conviction and enthusiasm that a couple of the others think maybe they can move up to the six. Grief is heavy. There is a reason we want to sleep. It is too painful to process, but I am managing to make progress with small steps.

# CHAPTER 43

# My Takeaways

In time for the holidays, I am sending the first distribution checks along with the box sets of seven memory books preserving everyone's childhoods. My relationships with my siblings are not hostile, merely quiet. For a year I have sent out letters on a quarterly basis informing them of estate business, but I feel there is one more that should be sent with these packages. I think a letter explaining in detail what it means to care for a person at the end of their life is fitting and will segue to a request my friends all tell me will never be taken seriously. Alas, it needs to be said.

The letter is gentle in its approach and thoughtful in its transparency. I explain about the accounting that will be finalized through the attorney's office before the end of the year, and I share details of what to expect in the future. I tell them the past several months have been spent sorting, scanning, and building new custom family albums so each sibling can have duplicate copies of our family photos, and I list for them the contents within the gift boxes.

The next portion of the letter appears here as it is written.

Finally, at this time, as we all begin to reflect upon Mom's life with the one-year anniversary of her loss looming on the horizon and the holidays coming, I hope you will remember the other life that was sacrificed in caring for your mother.

Yes, she was my mother too. And so I did my part. Fair enough to say, I did your part too as well as the parts of the other siblings. There is not enough time or paper to share the intimate details of what it really means to care for someone whose body begins to fail them while they wonder what is happening and fear the worst.

The entire time my goal was for her to feel loved, to feel safe, and never to feel alone while maintaining her dignity as I attended to her personal needs, all the while tackling the job of getting the house in condition to sell.

I remind them about how lucky we all are that I married a man who joined our family late but willingly used his skill set to do work on a house that had been badly neglected, thus saving us lots of expenses we would have incurred had we hired it out. I make the point that thanks to Greg we are all going to enjoy a much nicer inheritance because of the increased home value.

At the end of each sibling's letter, I customize a paragraph about how our mother loved them and what they meant to her even through her last months. Here I am especially careful to avoid inserting the words "when no one came to visit."

Especially moving is the paragraph to Brother Two, whom she had hallucinated about trying to fix a pail lunch for and fretted she couldn't get it right. I make sure he knows that all the things she ever hoped to do for him in her lifetime were also the last thoughts she held on to even when her life was ending. She was still focused on what he needed even in her dementia. In each separate paragraph to my siblings, I remind them that I am sure she will continue to look over them for the rest of their lives.

Before closing I invite my siblings, except for Sister Two, to do the right thing. I have to put it out there. Would they be willing to show their gratitude with a small portion of their inheritance so I can recapture some of the life I left behind, enabling me to take a year off from school to rebuild my future? Do I really think my siblings will show me a different side of themselves? No, not really. Do I think it will be a nice gesture for them to do something for me? In short, yes. To give up something they want to keep for themselves will symbolize a sacrifice on their part, I think. At the very least, I hope my request might lead to some dialogue.

Instead my letter to each sibling is met with silence. I check the post-office box every day for three weeks before realizing I have already received my answer. There is never a response about the memory books I toiled to create. There is never a word spoken about my request for more than they think I might be entitled to. There is nothing but the sound of tellers stamping those distribution checks that are quickly being cashed at the bank.

I know better than to ask for anything from Sister Two since she is still frothing over her advance cutting into her portion of the inheritance. I suggest only that she thank Greg, which she does in a very sweet letter arriving the same day she sends more hate mail for me.

It's okay, though. Everything I did for my mom was with

the purest of intentions, and everything I do for my siblings is done with the same heartfelt thought. I do not want to rob my siblings of their childhood memories. I would not withhold anything I found in that house that could maybe help them with their own grieving processes down the road. In my letter I simply gave them an opportunity, and they have confirmed what I always suspected. It is a peaceful way to part; we all know where we stand.

There are three impressions I take away before grief counseling comes to an end, which will give me strength long after we have said our last good-byes in the parking lot. First, people are meant to be in our lives for the amount of time we need them. Of course I wanted to keep my mother for longer. I felt the same way when my father passed away. But in essence my parents taught me everything they needed to, and what they left me with is all I really need to survive.

I have borrowed from my father his positive mental attitude, which has been an asset for me in making and keeping friends and building a stellar reputation as a role model for children. I have borrowed from my mother her sense of independence, which helps me to navigate rough terrain when there are no road maps to guide me. There was still so much more I needed from my mother, and I got what I needed to go forward in life in those five extra years we cherished together.

Sister Two offered me tremendous solace in a rare kindness she extended to me at our mother's funeral. She said that the longer I was here to take care of our mom, the more my mother realized I truly loved her and forgave her. This was the most gracious insight she could have shared because I would not have come to this conclusion on my own. But she knew. I am so grateful I had the chance to make things right, that

I came home and that I do not have to live with regret for missing the opportunity for us to heal.

The second thing I learn in grief counseling hits me like a ton of bricks: the marital strain that comes from caring for an elderly parent will take its toll. As soon as one of the other women reveals to us that she and her husband have been seeing a marriage counselor for two weeks, my ears perk up. I am very happily married to Greg today, therefore I have not shared the terrible episodes of stress that seemed to appear out of nowhere during the course of this story.

I finally theorize that the pain my husband must have felt from losing his first wife to cancer was probably ratcheting up a few notches every time he watched my mother step further into her decline. He was so jovial with her. He intended to be so strong for me. But he couldn't keep it up under all the pressure that was mounting for him both inside and outside of our home.

I was so glad to hear someone else say it was so—that marriages are susceptible under these extreme conditions—because for the longest time I felt completely alone in the knowledge that things could be better for my husband and me. After my mom passed away, we had the hard conversations and agreed we both have the commitment to push through. We found help. We talked. We practiced compassionate listening. We began to understand what we just went through. We were all torn up inside, and he never wanted me to see how much it hurt him because his focus was on how to fix me.

This brings me to the third insight I have gained from my grief counseling. Hospice grief counselors will liken the experience of being a live-in caregiver to that of a war-torn soldier in the trenches who sees all the action on the front lines. You will come out of it with the very same kind of post-traumatic stress that research shows can last for at least two years. Some of the women in my group are still grieving terribly after five and eight years. Grief is powerful and cannot be ignored. We can try to push it down, but it will bubble up to the surface again with our next heartache if we never confront it.

Taking on the care of a parent, especially when you have young children to look after as well, is a risk to the stability of any family no matter how strong it is. Yet, statistically speaking, we adult women over the age of forty-five are the most likely prospects our parents will have to get the care they need through the last years of their lives.

What I have taken away from the experience of caring for my mother are love and gratitude and a cat named Sissy, who is now attached to me like Velcro. I have also taken away fear that there will be no one to care for me when I am elderly. I do not have a daughter, and there is no guarantee that if I did she would want the job anyway.

I do not know what the answer is to how our society can care for our elderly in a better, more-affordable way. It is not right that the best facilities cost so much and that there are too many families who cannot afford this luxury.

I have found it is not the job of the neighbors, the church friends, or their best friends to care for your elderly parent. It is a bigger job than someone living outside of the home can handle with a life of their own to navigate. More and more families will become multigenerational when Grandma or Grandpa becomes too ill to live in their own home.

What I have taken away from the experience of caring for my mother is a hyper-awareness of how we treat seniors in our communities. The favorite place I took my mother for her first pedicure became my regular salon for years. But many months after my mother passed away, I watch a scene unfold from my chair inside the salon that changes how I support businesses.

On an unusually quiet Saturday morning, a man in his late fifties walks in with his elderly mother, whom he carefully situates in the waiting area while he checks on her ten o'clock appointment. The owner finds her penciled in for two o'clock. The son figures it is an honest mistake and asks how long it will take before his mother can get a manicure and a pedicure that morning, as he is willing to wait.

I am shocked to hear the owner say the salon is booked all morning. This is not one of their full capacity days, and I cannot believe this elderly woman would be turned away, not when this salon has built a reputation on accepting walk-in business. I want to cry right there. I know exactly what that man went through that morning to get his mother dressed and ready and out the door. I also know the excitement this little old lady must have had anticipating her beauty appointment. If I were thinking faster, I would slosh over the wall of my footbath to ask if she wants my seat.

In an instant the man and his elderly mother are gone. In a single day, my favorite salon has lost my future business. I cannot feel good about patronizing a place that has zero compassion for the elderly. The owner could have easily asked any one of us if we would be willing to give up our manicure appointment or could have squeezed her in between the next appointments. There are a dozen things he could have done differently. Now, instead of driving five blocks, I drive twenty minutes to my new favorite salon, and I am happy to do so even if I get stuck in freeway traffic.

From the experience of caring for my mother, I have

taken away a long list of items to do before I feel like my job of memory keeper is complete. I have the second set of boxes ready to send to my siblings, which include the digital copies I made of home movies and my father's audio recordings about his life, and the precious letters I culled from reams of notebooks written in my mother's own handwriting to each of us as small children so we would remember her love for us, along with her book of poems—I had a copy bound for each of them.

When it reaches my siblings, I will expect more of the same: nothing. It does not prevent me from doing what is right. I want them to have the memories I have restored so I know I have done everything I can to help them heal through the feeling of loss they must be suffering after our mother's passing.

I teach for one more year and then finally take some time for me away from school. I spend my sabbatical year writing this novel—something I start as a way to help me with my healing process. It has been cathartic to write even the most painful memories in parts six and seven. I still have not replaced Daisy, but Greg is laying the groundwork, and I suspect a new pup is not far off in our future.

After caring for my mother, I still see her everywhere, but it is now in the form of the many seniors I meet in waiting rooms of doctors' offices. I want to adopt them all. They are in varying stages of health, all too familiar to me. The elderly lady who should not be driving and can barely walk with her walker tells me her children are in Texas and she is managing to live alone for as long as she can because she has her cats to look after. I at once want to cry and hug her and offer to bake her macaroni and cheese while cleaning her garage, but I refrain.

I did it for my mother. If you are thinking about what the

experience will do for you, I promise you this: you will never regret the choice you make to care for your elderly parent. When it is over, you will humbly feel it was your privilege to be the one who was able enough to care for them. And from this blessed opportunity, only good can come into your life for the rest of your livelong days.

*This book was written in memory of my loving parents and for my darling husband, my biggest fan.*

# ACKNOWLEDGMENTS

There is nothing more exciting to a writer than enthusiasm from those who eagerly await your words on a page.

To my darling husband, who fueled my ambition by first building me a cottage where I could write and then doing most of my chores for the better part of a year so I could stay in my cottage as the months turned into seasons, I am one lucky girl. Mostly thank you for always supporting my creativity by loving all of my work.

When I finished the book, these three additional people offered input that was invaluable to me, giving me all the right encouragement to move forward: Jenene Nicholson, Tracy Stinson, and Jennifer McVey. Thank you for generously taking your time with the unedited manuscript and for all your notes and praise along the way. Every writer needs readers like you.

To my other lovely friends who have been in regular contact, excitedly awaiting news about the book's progress and cheering me on in my endeavors, a thousand thank yous for filling my heart with such joy: Wendy Ehrlich, Sue Fuller,

Melissa Germaine, Deb Leon, Gigi Mattos, Kathy Nelson, Maria Ribera, Allison Smith, and Joyce Walter.

To the professionals who endorsed this work, I am ever so grateful to you for your belief in me and my desire to help others who are at the front of their caregiving experiences: Stephanie Amsden, Dr. Robert Hendren, Dody Lapworth, Dr. Suzanne Pertsch, Leonard Watson, Catherine Raye-Wong. I am especially touched by your comments to me in your personal notes of congratulations.

Thank you to Jessica Gorham at Arbor Books for your flawless production work on designing my book.

And finally, what I have discovered through this process is that a good editor is much like a good stylist. Even if I were to put on the cutest outfit I own, someone with a keen eye for detail might add a scarf, subtract a bag, dart the blouse, cuff the pants, replace the shoes, add a fantastic leopard belt, and find the perfect shade of lipstick to bring out the flecks of cinnamon in my eyes. A good editor will make sure your best has gotten only better, crisper, tighter. A good editor will help you to emerge a stronger writer. Thank you to Elise Vaz at Arbor Books for tailoring my work with such style and grace.

# NOTES AND RESOURCES

## PART 1, Chapter 1: The Rift

1 Philip Moeller, "10 Tips for Caring for Aging Parents, Phillip Moeller," US News & World Report, July 18, 2011, http://money.usnews.com/money/blogs/the-best-life/2011/07/18/10-tips-for-caring-for-aging-parents.

The number of people taking care of an aging parent has soared in the past fifteen years. Phillip Moeller, contributing editor to US News & World Report, writes about achieving success and happiness in older age. The article lays out the financial impact of deciding to care for your parent as well.

2 Christine Dugas, "Caring for an Elderly Parent Catches Many Unprepared," USA Today, March 25, 2012, http://www.usatoday.com/money/perfi/basics/story/2012-03-25/caring-for-an-elderly-parent-financially/53775004/1.

Regardless of the ailment that renders your parent helpless, this article will remind you why it is so important to be prepared in advance. Christine Dugas writes about Money for *USA Today* and in this article interviews a daughter who is caring for her mother after a sudden stroke.

3   A. Barry Rand, "Caregiving Challenges and Rewards," AARP, November 8, 2012, http://www.aarp.org.home-family/ caregiving/info-11-2012/caregiving-challenges-and-rewards. html.

This article has heart and reminds us all that caregiving will impact everyone, from CEOs to moms sandwiched between caring for their own parents and raising their own children. This article introduced me to AARP's essential website. Download the "Prepare to Care Guide for Families," which has forms to keep you organized and resources you will need to feel less alone in your new role.

4   Mindy Fetterman, "Becoming 'Parent of Your Parent' an Emotionally Wrenching Process," USA Today, June 24, 2007, http://www.usatoday.com/money/perfi/ eldercare/2007-06-24-elder-care-cover_N.htm.

This is the personal account of the author's dealing with finally putting her mother in a home. It uncovers the financial choices available when considering assisted-living options, including what Medicare and Medicaid will and will not pay for. Mindy Fetterman is a personal finance reporter for the "Money" section of *USA Today*.

**PART 1, Chapter 4: The Solution**

Dugas, "Caring for an Elderly Parent Catches Many Unprepared." In this previously referenced article, the highlights to note are thus: "Those who move in with a parent take on a significant and sustained burden of care," and, "There is such a thing as caregiver burnout."

**PART 2, Chapter 6: The Awful Bath**

*Elder neglect* is a term encompassing multiple areas of neglect by caregivers or self-neglect. For really specific lists of what to look for, here are two sites to check out:

> Lawrence Robinson, Tina de Benedictis, PhD, and Jeanne Segal, PhD "Elder Abuse and Neglect," Helpguide.org, May 2013, http://www.helpguide.org/mental/elder_abuse_physical_emotional_sexual_neglect.htm

> "Preventing Elder Abuse and Neglect in Older Adults," HealthInAging.org, http://www.healthinaging.org/resources/resource:preventing-elder-abuse-and-neglect-in-older-adults/.

**PART 2, Chapter 7: The Fall**

**Prescriptions Chart**
At every single medical appointment you have, you will be asked to recount the prescriptions your aging parent is taking. It will be so much easier on you if you can hand over a small

laminated chart for the nurse to copy. Be sure to include the following:

- Patient information (name, date of birth, and who to contact if the patient cannot hear well enough to use the telephone, plus a phone number)
- Primary care information (primary doctor and his or her office phone number)
- Medical insurer (including name of health-insurance provider, phone number of insurer, and medical plan number);
- Prescriptions insurer (including the prescription plan number and the phone number for the prescriptions insurer)
- Pharmacy contacts (including address and phone number for each pharmacy where you would like to pick up your parent's prescriptions)
- List of medications taken including vitamins (include the prescription number for each, which will help you at the time of renewal; the strength, usually listed in milligrams (mg); the quantity of pills in each prescription; the reason the med is taken; and the location of the pharmacy where the med is filled
- Be sure to list your meds in alphabetical order and to include every renewable item you need from the pharmacy so you have a complete checklist and can avoid making a second trip.
- Add two columns for "renewal due date" and "date last filled"
- Finally add a header date so you know how current your chart is; title it "date last modified"

## PART 4, Chapter 14: Health, Safety, Style

*Elder abuse* is defined as the mistreatment of an older adult, taking many forms including physical, verbal, emotional, and sexual abuse; financial exploitation; and neglect.

There are several points from the article "Preventing Elder Abuse and Neglect in Older Adults" (http://www.healthinaging. org/resources/resource:preventing-elder-abuse-and-neglect-in-older-adults/, from HealthInAging.org, a foundation of The American Geriatrics Society) that are important to recognize. Please do make it a priority to visit this site for the details on the top nine warning signs of elder abuse.

**Adult Protective Services (APS)** is the first agency to contact if you suspect elder abuse (Robinson, et al, "Elder Abuse and Neglect").

### Difficult Siblings

The article by Mindy Fetterman referenced in Chapter 1 (http://www.usatoday.com/money/perfi/eldercare/2007-06-24-elder-care-cover_N.htm) is something I came across years after I cared for my mother. Hopefully it finds you before your experience begins, as I believe it will provide you with great insight and assurance that you are feeling tremendous stress from your siblings for a valid reason.

## PART 6, Chapter 27: Looking for Support

### Hospice Care

Since the time I cared for my mother, I have learned through my research that hospice care has become even stricter about making sure hospice patients are meeting the established guidelines for being a hospice patient and showing signs of continual decline; if they do not, some patients are being discharged after only several weeks. This is much different from my experience a few years ago. Each disease process has its own criteria that show the disease is likely end-stage and includes data to back this up.

This is one of the reasons my mother's arm measurements needed to be taken frequently to show she was losing weight and why there needed to be signs that she could not turn in bed independently. We had to demonstrate progressive decline. This was due partly to new Medicare scrutiny with the recovery audit contractors (RAC) who review charts and can ask for additional documentation to prove a person should still be in hospice care. This process is also true for any Medicare payments, not just hospice. Documentation must match up with criteria. It prevents Medicare fraud but also creates difficulty for families who are getting by with hospice support and are worried about hospice's needing to pull away. This almost happened to my mother, and I don't know how we would have survived without the support of hospice.

The following source explains the top myths versus facts about why some hospice patients are not kept under hospice care:

"Medicare Fee-for-Service Recovery Audit Programs Myths," Centers for Medicare & Medicaid Services, December 17, 2012, http://www.cms.gov/Research-Statistics-Data-and-Systems/Monitoring-Programs/Recovery-Audit-Program/Downloads/RAC-Program-Myths-12-18-12.pdf.

## PART 7, Chapter 34: My Privilege

**The Conversation Project** (theconversationproject.org) was founded by Ellen Goodman, a Pulitzer Prize-winning syndicated columnist who was left to make decisions about her mother's care that often left her feeling uncertain, unprepared, and blindsided. The Project is a campaign designed to encourage people to have honest conversations with their loved ones about how they want to spend their last days so they can have good deaths. Also see: Ellen Goodman, "The Most Important Conversation You'll Ever Have," Oprah.com, September 17, 2002, http://www.oprah.com/relationships/How-to-Talk-About-Dying-Ellen-Goodman-The-Conversation-Project.

All that was shared between my mother and me, some of which has not been recorded in this book, led to a very good death for my mother and brought tremendous peace to me that we had covered everything that needed to be said.

## PART 8, Chapter 39: Legal Documents Binder

### Four Legal Documents to Have in Place

There are many resources I use to cross-reference including the popular site SuzeOrman.com. On the site you can ask Suze a question directly or print many of the legal forms you will need.

Here are the terms you will need to understand as you plan your estate:

1. The difference between a *will* and a *trust*
2. *Durable power of attorney*

3.  A *pour-over will.*
4.  *Advance health-care directive*

See also:

Suze Orman, "Five Pieces of Financial Advice to Avoid at All Costs," Oprah.com, October 2012, http://www.oprah.com/money/Financial-Advice-to-Ignore-Suze-Orman-Financial-Advice/.

See also:

Dugas, "Caring for an Elderly Parent Catches Many Unprepared."

*For more information visit stefaniashaffer.com*